Ocean Voyaging

Ocean Voyaging

A Critical Discussion
of Modern Cruising Yachts and
The Technique of Ocean Sailing

David M. Parker

For Joanne

Contents

Introduction

Ocean voyaging has become more and more popular in the United States as well as abroad in recent years. More and more families, as well as single-handers, are setting out to cross an ocean or two, or to see the exotic places described by those early pioneers that have gone before.

Gone are the days of tarred rigging, flaxen storm sails, wooden ships, and iron men. The modern ocean voyager has at his disposal all the tremendous advances in yachts and techniques that technology makes ever more possible. In spite of these advances, however, we are somehow left with the stereotype of cruising yachts as heavy, outmoded, slow, and generally unsatisfactory vessels suitable only for crushing crabs along the coast.

In years to come we will see more cruising yachts built of fiberglass-reinforced plastic, aluminum, steel, and ferrocement, and fewer of wood. I, for one, welcome these advances. Many do not, preferring the "tried and tested" model for their dream yacht. At one time I also fought against the more modern practices with the fanatic light in my eye that tradition inspires. Years of experience have taught me the error in my thinking. Tradition is fine, but only when it serves better at sea than does innovation.

There are two main schools of thought in the cruising fraternity today, and the division is basically between the philosophies of the nineteenth and twentieth centuries. Some cruising men are guided mainly by the voyagers of the past and stick to heavy-displacement wooden craft encumbered with the inefficient sail plans of yesteryear in spite of the magnificent efforts of naval architects to improve the oceangoing yacht. They forget, these fanatics, that old Josh Slocum, Harry Pidgeon, and Alain Gerbault certainly would have jumped at the chance to sail in one of these modern, safe, and efficient yachts. These men were realists all, and any advance would have been most welcome to them. Indeed, Gerbault had a new vessel built for his last Polynesian adventure.

I was a traditionalist for most of my life, perhaps because I had read too well and too much of ancient voyages. When I was a young boy in Samoa I read endlessly of the exploits of small boat pioneers,

1

and I had the great pleasure of meeting Dwight Long, circumnavigating on *Idle Hour*. A few more cruising yachts happened by during my stay in Samoa, and they left a strong and lasting impression on me. I resolved to follow in the footsteps of my boyhood heroes, a resolve that has often been frustrated but never forgotten. As the years went by, it became traditional with me that a cruising yacht was of a definite form and character. After all, hadn't my heroes crossed the seas in such yachts? Boyish ideals are fine, but they also may be quite wrong.

The young seldom see the other side to any question, but as I grew older, and perhaps wiser, I became aware of another point of view. It started perhaps in England, where economic conditions after World War II made it difficult for the average cruising family to obtain beamy, heavy-displacement ketches of traditional pattern. But voyaging they went anyway, and many a happy voyage they made. The epic circumnavigation made by John Guzzwell in his self-built, Laurent Giles–designed *Trekka*, was an eye-opener. Trekka was of extreme light displacement with a fin keel and spade rudder. Eric and Susan Hiscock's two circumnavigations in a thirty-foot, narrow-beam sloop, *Wanderer III*, and Atlantic crossings by other adventurers in every imaginable type of little vessel showed that it was not so necessary as we once thought to have a heavy, cumbersome vessel in which to cross an ocean.

Today's harbors and anchorages are more crowded than ever before, and I doubt if a yacht such as Slocum's *Spray*, without an engine and lacking good maneuverability, would be happy any longer. Modern man, geared as he is to jet travel and telecommunication, would, I think, soon weary of lying doggo in port for a week or two waiting for a favorable wind to carry him out. He would probably rebel at taking to the sweep for long hours just to make a mile against currents. Often, though, when you ask him about the best yacht for world cruising, he is apt to describe something out of the eighteenth or nineteenth century! He wouldn't drive a 1911 Hupmobile to work, nor would he live in a log cabin. Why then does he choose an anachronism in which to sail? Perhaps we are all more conservative than we would like to admit.

Ask most yacht brokers for a cruising boat, and they will try to sell you a slow, clumsy, ketch or some sort of ship model that would look fine tied up to the yacht club dock. He is a victim of the same tradition as we, and besides, he'll never sell a crab crusher to a racing skipper! I have seen prospective voyagers standing smack in front of a CAL 40 with a "For Sale" sign on it bemoaning the lack of "real cruising boats" today. Well, I've sailed on forty-foot heavy-displacement ketches, and I've sailed on the Cal 40. When it comes to crossing an ocean, I'll take the Cal 40 any day! It's cheaper, given similar age, than the wooden boat. It's far, far faster. It's drier, safer, and much easier to maintain. Most important, it doesn't need a huge engine and fuel supply to get where it's going.

Perhaps as more voyages are made in modern craft and reported in writing, our images will change. But until then how does one decide what type of vessel he should have? As a sometimes reluctant convert to the "new school," I believe that if you know what is to be expected at sea and how a yacht can contend with the things that may happen, and if you are aware of the good and bad points of various designs and learn to recognize them, you will be able to make an intelligent compromise and choose the right yacht for your purpose and your personality.

This little book will, I hope, tell you how I would go about the task of selecting the hull, cabin layout, and rig; how to modify your boat as necessary; and how to equip, maintain, and rig her for ocean passages. I will let you in on how I plan a voyage and provision ship. I will deal with my "idiot system" of navigation, which is not elegant but always works, and I will describe several self-steering rigs that work at sea as well as in a test tank. A bit of speculative seamanship and some vignettes and excerpts from my log while sailing various types of vessels wind up my offering.

This is, then, a how-to-do-it book, but I truly hope that I do not give the impression that I think my way is the only way. My way is just one of many in the world of ocean cruising; it has simply been the best for me. My opinions, which I hand out freely, are nothing more than opinions. They may differ from views of other ocean voyagers, but I hold them honestly, for they spring from my own experiences offshore. I do not expect everyone to agree with all the ideas expressed here, nor would I wish them to. We are not all exactly alike, efforts of Dr. Spock, liberal politicians, television stations and the federal government notwithstanding!

After more than a hundred thousand miles have passed in my wake, I am aware that given the right conditions almost any sort of vessel can cross the ocean. What matters most is that a vessel be able to stand up to the unexpected and give pleasure to her crew. When all is said and done, isn't pleasure what we really seek?

1   Choosing the Hull Design

In order to get the right hull to keep you happy and safe off-shore, you must consider many factors carefully. It is not easy to change your mind once the decision is made. The primary considerations are seaworthiness, size, speed, comfort, ability to carry the necessary weight of stores and crew, ease of maintenance, and original cost—not necessarily in that order. Many so-called cruising yachts available today are not really fit for crossing oceans, mainly because they fail to meet acceptable standards on one or more of these criteria. They may be quite fast but lack the ability to carry sufficient stores. To some people ability to carry weight is of utmost importance, but this should not be so. A vessel may be capable of carrying weight but be prone to sitting around like an iceberg when the wind is light. Personally I feel the most frustrating experience at sea is a calm, and good light-air performance counts a good deal with me.

The general design philosophy by which the yacht is planned will govern many of the factors you will consider, so perhaps that should be discussed first. My own ideal cruising design has developed over many years of crashing about the ocean in a variety of yachts, some good, some horrible. Like most sailors, I borrowed a little here and rejected a little there, and after I had owned three yachts of highly different character and sailed them over the ocean, I sat down and designed and built the "final" yacht. Only time will tell whether I am right or wrong. I may well change my mind and build yet another final yacht some years hence!

I firmly hold that an ocean voyaging yacht is better of light to moderate rather than heavy displacement. Years ago it was fashionable to go voyaging in any ancient relic that could be bought cheaply. In fact, many of the so-called cruising boats available on the used market over the years seem to fit that description. Many lurid accounts have been published of the antics of these often unsafe, badly designed yachts. I am sincere when I doff my hat to those stubborn sailors who made world cruises in Colin Archer rescue ketches, Falmouth Quay punts, Block Island ketches, and the like. I imagine it was in spite of rather than because of their ships that they came through unscathed!

5

I recall a desperately hot and frustrating beat north from Kauai in one of these monuments to the nineteenth century. Out of kindness to the owner I will not mention her name. She was thirty-six feet long with a fifteen-foot beam, and she drew nearly seven feet with all the needless surplus weight that was aboard. She was a lovely thing to look at, as most ship models are. She had deadeyes and lanyards, double-blocked halyards, a clipper bow with figured trailboards, and turned taffrails. When the wind touched twenty knots, the racket from her rigging alone struck fear into the bravest heart among us. She would tack in a hundred and seventy degrees, which meant that the closest she could point in a seaway was about 85 degrees to the apparent wind. In 1812, when the type first appeared, this was not considered bad sailing, but today I consider it nigh unto treason!

We beat endlessly into eight- to twelve-foot trade wind seas (that's rough work with the cabin soaked in tepid sea water and the yacht shouldering the occasional breaking crest), and after ten days we had made good only about 120 miles to the north! My own comments at that point were not suitable for publication, but I wouldn't be surprised if some strange atmospheric disturbances were noted about then by a passing satellite.

By way of contrast, I made the same trek north in another type of vessel—my own sloop *Laguna*, my first love as far as ships go. *Laguna* was a moderate-displacement sloop-cutter of French construction thirty-five feet long, with a beam of nine feet and a draft of five feet five inches. She had a great fifty-two-foot spar stuck rather strangely through her middle. She was of normal wooden construction with nearly 50 percent of her weight in outside ballast. I had used her as an ocean racer for some years, and she had won her share of races, including the great "International Enchilada Derby" to Ensenada.

I had been told by sailors of the old school that she was no cruiser, being too light, too narrow, and too tall, and not having a diesel engine. As a matter of fact, the engine she had hardly ever worked at all, but I cruised many a happy mile without it. Perhaps if I had shortened her rig, put the ballast inside, and cut off her beautiful canoe stern they would have been less critical.

The trip north from Kauai to the horse latitudes about 34 degrees north was done hard on the wind in one tack, and it was done in eight days. (I still think that if you are forced to beat in the open sea you should do it fast and get it over with!) Strangely enough, when I returned from a pleasant voyage to Hawaii after three months' ab-

Laguna had a beautiful canoe stern. Note that the run aft is narrow and deep, causing amazing broaching tendencies!

A traditional cruising ketch of the old school. She is *Faith*, owned and built by Larry Baldwin.

sence, the same pundits were standing around saying she was too tall, too light, et cetera, et cetera. When I asked them how their summer cruises had been, I discovered that none of them had gone anywhere at all. Rather, they had sat around and talked about their great cruising boats while I had done a five-thousand-mile cruise in a yacht that was "no cruiser."

The traditional cruising ketch as found in American cruising lore just doesn't have it when going to weather in a seaway. True, it may be more comfortable than some light-displacement vessels, but then so is a hotel. A point that is perhaps lost on some is that the fast boat spends less time at sea, thereby reducing the duration of your discomfort, which any yacht at sea causes in abundance and which is apparently cumulative. Although the relationship between speed and comfort is negative (the faster you go, relative to sea conditions, the more uncomfortable you get), the fast boat gives you flexibility. When you want, you can slow down, and in good weather you can fly.

In addition to having weatherly ability, the light-displacement yacht requires less sail area, is easier on her rigging, is easier to maintain, and costs less all around to operate. Most important, the light-displacement vessel is a pleasure to sail. And, after all, it's for the pleasure of it that you go voyaging. If you say you are crossing the ocean to see strange and exotic lands you're kidding yourself. You can do that far better and more inexpensively by airplane, and you don't even have to invest in a boat. (You can do it in a great deal more comfort, to boot.) If, on the other hand, the sailing is more important than the seeing, and if you sail from a love of ships and the sea, you will want a ship that will really sail. The true source of pleasure in a passage is the performance of your little ship.

Just as an illustration of the heresy I have been pronouncing, you might read Erling Tambs's excellent account, *The Cruise of the Teddy*, and compare it with John Guzzwell's *Trekka Round the World*. While Tambs's easygoing account glosses over many of the hardships of ocean voyaging, it shows only too well the amount of sweat and muscle needed to voyage on an old Colin Archer lifeboat neither designed nor built for the task. Guzzwell's account, on the other hand, shows his pleasure in sailing his little twenty-foot yawl. Guzzwell is also a master of understatement, but I have never heard him mention anything but good concerning *Trekka*.

The modern ocean cruising craft will differ little from a good competitive ocean racer. Being free of the restrictions of the notorious racing rules, however, she can be as fast as her designer cares to make her. That may sound strange to those who have always accepted the idea that a cruising yacht is a slow yacht. Actually, since a racing boat need only beat her time allowance, she need not be fast at all. The racing boat is most often designed to take advantage of loopholes in the rule, sometimes actually losing speed but gaining valuable handicap. Quite often in ocean racing it isn't the fastest yacht that has the best corrected time but the most cleverly designed one. The cruising yacht, on the other hand, has only one job, and that is to get her crew safely from point A to point B and as swiftly and comfortably as possible.

It is perhaps difficult to find an architect who can design a fine cruising yacht, since his success depends so much on the racing records of his products. Some cruising yacht designers in America really design only coastwise cruising houseboats, suitable for the opulent yachtsman to show off to the gathered multitude on opening day ceremonies, but totally unsuited for voyaging. Marketing research has shown that the wives often choose the yachts, and far too many concessions are made to styling considerations at the expense of features that are necessary for the safety of the crew offshore. Fortunately, the yachtsmen with domineering wives who usually buy these design mistakes seldom get to sea seriously.

The modern trend toward tubby things with porches, verandas, picture windows, and high-bulwarked center cockpits leaves me with great pity for the poor souls afflicted with them. Can you imagine being hove to in anything more than a moderate gale with those picture windows standing exposed to breaking seas and that great freeboard, "absolutely essential for that apartment-like feeling of space below," acting like hundreds of square feet of sail that cannot be reefed? Not me!

I would suggest that if you want a yacht that's like an apartment, then buy an apartment—not a yacht—and live happily ever after! If the call of the sea is strong in your ears, then discard your wife if necessary and buy a yacht that will give you a fighting chance for survival should the need arise. Don't let a used car salesman turned yacht broker, nor an advertising writer, nor a comfort-seeking wife deter you from making an informed and logical choice.

A good sea boat will have moderate freeboard so that she doesn't sheer around when lying ahull in a seaway or when anchored. She will have a flush cambered deck or a deckhouse of minimum height so that seas breaking aboard are offered a minimal target for their destructive efforts. She will probably not have the space of a grand ballroom in her, unless she is rather large, but she won't endanger

A forty-foot fiberglass motor sailer with a center cockpit and a great cabin aft.

Note the flimsy taffrail and gingerbread windows.

you and yours in a blow either. Believe me, I would rather have a little less headroom and space while in port than have to patch up stove-in cabin windows in a gale at sea. Besides, as Nathaniel Herreshoff was once heard to remark, "If you must sleep standing up, then you must have headroom in your yacht."

I am sure that none of this will make much sense to the advertising writer, the average yacht broker, or the average yacht builder if he has never taken a knockdown a thousand miles from land or been forced to lie ahull to a force ten gale.

It seems to me that the modern ocean racing yacht as designed by Lapworth and Gary Mull in our country, by Cuthbertson and Cassian in Canada, and by Nicholson and Laurent Giles and partners in England are far more suitable with minor alterations for ocean voyaging than are some of the hideous creations now being foisted off as voyaging yachts.

In general design, then, I would lean toward moderation in all things. Highly original designs can sometimes be quite satisfactory, but more often they are not. The longest possible waterline per dollar spent is a good criterion in the absence of any other guideline. Forget the thirty-one footer with bunks for nine; you could never tolerate that many people on a thirty-one footer anyway. Find a design with a proven racing record, for she has had to sail under every condition the sea can throw at her to earn it.

The looks of a vessel are important, but your first viewing will probably be of the part that is least important. What you see above the water doesn't necessarily tell you what you're getting, because it is the *underbody*, not the topsides, that has to look good to make the yacht sail. Character yachts are so called usually because that is all they have to recommend them. I don't know how many yachts are sold to novices on the basis of their likenesses to ship models without the poor suckers ever having looked at the hull out of the water!

When you have made all the compromises and judgments, go ahead and buy. Find yourself an expert (someone who has crossed at least one ocean and is ready to do it again) and follow his advice as you modify and refine her for the type of voyaging you plan to do. Before you set off, however, I would strongly recommend at least a year of active ocean racing. Perhaps it sounds strange to tell a cruiser to go racing, but I have seen more voyages fail from lack of experience than from anything else. If you can stick out a season of ocean racing and still enjoy yachting, then there is real hope that cruising is your meat.

Seaworthiness

I take the term *seaworthiness* to include a number of things—first, the ability to stay afloat under adverse conditions; second, the ability to keep water out of the boat and off the crew; third, the ability to carry sail in a blow; and fourth, weatherly ability during a blow in rough seas. This last can at times be the most vital ability of all, considering the number of yachts lost on lee shores.

The ability to stay afloat is accomplished by first-class design and construction. This does not imply heavy construction, as one can stray too far in that direction and add weight that overburdens the yacht. Adequate reserve buoyancy is gained by moderate overhangs and sufficient freeboard for the displacement of the vessel. Beware of extreme overhangs and of the overly sharp or narrow sterns that are sometimes found in yachts built to the International Offshore Rule. Such designs lack good reserve buoyancy, are apt to pound at sea, and tend to be rather wetter than boats with more moderate overhangs coupled with a goodly sheer.

The cockpit, if any, must be self-bailing and as small as will minimally seat the crew. Beware of the flush deck with just a foot well. Although such a design does increase deck space, it is incredibly wet at sea. The wise crew spends little time on deck when at sea unless they are on watch, preferring to rest below where the risks of exposure are less.

Cockpit drains never seem to be adequate. On *Astrea*, my forty-foot ketch, I had four one-and-one-half-inch drains in a cockpit seven by four feet, and still there was always too much water sloshing around in heavy weather. On *Dawn Treader*, my most recent yacht, I have four three-and-one-half-inch holes leading directly from the cockpit through the transom. These have plastic flaps to keep following seas from entering, and they make her look a lot like a Flying Dutchman dinghy from behind. Looks be damned, I say. I'd rather have dry feet and a cockpit that won't take control of the yacht in heavy weather.

Cockpits should never open directly into the cabin, unless the cabin also is self-bailing. There should be a bridge deck or at least a bulkhead rising to the level of the cockpit seats. The companionway should be soundly built and through-bolted and fitted with sliding washboards rather than swinging doors. Swinging doors look very nice, but in a small yacht they steal cockpit space. They also seem prone to excessive leaking and to falling off when you lurch into them in a seaway.

Someone, someday, will invent a waterproof seat hatch for the cockpit, but right now they all seem to leak. In spite of complicated drain systems, gaskets, and other artifices, no yacht I have yet seen has cockpit lockers that stay dry. *Laguna* gathered about seventy-five gallons a day when hard on the wind offshore, and *Astrea* gulped down about fifty. *Dawn Treader's* seats will never leak—because she has no hatches in the cockpit. You may well say that *your* seats never leak, that you have turned the hose on them and poured buckets of water over them. But two days in the trades will find leaks you never even dreamed of. The only sure bet is to have some other method of getting to the stowage under the seats and to forget cockpit hatches.

Coamings should be from thirteen to eighteen inches high, measured from the seat. A cockpit without coamings, like those on Sea Witches, Sea Wolfs, and others with only footwells aft, is an absolute horror at sea. When the hobbyhorsing starts (and such yachts are prone to it), they scoop up astonishing quantities of water, which sluices down the deck and arrives at thirty miles an hour directly on the seat of your pants. I have a film taken on one of these vessels, showing a foot-high wall of water coming down the high side, with a crew member surfing along in his sleeping bag about to be deposited in the cockpit well. Even if you don't like the looks of coamings, at least rig temporary ones before going offshore. A slight outward angle to the coamings does a lot to ease the sore back that a few weeks at the tiller will give you. The angle, coupled with a generous cap rail, seems to help keep water from sloshing into the cockpit.

The cabin must be strongly built in relation to its profile height. Surprisingly, the cabin seems to be the Achilles heel of many an otherwise sound design. *Tzu Hang*, owned by Miles and Beryl Smeeton, was pitchpoled a thousand miles or so off the Chilean coast and lost her cabin trunk of heavy teak without a trace. (John Guzzwell, who helped repair her, tells me that thereafter they always referred to the six-by-six-foot hole it left as the "main hatch.") *Tzu Hang* was a well-designed and well-built yacht, immaculately maintained and well found. Her voyages both before and after her pitchpoling accident were adequate evidence of her suitability. After the crew had made their way to Coronel under jury rig, Guzzwell built a stronger cabin, which was badly damaged when the Smeetons set out once again to round the Horn and were rolled over while lying to a gale quite close to the position of the pitchpoling.

Vertue XXXV was struck by a freak wave while lying to a sea anchor in a hurricane off Bermuda, and her doghouse was split for several feet and a cabin window was stove in. The list is long.

The ultimate, of course, is to have no cabin sticking up there to be torn off, but this is not always possible in a small yacht. Instead, it is well to have a cabin well rounded at the corners and to have its sides at a good angle to the deck—45 degrees of angle is none too much. That modern menace, the doghouse or vomitorium, is best left ashore along with the Dutchman's anchor. The trunk must be well bolted through the cabin carlins if the yacht has wooden deck construction or well glassed in otherwise. The better rounded and moulded everything is, the less surface for the sea to react upon. Remember, the sphere is the best shape for strength.

Cabin windows are a constant problem in modern yachts because a plastic window is cheap and a good metal-framed glass window is expensive. Guess which one a builder will use if no one complains? It is better to have a lot of small windows or portholes rather than the large picture windows now offered by many designers. Of course, if you have a low cabin profile to begin with, the windows will probably be small of necessity. Take a look at the boats of Australia and New Zealand, and seldom will you find a doghouse or large windows on them. They are built to sail in the Tasman Sea, and the sailors and builders are no fools! Some voyagers, if stuck with large windows, install Plexiglas shutters about one-half inch or so thick. This can be effective, but it is only a coverup for bad design at best.

Hatches are seldom as watertight as they should be, but a double-scuppered coaming and a little ingenuity will usually dry them up. Skylights made of wood belong on air shafts, not on yachts. I remember the one on *Laguna* well. Every month or so I would get out my tools and "fix" the skylight. It was lovely to look at, and its pebbled glass panels lit the galley beautifully, but it leaked like the very devil offshore. If we were boarded by a sea anywhere on the forward quarter, the cabin became an instant shower bath. I even used to sleep in my oilskins offshore if our course was to weather. I tried canvas covers, rubber seals, prayers, and curses on the thing, and while it looked very nautical, it was a lousy shipmate.

The deck must be strong enough to withstand the occasional breaking crest that falls on it, and not so cluttered that the crew finds it difficult to work on dark, stormy nights. Decks on production fiberglass boats have been getting thinner and thinner, to the point where some of them feel like a trampoline if jumped on. This does not mean they are dangerously weak, but it gives me the jimjams to walk on one!

I favor the fiberglassed plywood deck on a wooden yacht because it doesn't leak. I had Iroko decks on *Astrea*, and they gave a wonderful footing at sea. However, they are murder on bare feet in the tropics, and they were always needing to be payed and caulked. Some Oriental builders favor a fiberglass deck with a teak overlay. Such decks are beautiful when they are new, but in time they develop the most astonishing ways of leaking.

The modern balsa-cored fiberglass deck as specified by Cuthbertson and Cassian and as built by Capital Yachts is wonderful. It is strong, light, and rigid. It allows more weight to be put into ballast or in stores. Perhaps Herreshoff was right when he observed that excess weight belongs only on steam rollers!

In fiberglass yachts as well as on wood ones the joint between hull and deck often causes trouble. In the case of wooden yachts look for a thick sheer strake of very hard wood. This will hold the fastenings better than will the sheer strake that is just another plank. In older yachts with leaks where the hull and deck join, it is usually necessary to replace the sheer strake in order to get a good seal. Trying to seal the joint with compounds or fiberglass usually fails.

In fiberglass boats the problem is usually due to shoddy construction and poor quality control. A generous use of bolts and epoxy bonding agents usually cures the problem, and it is easily done. Robin Lee Graham, circumnavigating on *Dove*, had so many problems with a hull-deck joint that he ultimately discarded the yacht and got another one in which to finish the voyage.

The form of the hull is important to seaworthiness and is a source of endless controversy. Any hull form is based on many compromises among speed, maneuverability, comfort, and so on in order to get the most seaworthy hull. How one stretches the compromise depends a lot on the personality of the owner. Some, like myself, will sacrifice much to gain speed and maneuverability, perhaps at the expense of a little comfort and weight-carrying ability. Others, advocates of the John Hannah school of thought, will sacrifice performance, comfort, and perhaps seaworthiness to get enormous weight-carrying ability. These compromises are best worked out by a competent naval architect in the planning of a new yacht. If a used boat is in order, a good marine surveyor can comment on most designs.

Shapes of cruising yachts vary from the extreme of Slocum's *Spray*, which was bluff-bowed with little deadrise, and which had a narrow run aft, to modern designs with fine bows, arc bottoms, and broad flat runs aft, sometimes with bustles or kickers.

I personally prefer a long waterline with the maximum beam rather aft of amidships, allowing the bows to be rather fine with little flare. This combination I have found to be good for beating in rough seas, as the bow has no flare to suddenly catch the boat as she creams into a wave. The long waterline makes possible higher easily driven speeds. Such boats usually have a rather flat, straight afterbody and relatively hard bilges. This helps the yacht surf more readily, I believe, and reduces rhythmic rolling, while adding to the stiffness that allows sail to be carried when it's blowing.

Astrea had such lines combined with a long, straight keel. She was a most comfortable yacht at sea, but was burdened with rather too much wetted surface, which made her hard to maneuver and frustrating to sail in light airs. She compensated by a really remarkable turn of speed when the gale warnings flew, but in the more than twenty thousand miles that I sailed her, she was only in gale conditions for a little more than six days!

Dawn Treader, as yet untried on an ocean voyage, is of similar but more radical form. She is of extremely light displacement and has a modern pendulum fin keel and a spade rudder. She should be much better in the usual winds one encounters while at sea, while I shudder to think of what may happen in a gale. If she is like others of her general type, she should be nearly supersonic! Hulls of this form lie to steadily and self-steer as well as or better than their long-keeled cousins. The low wetted surface of this type of yacht allows her to give to the breaking crests when lying ahull. *Trekka* lay to quite well, and her drift was square, leaving a noticeable slick to weather.

The bow should not be too V-shaped, but should be slightly rounded, or it will plunge deeply and will require excessive freeboard forward to keep the decks dry. It takes a good designer to make that compromise. The entries on a Cal 40 and a Cal 36, both designed by Bill Lapworth, look very much alike to the uninformed. The 40 is slightly fuller and a little less V-shaped below the waterline. The 40 tends to pound when going to weather in a chop, and the 36 does not. Surprisingly, though, the 40 goes like the proverbial train just the same.

When researching hull forms it is wise to seek the advice of an expert—not the kind found sitting at yacht club bars, but the kind found out on the docks working on boats.

A yacht must be buoyant if she is to be seaworthy, but buoyancy can be overdone. The famous Colin Archer rescue ketches suffered from too much buoyancy rather than too little. They would pop up and down like corks unless they were heavily laden, when they were no more buoyant than other yachts and had enormous wetted surfaces. Buoyancy is better attained by use of modern hull forms and light displacement. A light-displacement hull can be loaded below its lines without adding so much to wetted surface—and wetted surface is the name of the game when you want performance.

Boats lacking sufficient buoyancy for offshore work are typified by the six- and eight-meter boats developed under the International racing rule. Their offshore sailing characteristics most closely resemble those of a submarine. While they can be made seaworthy by use of watertight hatches and so on (Vito Dumas sailed an eight meter yacht single-handed across the Atlantic), they are not a great pleasure to sail with their streaming decks and cramped accommodations.

The ability to carry sail under gale conditions can be obtained by a number of means, some of which must be compromised for the sake of comfort. A beamy boat with a hard turn to her bilges will have good initial stability and will be stiff. She can carry a good press of sail up to a point, but if she doesn't have a great enough ballast ratio she may suddenly begin to lose righting moment and capsize. *Astrea* had only 30 percent of her weight in ballast, and she was very beamy. In a gale she often gave me anxious moments when she would heel beyond 50 degrees. At that point it always felt as if she was going all the way. She never did, although she did get over to 90 degrees more than once. The cure, of course, was to reef early and avoid the rush, but performance suffers when you have to reef too soon.

The narrow, deep craft with relatively slack bilges and a high ballast ratio will not be stiff initially, but as she heels she becomes more and more resistant to her press of sail. Her pendulumlike keel acts as a lever to restore stability. The tender, narrow boat will roll perhaps more than the beamy, stiff boat, but she will roll slowly and without the "jerk" associated with overly stiff boats. Obviously, the compromise between the two types of vessels is a delicate one. I would go for a boat a little on the stiff side and sacrifice a bit of comfort so that I could carry sail when it counts. The excess weight that seems to find its way into every cruising boat will help damp the sometimes violent motion of the excessively stiff design. There are those who claim that spread-out weight dampens the motion and those who claim that the weight must be concentrated in the middle of the boat to reduce motion. I really don't know the correct procedure. I do know that Sir Francis Chichester changed to a more concentrated weight distribution in *Gipsy Moth IV* and found the motion much improved.

Internally ballasted yachts are a horror that should be avoided at all costs. They usually lack weatherly ability and they are rhythmic rollers of championship caliber.

Two clipper-bowed yachts. Note the hollowed waterlines and the large

Another common design characteristic on so-called cruising yachts is that nautical monstrosity (or objet d'art, depending on your point of view), the clipper bow. While the fiddle head and trailboards of the traditional clipper bow are without doubt beautiful on a clipper ship, they are ridiculous on a yacht under sixty or so feet in length. A true clipper bow has hollowed waterlines below the load waterline and considerable flare above. On a small yacht there isn't enough length in which to fair the lines cleanly into the rest of the boat. The result is that at sea the bow plunges neatly into a wave — those hollow lines "cutting" the water just as they were designed to

18

degree of flare in the topsides.

do—and then the flared section comes into contact with the wave just like a wooden wedge into concrete. The boat shudders, loses two knots, smacks another wave, stops, and drifts off to leeward. It's called hobbyhorsing, and it's just about the most aggravating thing a yacht can do short of sinking outright. The yacht must be long enough to provide outstanding longitudinal stability to avoid sticking that terrible flare into wave tops. Clipper bows are not the only ones to hobbyhorse, although they almost always do. Any bow with too much flare and hollow underwater entry will do so if the yacht has a lot of rocker to her underbody and is too beamy and short.

19

There has been more nonsense written about the proper shape for the stern than perhaps any other part of the hull. Proponents of double-enders point out that the sharp stern "parts the following sea," thus reducing chances of being pooped, while the transom stern boys point out the great reserve buoyancy of that type. It is true that lifeboats have pointy sterns *and* that they are designed to endure heavy weather. It also should be pointed out that lifeboats aren't *going* anywhere! They need only sit around and survive until someone picks them up. As a matter of fact, lifeboats have sharp sterns because they often have to maneuver astern to pick up survivors, and the double-ender goes astern easily. The lifeboat stern is not dry in a seaway with a force six or seven sea running. When underway, the narrow run associated with the sharp stern raises a tremendous quarter wave and actually causes following seas to break far sooner than does a well-designed transom or counter stern. Whether or not the shape of the stern causes disturbance to following seas depends on the shape of the underbody, not the part you can see.

I have sailed on boats with short, sawed-off vertical transoms, canoe sterns, counters, and Colin Archer and lifeboat sterns on one occasion or another. *Laguna*, with her canoe stern, was pooped only once offshore, and that was in a force nine blow when I had slowed her down too much while running before the wind, and she was caught by a freak sea. I might note that at the time she was deep, five

Laguna had a moderate wineglass-shaped hull.

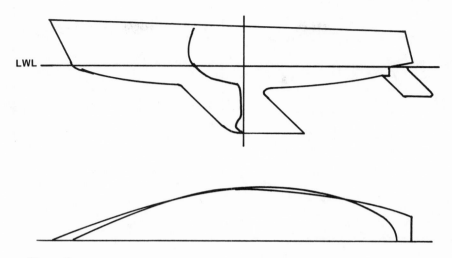

Figure 1.
Light-displacement hull form. Note low wetted surface, fin keel, spade rudder.

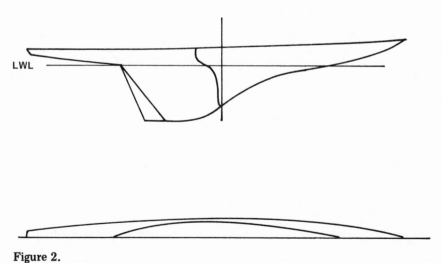

Figure 2.
A "meter boat." Extreme overhangs, short waterline, and narrow beam combine to defeat her as a sea boat.

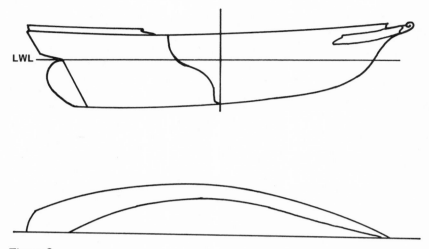

Figure 3.
Traditional clipper-bowed yacht. Note hollow waterline forward and heavy displacement.

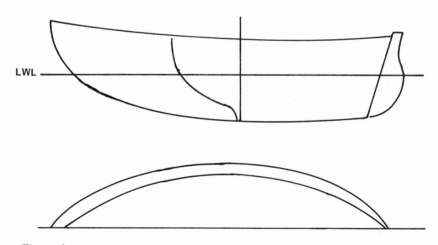

Figure 4.
Heavy-displacement double-ender of traditional design. Note large wetted surface, outboard rudder.

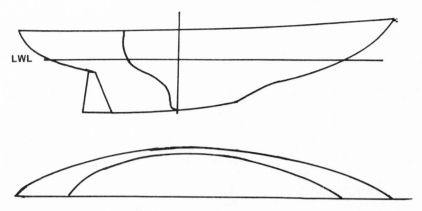

Figure 5.
Conservative canoe stern yacht. Moderate in displacement, the cutaway bow helps reduce wetted surface.

inches below her designed waterline, and had only about eighteen inches of freeboard aft.

Astrea had a broad semicounter stern with twenty-eight inches of freeboard, and she was never pooped even during her magnificent, frightening charge of 245 miles, noon to noon, on the fringes of a tropical storm in 1970. A thirty-three foot Colin Archer-type double-ender on which I sailed some time ago had thirty-six inches or so of freeboard aft and was of typical Norwegian construction. If she was running fast in force five or better, it was an instant cold sitz bath in the cockpit.

What is crucial in stern design, as far as seaworthiness is concerned, is the run aft and reserve buoyancy, which can be obtained either by good freeboard or beam above the waterline, or by the use of bustles or kickers below. Sharp or blunt, the stern must rise fully and smoothly to a following sea, or whoever is in the cockpit will curse the designer roundly. I personally favor the rather straight run aft from the midsection in order to provide a flatter quarter wave. The quest for the flattest possible quarter wave is, I believe, a major reason for the success of Bill Lapworth's designs. All but a few of them move quietly and efficiently, making relatively little "fuss." The more clumsy hull must heave to or drag warps to slow down, adding to the danger of being pooped, long before the modern, sweet-lined ocean racer will. A little reference to present day ocean racing may illustrate the point. These racers carry on with their heaviest

A modern spade rudder with a relatively straight run aft.

Moderate overhang and the use of a "bustle" give good reserve buoyancy.

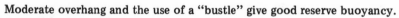

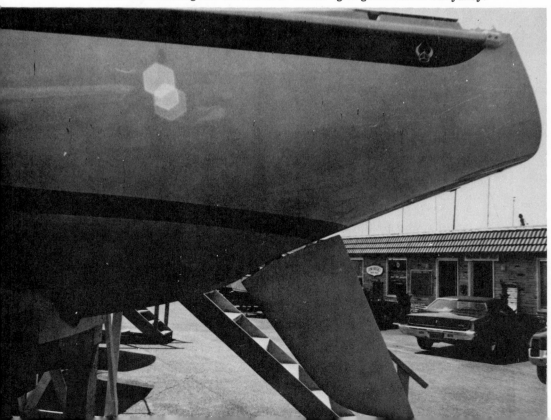

Dawn Treader gains buoyancy from generous beam aft. Note the extremely low wetted surface and flat run aft.

Conventional cruising stern. Note high deadrise, large wetted surface, clumsy lines.

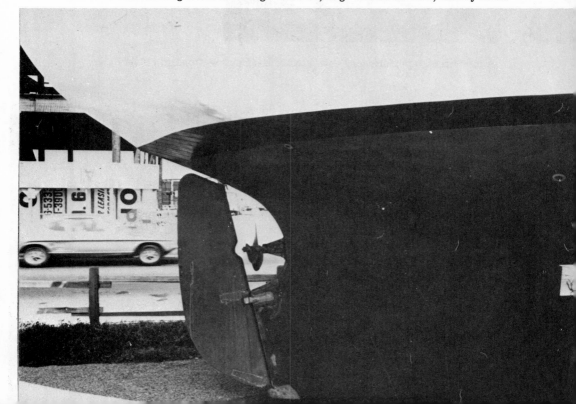

A modern high-performance entry. Note U-shaped sections and little flare.

spinnaker straining in weather that has the average "cruiser" dragging warps and praying for a break in the weather. And note—you will seldom, if ever, find a sharp stern in the racing fleet.

Finally, the larger the yacht you are contemplating, the more errors you can tolerate in hull form with regard to seaworthiness. A larger yacht will naturally have more freeboard and more waterline length to help out in tough situations, and she may have more stability than a smaller yacht. Her motion will be more kindly, due to her greater weight, in spite of design errors. On all other counts, though, absolute attention must be paid to seaworthy design.

Size

While the absolute size of your yacht is often of great interest to your fellows at the yacht club and to the dock walker with visions of glory in his eyes, it is actually less of a factor in voyaging yachts than one might believe. The yacht you select should be no larger than you need to carry the crew and necessary stores. Anything more becomes both a physical and a financial burden. Many a fine cruise has been spoiled by the tyranny of a great yacht and its endless demands for muscle at sea and maintenance in port.

The smallest practical size for an ocean voyaging yacht depends on the skipper and crew. Some folks seem to need "all the comforts of home." My advice to them is to *stay home*. Part of the fun of ocean sailing is to discover that you can be happy with so little when it becomes necessary.

The large boat must have large gear, anchors, tackle, and so on, and thus must have an electric windlass and other muscle-savers, which require batteries and a generator, which require a large engine, which requires a still larger vessel to hold it all, and then the vicious circle starts over.

I took *Astrea* to Hawaii in 1970. Although she was forty feet on deck, she was fifty-two feet overall, which was a bit much for a crew of two. I had been taken in by the need for an ever larger yacht. While I painted and cleaned, "fixed" the engine, sweated over sixty-pound anchors swinging on three hundred pounds of chain (they turned out to be too light), broke bobstays (sixty-five dollars each), shattered deck fittings (ever try to find a Merriman deck eye in Hawaii?), cursed the refrigerator (it took three or four hours of engine time to keep it cold for twenty-four hours), and struggled manfully to reef that terrible five-hundred-square-foot mainsail that was just barely adequate to push all the weight in equipment, I thought deeply about big boats.

I thought of my friend Ivo Van Laage and the nineteen-foot sloop *VLaag* he had sailed out from Holland, with not even a winch aboard, let alone any engine or refrigerator. But there we both were, me with an investment of forty thousand dollars and lots of sweat and calluses, and he with about one thousand dollars in his craft. The difference in price alone would have set me free to sail the ocean years and years earlier! When he and I would sit in the afternoons on *Astrea*'s fantail and play Baroque flute and guitar duets and modern jazz interchangeably (sometimes at the same time) I would think guiltily of work I had left undone, while he tootled away without a care in the world!

I used to enviously watch Wayne and Dottie Hagerman set out from their Rawson thirty *Willingly*, to do a little exploring while I "maintained my yacht" and listened despondently when they told me they had used only eight gallons of fuel in a year of cruising.

I thought much about John Guzzwell and his little twenty-foot *Trekka*, which he sailed around the world and which circumnavigated again after he regretfully sold her.

I remembered a day in San Diego when Eric Hiscock had kindly invited me to see his new fifty-foot steel ketch *Wanderer IV*. I had just got *Astrea* ready to cruise and was naturally quite proud. Hiscock seemed strangely nostalgic as we talked about the merits of our former yachts, and I sensed that he had rather more love for his old sloop *Wanderer III* than for his new yacht. After the Hawaiian cruise of 1970 I saw the reason. I would have given anything I had to get back to my old *Laguna* after five thousand miles on the man-killer *Astrea*!

Another factor that must be considered is the economic one. The purchase price is a small part of the actual cost of a cruising boat. I would consider that on *Astrea* I added roughly 35 percent of her original cost in preparing her for cruising. The larger the yacht, the larger will be the winches, blocks, stoves, refrigerators, and so on that she will require. The cost of marine equipment seems to increase as the square of the size. A stainless steel turnbuckle for *Astrea* cost fifty-four dollars. She was ketch rigged and needed eighteen turnbuckles. That's over nine hundred dollars! For *Dawn Treader*, on the other hand, I paid exactly one thousand dollars for a mast, all the wire, turnbuckles, halyards, blocks, toggles, three jibs, and a mainsail, as well as the boom and all the fittings! I shudder when I think of what all that gear cost for *Astrea*, which was only thirteen feet longer, was less safe in a seaway, had fewer berths, and went to weather more or less like a brick wall. I can tell you this, however.

The difference in cost would be enough to provision *Dawn Treader* for two or three years of happy sailing.

If one has a large family for whom space must be provided, then size will give it to you, but under any other condition I don't think size is worth the cost.

I don't believe size matters much as far as safety is concerned if the yacht is well designed, soundly built and equipped, and, most important, intelligently handled. Under most conditions you are likely to encounter at sea the small yacht is the equal of the larger one, not counting the roaring forties, where most sailors will agree that the *Queen Mary* is none too large!

As always, there are notable exceptions to these "rules." Consider that *Tzu Hang*, which was forty-six feet long, was pitchpoled once and was later rolled right over, being dismasted both times. Before you snort, "Bad seamanship or preparation," let me hasten to assure you that that was definitely not the case, nor was the design in any way unusual for a yacht her size. Shackleton had sailed the same waters in a twenty-foot lifeboat around the Horn from Antarctica to bring help for his stranded expedition. Bill Nance sailed *Cardinal Vertue* (a twenty-five-foot sloop) west about the Horn, and there have been others. Surprisingly enough, it has been the larger yachts that have gotten into trouble. Perhaps the old British saying "It's not the ships, but the men in them" is a lot more true than those who tout large yachts would care to admit!

The small yacht has its limitations when it comes to creature comforts, of course. Her motion will be quicker than that of the larger vessel of the same general form, although probably not greater. While her lighter gear is easier to handle, it is nonetheless mounted on a less stable platform. It is said by some that the small yacht is more fatiguing to sail, but I have not found it so. The human body is remarkably adaptable and will adjust to the quick motion of the small yacht as well as to the slower motion of a larger one.

Every time I approach an anchorage on a big boat I wonder: Will there be room to maneuver inside? Will those huge anchors hold the first time? Will the engine work? Then, after miscellaneous backing and filling, shouting confused and garbled messages back and forth from the bow, (where the anchors are) to the stern (where the helmsman is watching the scenery and talking to the crews of other yachts rather than paying attention to my frantic shouts), we are finally anchored. Back and temper are totally shattered, and I have made a proper ass of myself before the assembled multitude.

No, give me the little yacht every time; her light gear and easily handled anchors more than compensate for her drawbacks. Give me the yacht that needs no electrical anchor winches that may fail or set the ship afire (that's happened to me, as well), and I will sit relaxed at sea with the wind vane doing all the steering, play my guitar languidly, and listen to the radio. If I have to reef, I will reef a little sail, not a great cover from a football field, and twenty minutes after I come to anchor I will be less tired than the fellow on the large yacht who has been comfortable all the way over but who has just expended three thousand calories and most of his credibility with the crew getting anchored.

Speed

It is customary in the United States to advertise as a cruising boat anything that is slow, clumsy, or just plain unsuitable for racing. This attitude has led to a lot of misconception among those who set out to find a voyaging craft. The truth is that the only difference between ocean racing and ocean cruising today is that when cruising you strike the spinnaker *before* the mast comes down!

Speed is obtained primarily by the longest practical waterline length and by good design. It has been a practice in the United States to seriously underrig cruising yachts, thus making them really motor sailers, dependent on their smelly engines.

The speed of a yacht is theoretically governed by her bow and quarter waves at 1.34 times the square root of her effective waterline length. This means that the theoretical maximum speed of a boat with a twenty-five-foot waterline would be $1.34 \times \sqrt{25}$, or $1.34 \times 5 = 6.7$ knots. The best day's run for such a craft, then, would be 160.8 nautical miles. That's all well and good, but what happens in practice? Under ideal cruising conditions (best point of sailing, a whole sail breeze, and a favorable sea condition for twenty-four straight hours) a well-designed cruising yacht will average about .9 times the square root of her waterline length, or, in the case of our twenty-five-foot waterline example, 4.5 knots, giving her a day's run, noon to noon, of 108 miles. The underrigged vessel, or one of less than first-class modern design, will make good only about .6 to .75 times the square root of her waterline, giving a day's run of 72 to 89 miles. This latter class would include Carol ketches, Sea Witches, and other museum pieces.

If we were to take the ideal case and increase the waterline length to thirty-six feet, our maximum day's run would theoretically increase to nearly 193 miles.

At this point, someone is bound to protest, "My Crab Crusher 30 hits eight and nine knots all the time, when the wind blows!" I am quite certain that the electronic speedometer, the little liar, does say that. Of course, boat salesmen have been known to change the calibration on these beauties to make a crab crusher seem to be what she is not. Tell me the day's run, and I will tell you how fast your boat is. Averages count; flash readings don't. Any vessel will exceed its theoretical hull speed momentarily, particularly when starting down the face of a big swell in a blow. Here gravity helps get the bows up on the bow wave that previously had been limiting speed, and the yacht "surfs" for a moment, greatly exceeding her hull speed. Speedometer watchers should also be cautioned that the water near the top of a swell is moving in the direction opposite to that of a running yacht and that these surface layers of water run past the little impeller of the speedometer and cause it to overregister.

Some truly fantastic days' runs have been recorded in modern yachts of low wetted surface and large sail area. Lapworth's Cal 40 is a prime example. When you turn a Cal 40 downwind in a blow, it begins to hold sustained surfing charges down the swells. Its light weight and clean lines make it a delight to steer, and its spinnaker runs regularly exceed two hundred miles a day, far beyond the theoretical maximum. I do not believe that any yacht except the high-performance dinghy really holds a sustained plane in the same sense as a power boat does, but it is easy to believe the possibility on boats like the Cal 40 when she is charging along with the bow wave back at the chainplates and arching five feet above the deck line.

Speed also is related to seaworthiness. The slow boat is usually slow for adequate reason — her lines are not fair. This means that she will suck up half the ocean in huge quarter waves long before her sweet-lined cousins will, and she will begin to disturb the following seas to the point that they break and leave her likely to be pooped under conditions in which the faster boat is still surfing along and making miles to avoid a depression.

Comfort

I have never been on a yacht that was comfortable at sea, and I have never known an experienced sailor who was terribly concerned about comfort. Maybe that's why we go to sea — to get away from the enervating "comfort" of our civilization! In any event, if comfort is your prime criterion in selecting a yacht, then you should do your voyaging on an ocean liner, where there is comfort galore.

Most yachts can be made quite comfortable while in port, but at sea I believe the best you can do is to partially ease the discomfort. Best of all, make a fast passage and then forget the discomfort while you tell the other voyagers that you never got your feet wet, and that your yacht is steady as a rock in a blow.

Comfort at sea is relative at best, but the human body can take it. Just try to avoid starvation, exhaustion, and fatal injury. If you need more than that, perhaps you should stay ashore and collect stamps.

To avoid starvation the yacht must have accessible stowage for food and plenty of it. Most important, the cook must have a spot where he can do his job efficiently in any conceivable weather. A hot meal is a great morale booster when you are hove to in a gale.

That astonishing practice of putting the galley aft under the main hatch strikes me as being suitable only for handing up snacks and beer to those in the cockpit while racing or for cooking while tied up to the yacht club dock. Most cruisers, however, take advantage of the table and eat below, where the soup is less likely to be invaded by a wave top. Try cooking in a blow with an aft galley, and interesting things are likely to happen. Someone inevitably will slide the hatch open (you thought the hatch was always open?) and lurch with his wet sea boots onto your hand or into the stew and set himself on fire by treading on the stove. (Believe it or not, I have seen all these things happen in aft galleys.) Or a goodly sea is whipped which inevitably finds its way into the rice or into the rising bread. Aft galleys are sold to women on the basis that they are indeed convenient places from which to cook and yell orders to the husband at the same time, but offshore they are really less than efficient.

A lot of sailors hold that the motion is less back aft than it is forward. Well, perhaps, but it seems to me that it is the whole boat that must cross the waves, not just the front half. Both *Laguna* and *Astrea* had galleys located in the forward half of the salon, slightly aft of the mast. They both had head doors just opposite. The doors made a great place to lean — after I removed the doorknobs, which proved to be more deadly than a good left hook.

An added advantage of the forward galley is that if you have unannounced guests — and you often will when cruising — they don't climb down through the garbage dump and laundry to get into the main cabin. Rather, the cookery is located somewhat forward and hidden by a convenient bulkhead. The forward position seldom allows feet in the soup, and it is drier, although I once had a pot of spaghetti escape from *Laguna*'s stove and attack me clear back in the main salon one evil night in the trade winds. U-shaped galleys are quite comfortable; the stove is on one side, the sink on another, and work space on the third. The floor area for such an arrangement should be as small as possible so the cook can hold himself in place.

To avoid exhaustion, particularly with man-and-wife crews, I would say that some self-steering system is nearly essential. I have made my cruises watch and watch with a crew of two, and I wouldn't trade the experience for anything. But there's nothing nicer than standing your watch below at the chart table with a good book, taking an occasional look out the hatch for the odd freighter. (Self-steering systems will be discussed in Chapter 5.)

The motion of almost any yacht under fifty feet in length at sea will require a good bit of acrobatic ability and energy from her crew. There seems to be a rather constant effort to stay put. To those who believe that their legs will weaken and atrophy at sea, perform the following exercise fifteen times a day: climb up and down a well greased ladder about five feet tall, while a few of your friends rotate the ladder in a five-foot circle, while raising it up and down about six feet, dousing you with cold buckets of water. This will simulate the process of getting on deck and below while at sea.

After a spell of heavy weather a strange lethargy comes over me — that old enemy, fatigue. Fatigue will spoil a voyage by making you less observant and slowing down your mental and physical reactions. It reduces your motivation to reef when the time comes and may get you into serious trouble. Try to reduce fatigue by having a comfortable place to lounge about in the main salon and by having secure bunks where you can really sleep without having to clutch for handholds. The prudent sailor gets all the sleep he can, for he never knows when conditions may make sleep impossible for several days.

The constant blast of wind, so pleasant for day sailing, can wear you out on a passage. Avoid it by the use of good high weather cloths and dodgers. Keep as dry as possible by making certain that cabin windows and decks are watertight, a feat seldom attempted seriously in coastwise boats. There is absolutely no comparison between the leaking you see in soundings and that which you get offshore. And nothing is less conducive to restful sleep than a streaming wet bunk and clothing.

I don't know exactly how one avoids serious injury at sea, but I have never suffered anything worse than a broken hand and a finger or two and an occasional bruise. It goes without saying that you should use extreme caution around highly stressed parts and avoid inherently dangerous equipment. First on my list of things to avoid are reel winches that carry wire halyards. The brakes that lock the halyard aloft, often fail, allowing the winch, handle and all, to spin like the very devil as the sail comes down. Many crewmen have been cracked in the head by these whirling dervishes, leaving them unconscious for many hours. I have broken my hand more than once on these creations of the devil, and Merriman Bros.!

It is not uncommon for the helmsman to doze off and fall across the cockpit, cracking a rib or a skull on the opposite sheet winches. Proper design minimizes the number of projections a falling crew member is likely to crash into. A short life line also helps.

Removing all projecting doorknobs, handles, and sharp corners below and all toe stubbers on deck is a relentless project of mine on any yacht I sail. *Astrea* had a jib fairlead in the middle of the walkway aft from the foredeck. After four different people had broken toes on it, it gained almost international notoriety. Certainly the most uncluttered layout both on deck and below is the best insurance against serious injury.

Ability to Carry Weight and Stores

It is true beyond a doubt that a large boat will carry more weight than a small one, but some large boats lose performance more rapidly when they do. In a large vessel a good deal of the useful weight of burden is taken up with large engines, fuel, refrigerators, radios, batteries, generators, and other "necessities" that often afflict large yachts. When it comes time to put aboard stores, therefore, the yacht may already be below her lines. The smaller yacht is not so likely to be burdened with useless fillups and so can carry a higher proportion of her weight in stores. An added problem of the heavy-displacement vessel is that as you sink her below her lines with too much weight, you increase her already great wetted surface and spoil what little performance she had to begin with. Once you have spoiled a yacht's potential by overloading, she will really need the big engine and fuel supply. Many American cruising yachts are little more than motor boats with sails, presumably for the purpose of hoisting on nice days when a picture is needed to send home to Aunt Maude. But what happens when the engine runs out of fuel? Get a larger vessel. The old law of diminishing returns catches up sooner when you begin to overload a yacht than when you begin to rebuild a 1931 Essex.

Take another approach to the weight problem. Suppose you have a relatively light-displacement vessel. Since she will be designed to sail rather than motor, she will not need a monstrous engine and fuel supply to get her to her destination. (Wasn't that why we all bought sailboats?) Her size can already be smaller. Since she will be faster, she will spend fewer days at sea and thus need fewer supplies. Because she can be smaller, she will need less crew, who will need fewer supplies, et cetera, et cetera. But if you carry this to extremes, the exercise can get absolutely ridiculous, so another compromise must be sought. The point in question is where to make the compromise.

The size of the crew often dictates just how many supplies must be carried. I always figure on one-half gallon of water per man-day. That works out to about 5 pounds per man per day, figuring something for the weight of the tank. I like to carry 60 days' water for the whole crew, for a dismasting offshore can mean slow progress back to port. If I can eliminate one crew member by having an easier sailing rig or a smaller boat, I save 300 pounds of weight, not counting his weight, say 180 pounds; his gear, say 50 pounds; and his food and booze, say another 300 pounds. Believe it or not, if you look in Skene's *Elements of Yacht Design*, you will find that 900 pounds will sink our theoretical boat with a twenty-five-foot waterline about one full inch, regardless of her original displacement! You must make your own decision as to whether a crewman is worth his weight, or whether the 100 gallons of diesel fuel he replaces is worth more.

Perhaps a quick design analysis will illustrate my point. *Dawn Treader* is 27 feet long, 3 feet less than a Tahiti ketch. We both carry 65 gallons of water. My waterline measures $22\frac{1}{2}$ feet, while the Tahiti's is 26 feet. The Tahiti has 10 feet of beam, the same as *Dawn Treader*. The Tahiti spreads 470 feet of working sail, which is not nearly enough, so her designer recommends an engine to help out. *Dawn Treader* spreads only 340 feet of canvas and is somewhat over-canvassed. A Tahiti ketch will average about 50 to 60 miles a day under average sea conditions, while *Dawn Treader*'s type easily gets over 100!

The difference in space below is truly amazing. Six or seven inches of the Tahiti's beam is lost to her heavy planking and ribs. *Dawn Treader*'s hull is of $\frac{3}{8}$-inch fiberglass, so she loses only $\frac{3}{4}$ inch. The Tahiti has a designed displacement of a whopping 18,000 pounds, while her cousin tips the scales at less than 6,000. *Dawn Treader* could theoretically carry 12,000 pounds of weight before she had the same wetted surface (and horrid performance) as the Tahiti. Obviously, she will never get that much weight put into her, because she is a sailer and needs no engine to do her job. Thus the weight she can carry is useful weight — stores and water. She needs no large crew, since her gear is light and efficient, and the weight they would ordinarily command can be given over to such luxuries as musical instruments, diving gear, and a short-wave radio transmitter.

The great mistake in setting up a lighter-displacement vessel is to overload her with useless weight like refrigerators (which never seem to work anyway), oversize engines, generators, and so on, to the point that she is wallowing far below her lines, and then to shorten her rig so that she resembles a Tahiti ketch. She will then sail like a Tahiti, and it serves you right!

I would estimate that you could load down a good design about one inch for every five feet of waterline without seriously affecting performance, provided, of course, that ample freeboard remains. Heavy-displacement boats suffer rather more from this practice than do light boats, since they have greater wetted surface to begin with.

Maintenance

If you are on a budget, and most cruising folks are, it is wise to consider the cost of maintaining the yacht. I am something of a fanatic when it comes to maintenance. I care little what others may think, but I cannot rest easy at sea unless I know that I have personally checked everything on the boat and that everything is in first-class shape. A real cruising vessel should come into port after a cruise looking just the same as she did when she left. The streaked and stained look reflects on sloppy seamanship and a callous disregard for the only means of sustaining life on the sea. Have you ever noticed that it is these derelicts that usually provide the hair-raising cruising tales? The prudent yachtsman has a boat that looks as if it just came out of the builder's yard, and he seldom has any wild stories to tell, because his carefully maintained yacht has given him no uneasy moments.

Wooden vessels require more maintenance than do fiberglass ones, and iron boats apparently require endless maintaining. If you neglect a wooden hull, it will sink on you, while you can shamefully neglect a glass one, and it will just *look* as if its going to sink on you.

In terms of rigging and sails, the obvious choice is dacron sails and an aluminum mast stayed with stainless steel rigging. Today no one seriously considers cotton sails, which have a short life and a propensity for mildew. The wooden mast has an advantage over aluminum in that it perhaps can be bent farther before it breaks, but for maintenance it's terrible. Probably the greatest factor in the amount of upkeep a mast and rig will need is the relative displacement of the yacht. The heavy boat will have a bigger mast and rig and, because of its stiffness and weight, will be much harder on them mile for mile.

Varnished trim on a yacht looks elegant at a boat show, but you'll suffer dearly to keep it bright. At least every three months, and more often in the tropics, I found it necessary to renew *Astrea's* varnish work. Since there was at least an acre of the stuff on her, it seemed that no sooner was I finished with the job than it was time to begin again. How much nicer to use bleached teak for outside trim and have the elegant varnish work below, where it should last for years. Of course, there are those who say a yacht *must* have varnish or she becomes merely a workboat. To them I say that a little varnish, which can be easily done in an afternoon, is all a sensible cruising man needs to separate him from the ranks of fishermen.

Teak decks look grand, but they require more upkeep than do plain fiberglass ones. Also, fiberglass decks do not commit suicide when some guest drops fried chicken on them! Engines and various electrical gadgets will be covered in a later chapter, but suffice it to say that every mechanical gadget contributes to the time and expense of upkeep, and its value should be carefully considered and weighed against its maintenance requirements. I remember a wealthy soul whose cruising life was constantly made miserable by failures in his "essential" equipment. His air conditioner would break down at the most inopportune times; his engine would expire, sometimes forcing him to raise sail to make port before the bars closed; and the noise from his two diesel generators (one for backup) made the children's bedroom so loud they could not sleep despite extensive custom soundproofing. His tale was one of constant woe with his mechanical menagerie. Perhaps if he had considered a yacht instead of a floating hotel he would have been happier. I'm certain that a good mechanic could make an ample living just following him around fixing the weekly breakdowns.

Cost

The cost of a yacht is so variable that it's hard to say just when one has got his money's worth. Perhaps a good guide is to figure out how much you can afford, then cut that in half, saving the half for modification and equipment, and then buy the yacht. Many a cruising plan has foundered because the unwitting owner believed those advertisements that read "Sailaway, ready to go!" No yacht ever seems ready to go anywhere without extensive refitting, and the cost of equipment in smaller boats can easily reach or exceed the purchase price.

The used boat is often the best bet today unless you have a good place to build one of the excellent kit boats now available, or the skill and patience to build your own. When you buy a used yacht, the original owner has absorbed some of the cost of getting the vessel ready for sea.

Wooden yachts are getting scarce in this country, and today almost anything made of wood is foisted off as a cruising boat. The biggest problem with wooden vessels is the effect of aging and neglect. Many wooden yachts of sound design are just so deteriorated that it costs more than they are worth to get them into seaworthy shape. I've seen many would-be voyagers endlessly "getting the yacht ready," only to discover more things wrong as each part was uncovered and repaired. When bitterness and defeat set in, the yacht is sold at a loss, and the next poor soul takes over and begins again. I know of several of these "projects" that have had more than three owners in a ten-year period, and yet have never been to sea.

There are still builders who will undertake to build a sound wooden vessel, but the price is high. Some unscrupulous characters still build production wood boats in Taiwan, but the majority of them are of unsound materials and are dishonestly built at best. The designs of these atrocities are usually stolen or modified from a reputable designer's lines, while some apparently just "grow." These boats usually are sold with a good deal of traditional cruising claptrap and usually find their way to a yacht club dock in the hands of a weekend sailor who wants to be thought of as a voyager.

Then comes love! When a man falls in love with a yacht there is no price too high, regardless of the suitability of the design or construction. Some years ago I fell in love with a tall, slim, canoe-sterned French yacht whose price was considerably beyond my means (yachts, it seems, are *always* beyond my means). I used to go down to the landing and just stand there and dream of events that might make her mine. The years went by without any of the dreams coming true, and I finally bought another, newer, yacht. I was sailing her idly down the channels one afternoon, and what should I see but my old love tied loosely to a yacht broker's dock! I thought that I might see the owner there and explain my latest scheme to own her, so I tied up and hustled up to the office.

The owner wasn't there, and the broker explained that he had taken her in trade for a new yacht. I idly allowed as how I would trade my new fiberglass ocean racer and a few thousand dollars for her, just to tidy the place up, and to my delirious surprise he took me up on it! Although some may say that it's foolish to trade off a brand new fiberglass yacht for a twenty-year-old wooden one, I had what I wanted, and hang the cost!

I might add that old *Laguna* remains the finest thing in the way of a ship that I have ever sailed, regardless of her unending leaking, her squeaking in a seaway, and her maddening habit of broaching to when running under a heavy press of sail. She used to try to lose her gigantic mast at strange times and places, and she once took eleven knockdowns on a windy afternoon in the Alenuihaha Channel. Her engine seldom ran (she never really needed it anyway), and she was a champion rhythmic roller. Yet she never drowned any of her crew and never failed to turn heads as she charged through the racing fleet on a close reach. I raced her and cruised her many a happy mile, and no yacht will ever replace her, although many a finer yacht has been built, I'm sure.

Perhaps love is the overriding factor when deciding the value of a yacht. *Astrea* was obviously a better boat than was *Laguna*, but I sold her with relief and dry eyes, for she never really endeared herself to me. When you have studied all the factors, and balanced the virtues and vices, and heard the advice of all the experts, there will come along a craft that just "fits," and no amount of common sense, logic, engineering know-how, or divine intervention will keep you from having her. If you are one of those so lucky, cost is no object.

Multihulls

I suppose that no treatise on yacht designs should be without some salty comments at the expense of the multihull fraternity, but don't expect them from me. Like any other type of yacht, the multihull has both virtues and vices. While I have little offshore experience with the type, I have many friends who have. My comments are gleaned from their experience and some of my own, and any errors or omissions are my own.

The primary virtue of the multihull is an occasional astounding burst of speed. The prime drawback is that the multihull is not inherently monostable. It is just as stable upside down as it is right side up. Of course, a prudent skipper does not allow his yacht to get upside down in the first place!

The multihull configuration allows a tremendous amount of space to be crammed into a minimum length. It also has light weight and shallow draft and does not need a lot of sail area to get good performance as does a single-hull vessel. If soundly built *to the designer's specifications*, it is relatively safe and comfortable in a seaway, perhaps the equal of the conventional yacht in safety, and better in comfort. The drawback is excessive beam for its length, which makes finding a slip in the United States a bit of a problem, where every end tie seems already to have a multihull occupying it! Once away from the US, however, many simply can be run up on the nearest beach.

Modern laminated trimarans designed by Jay Kantola have arc bottoms and less extreme "greenhouses" for superstructure than do early trimarans, and many of the type have made fast, comfortable passages. By chance I have equipped several Kantola tris with self-steering gear, and the owners report that they self-steer well (better than a helmsman) on any point of sailing, an important consideration in any design. *Trollop*, for example, made Hawaii in twelve days in cruising trim, a feat hard to match in a good ocean racing sloop.

When five days out of San Diego bound for Hawaii in 1970 I happened to speak the Piver trimaran *Cetacean*, twenty-nine days out of the Galápagos Islands, just then quietly completing the first trimaran circumnavigation (for which the crew got precious little credit). I mention this because the trip up from the Galápagos to Los Angeles usually takes about sixty days and considerable use of the engine, and they had done it under sail in twenty-nine.

Even that bastion of tradition, the Seven Seas Cruising Association, now will allow membership by multihull owners. (I think that their opposition had sprung from distrust of the commonly encountered bearded, pot-smoking owners rather than from any real distrust of the design.) Of course, the ocean racing multihull is known for its fragility, and the even-year races to Hawaii are always good for a few laughs as the multihull fleet strews parts along the course.

As I see it, the secret to fast, safe multihull passages lies in sound design and construction and extreme consciousness of weight. The hulls must not be allowed to sink below the designer's marks or wetted surface will increase, bringing a disastrous loss of performance. The conventional craft can be treated much worse in this respect and still salvage some of its performance.

2   Construction and the
        Interior Layout

Yachts traditionally are built of wood, and there are some who say that if God had intended boats to be made of fiberglass he would have provided fiberglass trees. And, they might add, ferrocement trees!

Having sailed on all but ferrocement vessels, I can say that there are good and bad points to each. There is no greater source of pride than a fine wooden yacht with gleaming enamel and varnish. She calls forth images of the sea in the "good old days." I recall that *Astrea*, built of wood, was the source of many a favorable comment from passing fiberglass yachts as they were off for a sail while I was busily sanding and painting her elegant hull. There are those who say that a hull must be of wood because it can easily be repaired with native materials anywhere in the world. That's true, but it will *have* to be repaired far more often than will a well-built glass hull.

The great thickness of a wooden hull makes it quieter at sea, but it also steals accommodation space. Forty-foot *Astrea* had about as much space inside her as does the average thirty-five-footer of the general type in fiberglass.

Fiberglass hulls are said to sweat, and they do, as do steel, aluminum, and to a slightly lesser extent, wood ones. The difference is that a wood hull usually has ceilings that hide the sweating. In addition, sweating may be conducive to rot in wood hulls while it doesn't damage fiberglass ones.

As mentioned in Chapter 1, maintenance is much less critical with fiberglass construction. You can neglect a glass hull shamefully and it remains pristine and unchanged beneath its coat of grime. Let a wooden hull alone for a few months and it will begin to deteriorate.

My own preference changed rather abruptly to fiberglass one dark night in Lahaina, Maui. The lights of Lahaina seem to form a range for the narrow entrance channel. If you are unwise enough to follow them, however, you wind up on a reef about fifty yards north of the actual channel, which is poorly marked and about twenty feet wide.

Just after dusk several of us noticed a Cal 34 approaching the entrance. The Cal 34, a fiberglass sloop designed by Bill Lapworth and produced by Jensen Marine, is not known for its strong or thick hull. In fact, I had been heard to refer to it as "just Tupperware." If you walk up to the side of one of these you can readily push it in a little. This naturally horrifies any advocate of stout wooden hulls.

Consequently, after the usual flashing lights and screamed warnings from those of us within the harbor, there was a resounding crash from the direction of the reef and the Cal 34 was stranded in two or three feet of water. As often on the lee side of these islands there was a good four to five feet of swell coming easily over the reef, which extends about a third of a mile out from the beach. These swells were now picking up the helpless ship and driving her relentlessly over the coral heads toward the distant sea wall.

Bill Dunlap, owner of a fiberglass Columbia 36, and some others instantly went out in dinghies or by swimming to see what they could do, but John Guzzwell and I said rather gloomily that there wasn't much to be done, for she'd be crushed like an egg anyway and since the crew was already ashore by now we'd be wasting our time going out there.

When the stranded boat had finally made her agonizing way all the distance to the sea wall, coral heads and all, everyone was astonished to find her half full of water but unholed. With the help of a local sports fisherman, lots of line, and several stout souls hanging from the masthead to heel her over to the horizontal, she was dragged out the same way she had come in, over the coral heads, and brought safely to harbor at last. John and I sat soberly in his dinghy and reflected on the chances of our yachts under such conditions. While I considered *Astrea*'s construction to be unequaled in any conventional yacht, and while I knew for a fact that John's *Treasure* was built by the finest shipwright in the world today (John would protest modestly but I am not alone in calling him the finest), we came to the conclusion that we both would have lost our homes and kingdoms before they had ever reached the sea wall.

On that day I began to look at the Columbia 36 with considerable respect. At the end of that cruise I sold *Astrea* to a prospective cruiser (she is still sitting at a dock with her great spars naked and yearning to be off to sea again) and set about designing a fiberglass ship of much more modern design.

In searching for a fiberglass boat of suitable construction for cruising, the most important step is, of course, to find a fine designer and a reputable builder. In this day of production designs there is no excuse for having a yacht that does not sail well and look good. Advertising claims to the contrary, not all makers build "the finest boats yet constructed." Ask for specifications of the layup of the hull, for it is not just mass and thickness that give strength, but proper materials, engineering practices, and, most important, quality control.

I favor the hand-layed hull over those built with a chopper gun, because the resin-glass proportion can be better controlled. Boats built with a high proportion of resin to glass are brittle, and the laminate does not develop as much strength as does one having a relatively high proportion of glass fiber. With regard to rigidity, a hull made of matting alone with its random direction of fibers will be quite rigid and thick; however, it should have layers of heavy woven roving to give it impact resistance. Each manufacturer has his own preferences as to how rigid or flexible his hulls are to be.

Today's hulls, provided they are honestly built, are more than adequately strong for the jobs for which they are intended. But are they adequate for long-range cruising? I would say that most are, but I would always do a little reinforcing here and there for added insurance and peace of mind. This work is simple if the yacht is built without that infernal molded interior liner pan, which many manufacturers use in order to increase production and save money. The "pan" is the inner liner of the hull and contains bunks, tables, galley, and so on, all in a one-piece molding. All the drawers, cupboards, and bulkheads are then farmed out to a woodworking production line and simply bolted into the appropriate places. All well and good, if the layout and hull reinforcing are just what you require. But it's a horror to try to change anything beyond the superficial.

Most weekenders and ocean racers do not have the best layouts for a cruiser, and while some builders offer two models of the same design, the models often differ only in that the cruiser is provided with rather more varnished trim below, a set of curtains (useless at sea) and cloth rather than plastic upholstery material (good at any time). And the cruising model may lack some of the bunks that make many modern yachts true floating dormitories.

Remember that most modern boats, whether sold as racers or cruisers, were designed for racing on weekends, not for crossing oceans. The ones they sell as cruisers just didn't make out too well as racers. They are nearly all built on racing hulls and advertised as being slightly longer or shorter than they really are to hide their origins. There's nothing wrong with using the same hull, but why lie about it? Then they make up a new deck and interior moulding,

Hull-deck joints could well do with two or three layers of fiberglass tape.

The completed deck gets two layers of heavy matting and a top layer of cloth to aid in finishing.

Treasure, John Guzzwell's new yacht. Note central cockpit with permanent dodger and self-steering vane.

just about all of which, I assume, are made to please the distaff half of the family. They generally have extra high freeboard and a center cockpit with a master bedroom aft and the rest of the accommodation forward, pinched up into the bows, leaving the beamiest part of the boat occupied with cockpit drains, engines, and tanks.

Did you ever think about why there are so many bunks and so few lockers and drawers on these things? It costs about twelve dollars to build a bunk, but it costs about twenty-five to build and install a good drawer. Add a little advertising and you will know the source of that aggravating question that always identifies the novice, "How many will she sleep?"

As I said, if the yacht has no liner pan, you can reinforce her hull if she needs it and put in a bulkhead here, rip out a bunk there, and generally change her around to suit your needs. Most smaller coastwise yachts now sold will need better galley facilities, more accessible storage, and a good sturdy chart table with an icebox under it. They will also need modifications to their rigging and rudders to be truly suitable as independent long-range cruisers.

Wooden construction appears to offer an easier job for the would-be modifier, but this can be an illusion. I would not have believed it myself, but it is far easier to make a pattern and glass in a

45

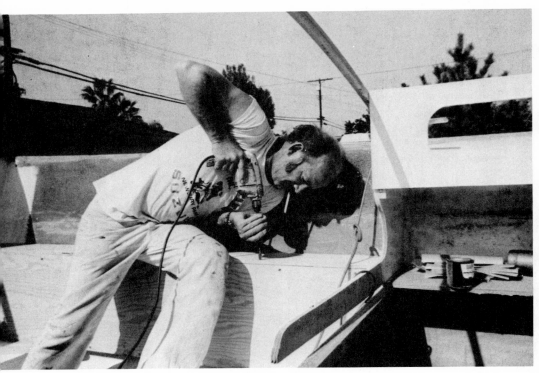

It is a simple matter to add a modification here and there.

A dinette appears where there once were bunks.

bulkhead on a glass yacht than on a wooden one with its shelf, clamp, and bilge stringers all getting in the way.

Longevity has always been a serious question in the mind of anyone buying a yacht. Wood yachts are said to be long-lived, and they are. Their life depends, however, on a slow, metamorphic process whereby they are constantly being rebuilt bit by bit as a fastening here or a plank there rots or fails and is replaced. Some say that a fiberglass yacht will slowly become harder and more brittle as the plastic polymer chain cures over the years, and that someday you will hear a great cracking sound and the yacht will turn into a pile of rags and powdered resin before your eyes. Well, I've seen a lot more unsound wooden vessels twenty years old than I have fiberglass ones, and if you added up the cost of maintenance to the wooden boats you could probably buy a new glass one for the price. That fabled self-destruct just never seems to happen. As an off-hand thought, though, I wonder what on earth I would do with a yacht that would last fifty or so years; I won't last that long myself.

In terms of construction cost, the fiberglass yacht comes out way ahead in initial outlay. Wooden yachts are built in the United States today only by the custom builder, and the good white oak and Honduras mahogany needed for that fine work is getting prohibitive in cost. The fabled Tahiti ketch that could be built for $1,500 in the thirties now would cost about $30,000 if made by a good yard with first-class materials and a diesel engine! Although wood soon may be quite out of reach for all but the most affluent, some chance still remains for those who prefer the warmth of wooden hulls. The New Zealanders have come up with a three-skinned laminated wood construction that is strong, light, and cheaper than conventional wooden construction. Guzzwell's *Treasure* is of this build, and she is magnificent, sheathed in fiberglass, longitudinally framed, and truly one of the finest yachts I have ever seen.

The sandwiched hull of some modern ocean racing production yachts, built with fiberglass layup surrounding a parquet of balsa wood squares, results in a light and rigid construction. I have some doubts, however, as to its suitability for long-range cruising, since often the skin is a little too thin and may suffer damage when brought up against piers and docks. This is not to say that slightly thicker outer skin wouldn't cure the problem, but I wonder if the quest for light weight in ocean racers sometimes isn't carried a little to extremes, as is the trend toward excessive weight among cruising craft.

The ferrocement revolution is still new in this country, and I

The galley is roughed in, lying in the port forward quarter of the salon. A quarter berth extends back under cockpit at left.

Every piece of plywood must be thoroughly covered with primer to help prevent checking.

The cockpit has angled back rests and is long enough to sleep in.

A light plywood deck will be laminated on these light molds and covered with three layers of heavy glass.

The starboard side of the cabin contains a dinette with a folding table and chart-table–icebox, right. Note the light deck framing possible with cold-molded plywood deck.

would estimate that fully two or three hundred hulls are started for every one that ever is launched. Ferrocement offers the stuff of dreams to the unwary yachtsman. You can save 20 percent of the cost of a wood hull by building in ferrocement, say some (Bill Garden says about 5 percent), and eager amateur boat builders rush out and clutter up their yards with miles of construction rods and steel mesh. After they have plastered, compacted, filled, and faired those reluctant bilges for the umpteenth time, they find that the hull is only a tiny part of the cost of a cruising boat and that the majority of things that go into a yacht cost the same for wood, fiberglass, or ferrocement. They often find, too, that they don't need any ballast to get her down to her lines and that it's hard to go back and put in something you forgot in the construction of a concrete hull.

In the unlikely event of a launching, the builder learns some things that weren't pointed out in those glib brochures. Concrete and zinc set up a bubbling reaction, which, if not chemically prepared for, makes the hull porous with the result that the boat slowly sinks. Improper compacting and curing results in essentially the same thing. Finally, how do you survey the structure of a ferrocement boat when it's hidden under all that concrete caulking? I refer, of course, to the steel that is actually the ship's structure. No survey, no insurance. No insurance, no sale in most cases, unless you can get cash. Add to all this the fact that I have never yet seen a ferrocement yacht that looked like much aesthetically; most of them seem to me rather lumpy and finished off with fir, redwood, and other nautical unlikelihoods.

Of course, I have no doubt at all that the kinks in this construction method will be ironed out as time goes by, as indeed they were with fiberglass, but it will remain an axiom of the sea, and perhaps life in general, that you seldom get anything good for nothing.

No matter whether you favor wood, steel, aluminum, fiberglass, or ferrocement, seek the advice of a good marine surveyor *before* you buy. Be honest in telling him your requirements and what you want to do with a boat, and *listen* to what he has to say. *Do not listen* to anything but the price from most yacht brokers, since most of them are salesmen rather than sailormen anyway, no matter how honest they may be. Make comparisons objectively by writing lists of the bad and good points of the strength of construction, need for modification, and ease of repair and modification, and try to put a dollar value on each. It will soon become obvious which boat is for you.

Layout Below Decks

The various layout schemes that are possible and practical are almost endless, but some strike me as better than others for voyaging. Limiting factors to consider, of course, are the size of the crew.

I consider the ideal vessel for two people to be between thirty and thirty-five feet; for three, up to thirty-eight feet or so; and, while forty feet will accommodate more than four compatible souls, I strongly recommend that no more than four sail in the same vessel regardless of her size. It has been said by some wag that a boat shrinks one foot each day at sea, and I have found that to be too small an estimate with some crews.

The ideal is a layout that allows each crewman to perform his necessary tasks efficiently without disturbing the bailiwick of another or awakening a sleeper. The galley must not intrude on the navigator's area, nor the bosun's stores, nor the bunks of the off watch. One wretched night on a badly laid out forty-footer (she was adequate for a crew of two but not for the six we carried) I had my bedding set afire by the cook stove because the galley table was right at the end of a settee bunk, and there was no half bulkhead separating them. Every time we breasted a good swell, I would slide aft on those treacherous Naugahyde bunks, and my feet, blankets and all, would arrive at the forward burner of the stove.

First locate the high-priority items in their optimum locations, and let the others fall where they may. The priorities, of course, are up to you.

I prefer to have the galley in the forward section of the salon or, if the yacht is long enough, in its own section forward of the salon with the head opposite. This allows room for a quarter berth on one side aft, and for an adequate chart table on the other with either a heavily insulated icebox or storage for bulky objects beneath it. Having the quarter berth on one side allows you to eliminate one of the cockpit seat hatches that always leak so badly. It is a good idea to put the quarter berth on the port side and eliminate the hatch on that side, because if you are hove to on the starboard tack in heavy weather (which is good practice because you have right of way), then the low side where water is apt to collect has no hatch for it to run into. The galley will be on the side opposite the icebox in order to better distribute the weight.

I like my chart table–icebox combination in the starboard aft corner of the salon. When I take my celestial observations from the hatch, I don't then have to ramble all over the cabin with sextant, stopwatch, and radio receiver. I simply sit down at my chart table, work up my figures, and plot my line of position without awaking the sleepers (who always seem to be in the main salon rather than in the forepeak). Another advantage to this location is that wet blocks of ice can be lowered almost directly into the ice chest rather than tracking water all down the salon. Ice hatches on deck are a fine thing for those who never go to sea, but offshore they always wind up allowing a lot of sea water to find its way among the steaks and milk.

The chart table should be permanent, and to me it takes priority over all else except the galley. I spend more time at the chart table than in my bunk. The table should be at least thirty by thirty inches and should have high fiddle rails, the front one of which should be hinged to fold down away from the table so that you can work on oversize charts without folding them or capture the odd pencil that works its way into the corners.

Bunks are a perplexing problem in modern yachts, mostly because there are so many. I personally prefer the quarter berth, six feet, four inches long, with half its length back under the cockpit so that it makes a nice lounging spot when not in use. Sleeping there allows the skipper to be readily available to the deck without waking others while lurching his way through the cabin. Since half of a quarter berth resembles the nether end of a coffin, it is hard to fall out of even when it is on the high side. Some advocate a bunk around twenty or twenty-two inches wide, but I like one nearer thirty or more. I just get too claustrophobic in a narrow berth. Besides, all the pillows, duffel bags, and so on that collect on berths can be laid along one side to provide great protection from the side of the hull. In the case of feminine company aboard, a wide bunk has other obvious advantages. If a ship is broad and deep enough, I like a pair of settees in the salon facing each other across a table with pilot berths above and behind. There is nothing more secure and sea-worthy than a nice permanent bunk that can stay made up, with its high leeboard and feeling of private domain. Besides, there is room for some sizable drawers beneath them.

If your ship has one of those dinettes that are so nice in allowing easy passage through the yacht, you will still want at least one permanent berth on that side of the ship for the off watch to use. The dinette is a nice feature, but if you try to change it back and forth from table to bunk at sea, you will probably take to eating in the cockpit or at the chart table.

The V berths up in the forepeak on small boats are seldom used at sea, most crews preferring to "hot bunk" back in the salon where it is less cramped and noisy. In fact, on many small yachts with small crews the forward berths are eliminated and the space given over to storage bins—easily removable for that day when resale comes along. Folding and swinging berths should be avoided. They are usually left down if they are to be used, so why not build them in? If the yacht is so small that she needs auxiliary berths, perhaps she is too small for your purposes.

The next item has different priorities depending on the available space, but for me it ranks low on the scale. That is the head. I am often astonished by the volume of space given over in small yachts to a gadget we usually use for no more than ten minutes or so a day. A yacht I once saw had three heads, two with showers, all jammed into a very cramped forty-two-foot layout. Incredibly, the boat had been designed specially for the couple who were its only crew. Perhaps they had forgotten the difference between houses and yachts, or perhaps they both suffered frequent colonic emergencies, but I think I would choose to wait ten minutes and give that valuable space to a good bosun's locker, better chart stowage, a radio cabinet, or even a flag locker. Some insist on a wash basin and even a shower in the head. This is fine for luxury, but it certainly isn't necessary.

When cruising, fresh water is a luxury, and most bathing is done with a sturdy canvas bucket on deck or with a sponge and a steaming teakettle of salt water below. While that shower bath will help sell the ladies on sailing, it sure will disillusion them if they try to use it at sea. Imagine standing all soaped up in a slippery shower pan, surrounded by a cold and clinging shower curtain, while your yacht rolls 45 degrees in each direction and pitches five feet or so. It's a great way to break bones, but its a lousy way to stay clean. Some people who are not yet wise in the ways of the sea seem to think that a yacht at sea behaves in exactly the same way that it does tied up to a slip in a calm harbor. When cruising I prefer using the sink in the galley to that in the head for washing up (I always have a salt-water pump there), perhaps because of the cramped space in most heads and the inevitable odors that small compartments are heir to. If the head is kept small and located forward, it will steal little from the rest of the accommodation. Perhaps Americans suffer from bathroom fetishes, because most foreign yachts have strictly functional heads, and not too many of them, either.

Hanging lockers are a problem, because while they are essential to those who live aboard dockside and work in offices, the clothes in them wear out at sea from the constant friction of swinging against the sides of the locker. Since I have had my bout of living aboard while holding a job ashore, I no longer would give one of the things space. What would have been a hanging locker on *Dawn Treader* is now a sail locker, and very handy it is, too. Instead of the swinging door, she has a permanent waist-high bulkhead, allowing a grand place for cases of canned goods, toolboxes, some sails, and the occasional pair of lobsters you don't want crawling around in the cockpit.

Clothes are a minimal concern when voyaging anyway, consisting for me of two pairs of dacron-polyester shorts and a few colored short-sleeved shirts in the tropics, and two pairs of long pants, a few wool sweaters, and a heavy jacket elsewhere. One outfit I wear, the other I wash, and when one wears out, I replace it at the next port. A thousand miles from shore no one's looking anyway, I also carry heavy foul weather gear.

Anything not stuffable into monkey hammocks or small bins can be laid out under the bunk mattress for "ironing," and an astonishing amount of junk can live beneath your mattress without causing discomfort to a true sailor! Charts, for instance, live very happily beneath bunks without being rolled.

Tastes for stowage arrangements vary. I prefer bins of moderate size with oval holes in the fronts of them and an ample number of small to medium-sized drawers. I am aghast at the cupboards with swinging doors set athwartships with which so many yachts are equipped. Every time one of these is opened at sea, if it lives on the high side, a torrent of surprising things lands on the sleeper in the lee bunk unless a high fiddle is installed inside the cupboard. If you're going to install a fiddle, why not dispense with the door and its expense and build a bin with a grab hole in the front? It will hold more, although things are not so easy to find as they are when spilled on the floor and in your mate's bunk. Drawers are expensive, and they are heavy, but if equipped with notches in the proper places they won't spill things so readily as a cupboard. For small, fussy things like knives, silverware, matches, tools, and so forth, drawers are fine, as they are for charts. A common dodge is to go to an unfinished furniture store and buy a few small dressers or night stands and then fit them into an unused bunk space by cutting them down as necessary. Of course, you can employ a shipwright or build your own as well.

The layout should not be allowed to get too wide in terms of floor space. This is definitely contrary to what yacht advertising has to say about the matter, and to what the woman as decorator may think. The reason is simple. The speed of a falling object increases as the distance it falls becomes greater. It's a lot easier to add to your collection of bruises falling across a wide cabin than across a seaman-like narrow one. If you plan on a little dancing from time to time when in port, do it at a nice hotel with a good band.

As in any good subway car, there should be plenty of grab rails strategically located so that you can do your Tarzan act while making your way through the cabin.

Decks below should be of a serviceable nonskid variety, either teak or fiberglass with a good "tooth" to it. Rugs and carpets below serve well in port, but they are apt to be treacherous at sea if they are not well fastened down with screws and cup washers. With the submarinelike action of sea boats, and the streaming oilskins that will be brought below, most carpeting rapidly gets soaked with sea water. Once it has done so, it becomes the very devil to dry out. If the ocean calls, carpets are best left back home along with the pet parrot and your Saint Bernard.

Ventilation is crucial in wooden vessels, since they will rapidly rot in the tropics (and elsewhere more slowly) if fresh air is not circulating through all parts of them. The fiberglass vessel needs ventilation, too, but the need is more for comfort and freedom from

The keel is set up, ready to receive the hull.

The hull is lowered onto the waiting keel casting. The joint must be well bedded with compound.

The keel is painted.

Ready to launch! Note the ventilated rails and outboard chainplates.

mildew than from any danger to the yacht. The natural circulation of air is from the companionway forward when under sail, due, I suppose, to the natural shape of the boat and to backdraft from the mainsail. Every effort must be made to utilize this flow and to augment it if possible. There is one case when the natural flow of air is reversed, and that is when you set up a windsail in the forward hatch (known as island air conditioning).

Large mushroom vents in the extreme ends of the vessel operate on the principle that warm air rises, and it is wise to put a grating in the cabin sole just as far aft as you can so that circulation is assured through the bilge. (This grating also serves to catch the worst of the oilskin drip from those entering the cabin in heavy weather.) All cupboards and bins must have rows of large ventilating holes at both the bottom and top of each or the contents will mildew rapidly. One or two holes in the middle of the door do not ventilate any better than does opening one window in a house.

The question of the proper place for the cockpit has been bandied about considerably and is mostly a matter of preference if the yacht is of good size. There seems at the present time to be a recurrence of that 1925 fad, the center cockpit. Center cockpits are nice, but if the yacht is less than about fifty feet long, they steal accommodation space at the beamiest and deepest part of the vessel, where it can ill be afforded. The midship cockpit is said to be drier than an aft one, but since aft ones are dry anyway if they have adequate coamings, I cannot see the point. A center cockpit reduces the changes of picking up loads of water if pooped at sea, but with its "pagoda" and high freeboard it raises the profile to sometimes dangerous heights. Going to windward, of course, the center cockpit is wetter than an aft one unless it is fitted with a windshield from the nearest Chris-Craft power cruiser, and then it looks like one.

Some salesmen claim that the center cockpit "divides" the accommodations, giving privacy. Well, I believe that if you are going to be with someone you don't like or someone with whom you are that modest, then you shouldn't be cruising with that person anyway. Privacy at sea is obtained by mutual respect among members of the crew. We all use our "blinders" when modesty requires, and we never interfere with the personal domain of our mates.

In addition, a divided accommodation does not allow a free passage of air through the vessel, and she may become intolerably hot in the tropics.

In a motor sailer, a center cockpit can be used to cover the engine and tankage and so forth, but remember that when such

The mast being stepped. Note high camber of the decks.

Dawn Treader is launched. Note extreme beam, narrow deck house with angled sides.

things are aboard, there is less space for creature comforts like adequate bunks, lounging space, and galley. For coastwise cruising, the center cockpit offers good height from which to take bearings and a grand place to lounge about under a boom awning with an occasional martini, kept chilled by the refrigerator powered by the great diesel engine.

The aft cockpit has another advantage that few inexperienced yachtsmen will appreciate. It allows the tiller or wheel to be coupled efficiently to the rudder, either directly or through gears. The center cockpit usually requires either one of those nautical horrors, cable and pulley steering (grossly unreliable and hard to repair at sea), or complicated and only slightly more reliable hydraulic steering.

3   Rigs and Rigging

Choice of the right rig—sloop, schooner, cutter, or ketch—is largely a matter of personal preference, but each has its good and bad points. I have sailed with all these rigs for long ocean passages, and I prefer the modern sloop rig as developed by the ocean racing fraternity, often used with a second headsail while reaching. This rig combines the advantage of the efficient Bermuda sloop rig with the versatility of the cutter.

The consideration of gaff versus Marconi rigs hasn't even entered my mind recently. The gaff rig has such tremendous weight aloft and lack of efficiency to windward that its good results off the wind just don't compensate for its drawbacks.

The size of the yacht must be considered in choosing the most efficient rig. When the yacht requires a sail area that makes the main so large that it cannot be handled by one man, it makes sense to use one of the double-masted rigs. With regard to keeping the sail area minimal, however, it is easier to get a light-displacement hull these days, so perhaps the days of the ketch, yawl, and schooner rigs are numbered as far as small yachts go.

In considering the limiting size for a sail, most will put the upper limit at about three hundred square feet. That's about as much as one man will ever want to handle on a dark and stormy night alone. Light-weather headsails may be considerably larger, providing you don't leave them up too long, at which time they can become a real problem in a blow.

Rigs

Let's consider the merits and drawbacks of the various rigs, starting with the least efficient. That brings us to the ketch. This rig has been highly touted as the ideal cruising rig, and for broad, beamy hull forms lacking great weatherly ability that could be quite correct. The great advantage of the ketch is on a beam reach. She spreads a lot of canvas if you add a mizzen staysail, and it is a low-aspect-ratio rig when you consider the whole sail plan rather than single sails as the wind does while passing over it. This is great on a reach, because the heeling moment will be small. When you are on any other point of sailing, and most cruising always seems to be, the ketch is a big loser. That very fine low-aspect reaching rig is nearly hopeless for going to weather. The sails are trimmed in the following order: first the mizzen, which should be amidships; then the main, which cannot be amidships on most ketches without backwinding the mizzen; and then the staysail, which must not backwind the main; and finally the jib or genoa, which should not backwind the staysail. The net result is that the back half of the yacht is hard on the wind, and the front half is on a close reach. This is not conducive to efficient weather work. When you turn off the wind to run, things are equally bad. That mizzen has to come down or it blankets the main, the most efficient sail, and causes it to flutter and sometimes do a Chinese jibe all standing before the yacht is even by the lee. Those two neat, small headsails, one usually on a jib boom, combined with the main are just not enough to move her along as they would if all the canvas area was in only a main and a jib.

It is said that the ketch will sail herself under more varying conditions than will a sloop or cutter. That was true back in the days when yachts were designed by "eye" rather than in the testing tank. A good modern hull is well balanced and does not need a spread-out sail plan to allow the skipper to "cheat" the trim of jib and mizzen to get the beast pointed in the right direction. I have been on ketches, including my own, that would self-steer rather well, but it is nearly always at the expense of speed and efficiency. Most self-steering ketches have the sail trim so scandalized that they are really hove to with the main drawing, and thus forereach in more or less the right direction, though rather slowly. Of course, with some other ketches I have sailed, there was little difference in speed between flat-out charging and hove to anyway. If you want to use self-steering as a criterion, any modern sloop will self-steer as well as most ketches.

It is a simple matter to reduce sail with the ketch rig. Just step back and down the mizzen, or go forward and drop one of the two jibs, and you have lost a lot of sail area. Here the problem is that usually at sea you have the mizzen down anyway if you are running or hard on the wind. One of the jibs, usually the staysail, is often down, so you go up and reef the main just as you would on a sloop, except that on a sloop *you haven't had to mess with the two previously dropped sails*. It has been said that the other alternative is to drop the main first in a blow and carry on with the jib or jibs and the mizzen. This works out well except when running dead before the wind or when hard on it. On the wind those small, low-aspect-ratio sails just never have a chance, and when running the slewing force of the mizzen can make the yacht nearly impossible to steer.

While certainly more combinations of sail are possible with the ketch rig, they are all less than efficient.

Some pundit will always arise to tell me that *Windward Passage*, *Blackfin*, and the like are ketches, and that they go like hell. That's absolutely right, but these boats are specialized racing vessels and use the ketch rig for the racing handicap it allows them and to provide a place to hang up a mizzen spinnaker. My mind boggles when I think of the probable performance of either with a sloop rig.

I consider the yawl to be simply a sloop that has successfully cheated the rating rules and has some unmeasured area in which to hang mizzen staysails. It also has a good place for the watch to hang onto at sea and a good place for the ship's bell.

The schooner is without doubt the most inspiring and beautiful rig of all, and it has not been given its due in the rush into the twentieth century. The staysail schooner rig, if the masts are not too far apart, goes to weather almost as well as the modern masthead sloop. Many have been the times that old *La Volpe*, a forty-five-foot Angleman staysail schooner of ancient vintage on which I go racing sometimes, has aroused enraged comments from sloop sailors because of her weatherly ability even in our usually light southern California breezes. Some people claim the schooner is not a good cruising rig with its acres of canvas. It is true that the fisherman staysail, the golly-wobbler, and the like would be a bit much for a man-and-wife crew, but if she is allowed only her working sails she comes out about the equal of the ketch as to ease of handling. The great advantage is that hull for hull and sail area for sail area she will beat the ketch all hollow going to weather. Alas, there is no rig that I can think of that is worse than a schooner dead before the wind! Most schooner skippers just head up a bit and make long tacks downwind on a broad reach, thus allowing her to use her fantastic reaching ability to its fullest. There is still nothing that brings back memories of my boyhood like the sight of a staysail schooner jammed on a close reach with her fisherman staysail straining and a broad wake stretching aft behind her. There is simply nothing that I have yet found that matches the thrill of sailing a really good schooner. I don't think I would choose the rig for strictly cruising unless I needed a vessel more than fifty feet or so in length, because anything less is apt to be something of a ship model rather than a ship. Besides, there are few of the breed left today.

The true cutter, with its moderate-sized main and two generous jibs, is little seen today, having been replaced by the (barely) more efficient sloop. Most older cutters were not as good in weatherly performance as the sloop, but they were capable of more sail combinations to meet differing weather conditions. They would also self-steer better than yesterday's sloops, but mostly for the same reasons as the ketch rig. Even the modern sloop now carries a second head-sail while reaching, if only to make up for the mainsail area lost to the modern International Offshore Rule, which favors large genoas at the expense of the main.

By far the most common rig today is the modern masthead-rigged Marconi sloop. She is apt to have her mast nearly in the middle, or at least 30 percent of the distance back from the bow. This is to increase the maximum allowable size for the various jibs and spinnakers needed to win ocean races. That's all to the good, however, because speed never hurt a cruising boat either. The rig is the most efficient of all the common rigs in weatherly work, is adequate on a reach, and really shines downwind, especially if a spinnaker is set. Most old-time cruising men shudder at the thought of a spinnaker, but those without prejudice go ahead and make fast passages with them. *Magic Dragon* used a spinnaker nearly constantly in the fantastic passage she made under self-steering from England to Barbados.

The sloop rig is simple, requiring a minimum of wire and rigging. It is easily stayed with the mast in the middle of the boat, and with the masthead rig there is no need for running backstays or other complication. Reducing sail is a snap in a well-rigged sloop. You can either reduce the size of the jib first by changing down to a smaller one or roller furling the one then set, or you can reef down the main, using either roller reefing or tie reefing and finally striking the main and sailing along with only the jib. The centrally located sloop rig is far better able to balance up under either jib or main alone than is any other rig. All around, if the hull has the proper form for efficient sailing, why hamper it with any but the most efficient rig? The great fault with the sloop rig is that the mainsail may become too large for comfort if the ship exceeds forty feet in length and if the crew is one man and a wife who is less than an Amazon. It is surprising, though, that the legendary Cal 40 goes perhaps twice as fast as does a 36-foot Hannah-designed Carol ketch while having only about one-half the working sail area. She has only one mast to care for, one set of rigging to maintain, and only two sails instead of four to adjust, reef, and generally mess with. If you think of cost, maintenance, and performance, the sloop wins every time. If nostalgia alone motivates you, I would suggest a trip to the ship room of the Smithsonian Institution rather than life on the ocean wave!

Rigging

While the modern ocean racing rig has much to recommend it, it has certain weaknesses as commonly found in California-built production boats. This is due to two primary factors—speed and greed.

Speed is what the ocean racer demands, and a lighter mast and rigging have less wind resistance and weight aloft. This, of course, helps the performance of the yacht, especially to windward. This demand for speed is eagerly accepted by the greed contingent, the production yacht builders. If an occasional mast goes by the boards it is easy to cry bad seamanship and rest assured that the owner has insurance. That may be well and good for the weekend racer, but it can be disastrous for the ocean voyager. He generally has no insurance because of the prohibitive premiums charged for ocean cruising policies, and it wouldn't do him any good anyway if he's a thousand miles from shore and has only five hundred miles' worth of fuel left. Under the circumstances of most dismastings, the engine and its vulnerable batteries are likely to have gone long before anyway.

It is not difficult to strengthen the rigging so that it provides a greater margin of safety than is usually allowed on a racing craft. If the mast is of ample sectional dimensions, the rigging wire, which should be of 1 X 19 stainless steel, can be made a size or so heavier. This really adds little absolute strength at first, but it allows a safety margin for some of the effects of aging and lack of inspection and maintenance that cruising yachts seem to suffer. The forestay should be the thickest wire on the boat. It takes all the chafe from the luff hanks of the jibs, and if you lose a mast at sea, you're infinitely better off if it falls in any direction other than back into the cockpit. (See the accompanying table for the breaking strengths of wires.)

Novices commonly go out and buy oversize turnbuckles before setting out on a cruise but keep the same small wire they had before. I believe, on the other hand, that the wire should be equal to or stronger than the turnbuckle. If the rigging breaks down at sea, it will break at the weakest point, and would you rather replace a turnbuckle from the relative security of the deck or replace a wire at the masthead? A turnbuckle can be replaced by several turns of flexible wire or by many turns of parachute cord and such a jury rig will last a long time at sea. I once used thin flexible wire stolen from the top-

Breaking Strength of Stainless Steel Wire in Pounds

	1 × 19	7 × 19
$\frac{1}{16}$	550	480
$\frac{3}{32}$	1,200	920
$\frac{1}{8}$	2,100	1,900
$\frac{5}{32}$	3,300	2,500
$\frac{3}{16}$	4,700	3,800
$\frac{7}{32}$	6,400	5,200
$\frac{1}{4}$	8,200	6,600
$\frac{9}{32}$	10,300	8,000
$\frac{5}{16}$	12,500	9,000
$\frac{3}{8}$	17,500	12,000
$\frac{7}{16}$	23,500	16,300
$\frac{1}{2}$	29,800	22,800

ping lift as a jury turnbuckle on *Laguna* for more than a thousand miles after one of her numerous attempts to shed her overly tall and thin sectioned spar.

The modern practice of omitting the lower aft shrouds and, in some cases, the forward lowers as well is fine for racing, but for security at sea I prefer both sets of lower shrouds.

Similarly, I prefer two sets of spreaders. A look at Skene's book (which no prospective cruiser should be without) shows that with a masthead rig having one set of spreaders the load on the upper shroud is 38 percent of the total load on the mast (which will be equal to the restoring force of the hull and ballast). When you use two sets of spreaders, the load drops to 20 percent. (However, I would rather not lose the upper shroud if I can help it when at sea, as I did it once on *Laguna*. Replacing that shroud requires going aloft on a wildly swinging mast, which has now lost a good deal of its supporting structure. Better to lose a lower. You can heave a line over the spreader, cinch it up with a handy billy, and never have to go aloft.)

Astrea, with her fifty-seven-foot main spar, had only one set of spreaders. She required jumper stays to keep her solid spruce masts from whipping, and her wire was of a size that required turnbuckles from a heavy cruiser to match its strength. How much nicer to have had two sets of spreaders, a stiffer mast, and smaller, cheaper wire!

In a multimasted rig it is wise to have the main and mizzen masts stayed independently of each other. *Astrea* did not have this rig, and I learned some valuable lessons from a five-thousand-mile cruise I made in her before I changed it. When she would crunch hard into a wave the whole rig would attempt to keep on going (Newton had some things to say about that) in the same direction. Since the main had its backstay attached about halfway up the mizzenmast, the aft spar would turn into a thirty-five-foot longbow. It's amazing how much stretch you can get out of three-eighths-inch stainless wire when a 28,000-pound cruising boat decides to stop while its rig tries to continue the voyage. I sat for days in heavy weather warily watching that whipping mizzen, fascinated like a rabbit confronted by a cobra, knowing that if it should fail, it was the sole support of the mainmast. "As the main goes, so goes the mizzen," we used to greet each other when the weather was lighter. Needless to say, when we made port I stayed the masts independently.

Whether to choose an aluminum or wood mast has become academic in California, because enough good spruce to make a wood one costs a small fortune. The wood mast has many advantages, not the least of which is its ability to flex and bend rather severely before it breaks. *Laguna*'s mast was wood, and I believe she would have broken an aluminum one on several occasions when she broke shrouds. As it was, nothing other than my pride was permanently damaged. The aluminum mast is light and rigid compared with a wood one of the same strength, and it does not require endless varnishing. Tangs and beckets can be welded to it if desired, thus eliminating the danger of the fastenings pulling out of wood. An aluminum mast will break more easily than wood, however, if it is allowed to get out of "column" (meaning if it bends too much). Aluminum spars also are noisy. Let a capful of wind come up in most marinas and the most incredible din of slapping and clattering halyards is heard! This can be remedied by always tying the halyards away from the spar.

You must also decide whether to use roller reefing or old-fashioned slab reefing. If you have a few hundred dollars to spare, roller reefing is convenient, because you can roll up any amount of sail you want. You will have reef points in the main in addition, for of course, the times when the roller gear won't work. With today's mains, which are cut with a lot of draft, roller reefing spoils the shape of the sail if very much more than a foot or two is rolled in. Of course, you can carry along shaped battens and things to stuff into the sail as you roll it up, but that tends to defeat the principle that roller reefing is supposed to save labor. More and more skippers are using various modifications of old-fashioned slab reefing.

A modern quick reef or jiffy reef operation is quite simple. First reeve off a light line from a dead end on one side of the boom under and slightly aft of the clew reefing cringle; run it up through the cringle and then back down to a cheek block in the same position on the other side of the boom. Run the line forward along the boom through a few fairleads either to a small reefing winch or merely to a cleat on the boom near the gooseneck. This operation is done in port, not just when you are ready to reef down. When the time comes to reef (and the time to reef is whenever you begin to think about whether it's time to reef), haul the jib to weather and heave to, if on the wind, or simply haul a little main sheet if before the wind. Grab your reefing pennant from its cleat near the gooseneck and either crank with a winch or haul by hand until the cringle is down to the boom. Actually, the boom is being hauled up to the reefing cringle at the leach. When hauled down, the pennant (or reefing line) should form an angle aft from the cringle so that it acts as an outhaul as well. Once this is done—and it takes less time to do it than to explain it— lower away on the halyard while bowsing down the tack cringle with either a short length of line or a pennant rigged like the one aft. You can then tie in the reef points at your leisure or, as many skippers now do, let them go. If off the wind, the little extra fullness that this reef allows is all to the good. Hard on the wind the boom will be inboard, and you may tie off if you wish to give a better set to the sail. The old cotton sails would not stand this sort of treatment, but modern dacron takes it just fine. Even on *Astrea* with her huge main, I could turn out all standing and pull down a reef on her twenty-foot boom in about five minutes without a winch and without calling out a single hand from below.

The roller furler sometimes requires a hand at the clew to haul aft to avoid wrinkles, and this means that you must come hard on the wind to reef. Not so with the old-fashioned system, with which you can reef under most points of sail, without topping lifts, and do it more quickly.

Headsails usually are not reefed but are taken down in good time, before conditions get so bad that they blow out of their luff tapes. It is possible to reef a headsail if it is set on a boom, but most of these boomed headsails have so little pull that it hardly matters whether they are reefed or not. *Astrea* would perform just the same whether her jib-boomed foresail was set or downed. The sail was worthless ex-

69

cept as a club to try viciously to sweep me off the foredeck whenever I was there, whether to reef the main or merely to sit out on the bowsprit and admire the view.

More and more coastwise sailors are turning to roller furling headsail rigs, as are some offshore types. As sailmakers get more familiar with cutting sails for such rigs I believe that most of the problems will sort themselves out. What a labor-saver it seems to have only one headsail to worry about. Just unroll the right amount, and if she blows, reel in a foot or so. It sounds easy, but doesn't always work that way. Unless the sail is expertly cut, it won't be shaped right at any extension except full out, and its sheeting point may vary considerably as it is reefed. These matters are small ones but are worth consideration if efficiency is your goal.

Large headsails on roller furling rigs present some dangers as well. The worst is that when rolled up on the stay they make a pretty large bundle. If you should happen to have to lie ahull to a gale sometime, that bundle of sail will try to unroll and will shake the yacht like a terrier shaking a rat. This puts great strains on the rig as well as forcing the yacht's head downwind from the square, smooth drift you want. Sometimes when running, unless the sail is set on a rotating headstay rather than on its own stay aft of the headstay, it will foul the headstay when you attempt to roll it in, tearing the sail. On the other hand, rotating headstays carrying roller furling jibs have been known to give way under strain at inopportune times. I think I would rather take my chances striking jibs and tying them to the toerails than tempt fate with a roller furling gear, unless it was one that could easily be taken down in case of emergency. Most cannot be taken down quickly, since great tension is needed to make the sails on them set properly, and they are often set up with a wire and a turnbuckle. If you can get the thing down easily, will it be easier than taking down an ordinary jib?

I consider blocks and winches to be parts of the rig, rather than yacht equipment, since they often dictate just how much sail can be comfortably carried. The winches should be as big as you can afford. A good winch has roller bearings or needle bearings at the top and bottom of the drum. It has a heavy, forged shaft, and it is so constructed that the metals in it will not begin electrolytic action even when they are soaked in sea water for days at a time. The only brand of winch I have yet found (although I haven't tried them all, by any means) that doesn't bend just enough to bind on the bottom of the drum when the pull really gets hard is the Barient. You may say that a little binding is no sweat, but under the kind of conditions in which such bending is likely to occur it can't be permitted. The Barient winch is quite costly, but it is so efficient that you can use a size smaller than required in another make and still have ample reserve power. Some winch manufacturers have obviously never been to sea, or they wouldn't combine brass, stainless steel, aluminum, and phosphor bronze in the same piece of equipment. Alongshore the seas don't get into the winches so badly, and the winches are also hosed off fairly often with fresh water. Sir Francis Chichester wrote at length of the electrolysis that made his winches useless during his circumnavigation.

"Small blocks and large line to you!" reads the old sailor's curse. He might have added, "Nonroller bearing blocks as well!" Having large-diameter sheaves and roller bearings in your blocks means that friction, and thereby the amount of pull required to do any particular job, is reduced. It becomes obvious, then, that spending a little more on blocks (which are cheap anyway) beats spending a lot on winches. It used to be that no yacht was considered to be well equipped without wooden shelled blocks, and beautiful things they are, too. In recent years, however, the price of these beauties has become prohibitive, and today we must content ourselves with plastic imitations, which, incidentally, are just as strong and just as efficient if roller bushed, and lighter as well.

Masthead sheaves should be large, at least thirty times the diameter of the wire they carry, or they will rapidly wear out the wire. If the sheaves are metal, it should be the same metal as that of the halyard. Otherwise you invite electrolysis. Some may think that not much sea water finds its way to the masthead, but one December on *Astrea* I was perplexed when the main stuck halfway to the masthead. No amount of tugging or swearing would budge it. After trips aloft (I had no other masthead halyard at the time), swearing and cursing the gods, we found an even taller ship in the same anchorage (she was Ernest Gann's old *Black Watch*) and used her main halyard to hook through our own and then winch it clear of the masthead sheave where it had jammed. *Astrea* was at that time less than a year old, but her aluminum masthead sheave had reacted badly with her stainless steel halyard and had simply disintegrated, letting the wire jam itself between the broken sheave and mast well. Needless to say, I soon had a second halyard rigged at the masthead and replaced that sheave with one of stainless steel. A phenolic one would have cost one-tenth as much as the stainless, but I was afraid it wouldn't be strong enough.

Toggles must be used below every turnbuckle, or they will not lie fair with the shrouds and stays. This in turn will place undue stress on both the turnbuckle and the connection between the wire and the turnbuckle. A majority of rigging failures can be traced back to a failure to use toggles.

One of the best ways to get a good argument going among cruising men is to ask what is the best way to get the wire connected up to the mast and the turnbuckles. Some opt for eye splices, some for hot poured sockets, some for nicropress fittings, a few for modern swaged terminals, and a few for other types of terminals. Wire splices are fine, but they are expensive and difficult to make in 1 × 19 stainless wire. They also lose about 25 percent of the strength of the wire.

To make a hot socket, the wire is pushed through a special fitting with an eye in it, and then molten zinc is poured in to make a very strong fitting. This system is undoubtedly the best when you are using galvanized plow steel rigging wire, but with stainless steel wire, electrolytic action is set up between the dissimilar metals. The humble nicropress fitting can be put on anywhere by anyone with a strong arm and a clamping tool. It is sturdy and seldom fails unless the wire of the eye is pinched during the clamping operation. The thimble over which the eye is formed must be of the extra heavy pattern and in stainless steel. I saw some thimbles on an old six-meter yacht that were filled with a bushing just large enough to allow the pin to pass through, and such types would be ideal. The idea is to avoid creating stretch by allowing the thimble to change shape.

With the modern racing yacht has come the common swaged fittings which were developed for aircraft control cables. They are beautiful, strong, and neat. And they are treacherous at sea. I have broken at least ten of these beasties offshore, and the result has been nearly disastrous more often than I care to think about. They have never broken aloft, but always at deck level where they attach to the turnbuckles. What happens is that as rain or spray hits the wire, it runs down to the swaged fitting. The fitting admits a small proportion of the water and rusts the stainless wire. (Yes, stainless wire rusts.) The rust, as it forms, generates terrific pressure, which in turn cracks your fifteen-dollar swage fitting, and away goes your fifteen-hundred-dollar mast. To prevent such disasters, you can soak the swaged ends of the wire in hot (nearly boiling) fish oil, and then paint them thoroughly with a rust preventive paint to seal out the water, and they will serve well. Or you can swage the fittings aloft and use some alternative method below.

The "Norseman" fitting is little seen in this country, but it may be the answer to all the questions about rigging terminals. These fittings are of stainless steel, and they come apart ingeniously to admit the end of the wire, which is then set up tight by screwing the two halves of the fitting together, thus locking the wire in place. All you need is a wrench. The advantages are that they can be taken apart again and again for inspection; they can be reused apparently indefinitely; and they are neat and not at all bulky. They are more expensive than swaged fittings and seem to be available only from England, but they certainly give me peace of mind. They keep over 95 percent of the strength of the wire, which is better than any other method.

Chainplates on modern fiberglass yachts are often rather light and flimsy-looking when compared with those on the traditional cruising vessel. The reason for the discrepancy is the difference in weight between the two types of boats. Because the light-displacement boat puts much less strain on the rig, it can get by with much lighter plates. There should be a chainplate for each shroud. I get a little nervous when I think of the intermediate and upper shrouds, on which the integrity of the mast depend, both fastened to one chainplate. The chainplate is usually made of stainless steel, although other materials will also serve. Most modern yachts have the plates passing through the deck and fastened to bulkheads below. This system allows the shrouds to be set up on a narrow base, which in turn allows the genoa to be sheeted at a smaller angle. For extra peace of mind, I would fasten a set of plates to the outside of the hull. They would not be so pleasing to look at as the internal arrangement, but the greater base allows a longer spreader and reduces the compression load on the spar. The extra margin of safety allowed is more important than looks.

The solid or rod rigging favored today in ocean racing is not suitable for ocean cruising, fine though it may be for racing. It needs to be magnafluxed regularly to find the microscopic cracks that develop in it. This is hard to get done in places like Nuku Hiva and Tonga!

Chafe protection is still important, but you almost never see those romantic-looking balls of baggy wrinkle in the rigging any more, due to the durability of today's sails. The aft lower shroud and the upper shroud can be covered with a tube of slick, close-fitting plastic tubing, and the aft side of the spreaders can be covered with pieces of sheepskin. I have made open-water passages without either, and the result was a shiny line on my mainsail where it rubbed each shroud and the spreaders when running. I found a few broken threads in these shiny patches, but not enough to endanger the sail under most conditions. (I always have my sails made up with a triple or quadruple row of stitching anyway, if they are intended for cruising. I don't really know if it's worth the extra expense, but it makes me feel better.)

73

In order to protect the crew from the boom should the topping lift part while the sail is furled, each boom should have a permanent boom gallows of robust construction. I make mine of two pipe stanchions at least one and a half inches in diameter, through-bolted to a two-inch-thick piece of teak or mahogany. Three notches for the boom, well covered with leather, allow the boom to be stowed to the side of the centerline of the cockpit so that it doesn't crack someone in the head. Having a gallows makes it a cinch to furl sails at sea, and it's a grand place to lean while taking sights.

4   Equipment

Modifying and equipping the cruising yacht can be seriously overdone, in my opinion, but this is not to say that there aren't lots of things to be done that will make the voyage safer and more pleasant. Many would-be voyagers spoil their chances for a successful voyage by putting aboard useless things that are beyond their mechanical competence to maintain, and thus lose a lot of the pleasure to be gained from the voyage.

As you can tell by now, I am a firm adherent to the "bare knuckles" school when it comes to what should or should not be included in a cruising yacht's equipment. I have sailed the ocean in high luxury with electric refrigerators, radios, and generator sets, and I have sailed with kerosene lamps and no engines. Surprisingly enough, the most pleasant and satisfying have been those with minimal mechanical and electrical equipment. After a week at sea, particularly if the course is at all weatherly, a good deal of the electrical gear will be out of commission from the damp anyway. When you most need the engine, if it has no hand-starting capability, it is usually hard or impossible to start because the batteries, which serve so well for a weekend of coastal cruising, have deteriorated from tropical heat or from soaking in sea water. It is absolutely amazing how much so-called "marine" equipment just won't work at sea! Recent tests show that many life rafts won't inflate with their sophisticated CO_2 bottles, but have to be pumped up by hand. The signal flares don't light, the radar reflectors don't reflect, the radios have only a twelve-mile range, and the refrigerators won't cool the box. The list goes on and on. I have found through sad experience the danger of dependence on anything other than the simplest and most reliable systems of getting things done at sea. I now stick to time-tested, manually powered devices and things that burn kerosene and shy away from all else.

On a voyage home from Hawaii I was skipper on a modern American cruising yacht. It was a beamy ketch, of course. Possibly as an excuse for not going sailing, or possibly through bad advice, the owner had spent nearly ten years "getting ready" for a sail to Hawaii. The boat had a fine diesel engine, fuel tanks for two hundred extra gallons (she needed that, and more), and all electric lights. In addition, of course, she had electric bilge pumps, an electrically pumped stove, and an autopilot. She had four radio transmitters, two sextants, two signaling pistols, and a huge supply of tools and spare parts for everything possible—spare tillers, spare rudder, and sheets of plywood to patch the hull if needed. She did *not* have a timepiece, and she had no barometer, the most important instrument for a Pacific trade wind passage. The engine had two burned intake valves and two vulnerable alternators located under the cockpit deck, which was removable and leaked like sin. By the time the owner had made the run downwind to Hawaii the engine would not start, because the batteries were full of salt water from the constant cockpit leaks. By mistake she sailed past her harbor and had to be towed in ignominiously by her nose, since she wouldn't sail well enough to weather to be able to beat back to the harbor entrance against the stiff trades. She also was full of rot, because a great number of compartments had been built in, destroying her ventilation. All and all she floated better than twelve inches below her designed waterline and had the wallowing feel of a swamped dinghy when you stepped aboard.

After we had reluctantly started for home in the thing, her overabundance of equipment began to make itself felt. What little sailing ability was designed into her was lost to the tremendous unbalanced extra weight she had aboard. When on the wind in twenty knots, she would heel so far that the lightboards located four feet up the shrouds would go under, putting out her electric running lights. She needed her engine to make reasonable progress to weather, but it, being in disrepair, failed. So there we were. We had eighty or so gallons of water that we couldn't drink because the pumps were electric. The stove, likewise, could not be used because although it burned kerosene, it required an electric pump to pressurize the fuel. The radios also turned out to be electric. We drank water through a section of fuel hose, now useless with no engine, stuck into the tank filler like a straw. I blew mightily into the kerosene tank and quickly slapped the cap back on to pressurize the stove. All in all, it was an incredibly frustrating voyage.

How sad it was to realize that the efforts of her owner to improve her had really defeated her. Radios, electric pumps, and electric lights are fine, but they require much more than their own weight because of the batteries and generators they need. They also require a reliable backup manual or kerosene system. If weight is critical—and it is—why carry two systems in order to account for the almost certain failure of the electrical one? Besides, if you are going to finish the voyage with kerosene lights and hand pumps anyway, why give the electrical gear space aboard? Take the money and buy a few good sails and a few coils of line or a spare anchor and gear.

This is not to say that modern conveniences are necessarily bad at sea. It is only that if they cannot be made reliable, and they have not up until now, then they should be employed only if you have the space and the money to support such toys and if you have solid, reliable backup, or, really, *primary* systems.

Because of the corrosive propensity of salt water, the environment in the bilges of a small yacht at sea is just about the worst possible for mechanical equipment. Add to this the fact that industrial designers, not sailors, design most yacht equipment today. What works well and reliably at a dock in Marina Del Rey may well not be up to the job when in the totally different world offshore.

When you get right down to it, a voyaging yacht is a space ship without oxygen tanks. Your safety depends on self-reliance and the reliability of your equipment. More often than not these little space ships are kept in orbit more by the muscles of their crews than by the electrical and mechanical equipment they carry along. Put aboard contraptions for comfort and convenience if you wish, but not at the expense of the old reliable hand-powered things that may well save your life.

Auxiliary Engines

Since the development of the modern lightweight diesel engine, few sailors want anything else aboard because of the inherent safety of diesel fuel. For small vessels perhaps no engine at all is the best policy if the length overall is less than thirty feet. In a larger yacht an auxiliary engine is desirable, mostly for maneuvering around anchorages and for convenience. There is no excuse today for a yacht to use her engine at sea except to charge the batteries. If she needs it to make a passage, she is really either a power boat or a motor sailer, neither of which has a place offshore, in my opinion.

If you are going to give an auxiliary space aboard, it should have the ability to get you out of a tight spot. An ideal auxiliary will use a reduction gear and a large, slow turning prop that will push you against a good current and a headwind chop at about three or four knots. If it won't do that, perhaps it is merely excess baggage.

In terms of reliability, most modern diesels are good, provided they are properly installed and properly maintained. The exhaust line must arch high above the waterline in the center of the boat before it starts its run aft. If it does not, water will find its way into the valves when the vessel heels or when a high following sea is running. If that is not possible because of space limitations, then a large valve will have to be put in near the end of the exhaust line. Just be sure to open and close it daily so that it won't freeze up.

The fuel system will require much better filtration than is supplied with the engine. So far as I know, Gardiner is the only company left in the world that makes a true marine diesel engine. The rest are either automotive or industrial engines somewhat modified for the sea. You will need at least two water stripper filters, such as those sold by the Fram Corporation. They should be the largest you can get into the available space and should be installed in addition to the ones supplied with the engine. The smallest quantity of water can utterly destroy the fine injector system of the diesel, which is set up to very fine tolerances. In fact, tolerances in the Bosch injector system of a diesel are such that only specialized repair stations are capable of effecting repairs to the fuel system components. It is wise to carry a spare injector pump–distributor system if your engine has one, as well as a spare injector or two.

The General Motors diesel system seems to be ideal for larger yachts. This is a two-cycle diesel that therefore has no intake valve. This saves parts and reduces the chances of failures. The system uses no injector pump–distributor as does the Bosch system but has a cam-actuated injector pump for each cylinder, installed just about like an ordinary spark plug. This makes it a simple matter to adjust or replace, an important factor in a seagoing craft. Perhaps the nicest thing about the "Jimmy diesel," as it is called, is the fact that if it runs out of fuel it does not have to be primed and the system bled down for air as do the Bosch injected systems. Just push the button for a few seconds and it starts right up, and it is self-bleeding all the time. These engines are just about infinitely replaceable. You can change the cylinder liners without buying a new block, and the parts are easy to get all over the world. They also are quite reasonable and do not require more than passing skill as a mechanic to install.

I suppose everything good has drawbacks, and the Jimmy has some, too. It is extremely noisy, having both a singing two-cycle exhaust bark and supercharger whine and a general mechanical racket. To deaden the noise you will need mufflers three to four times the capacity normally required and good sound deadening in the engine room. The Jimmy will burn a little more fuel than will a Bosch-injected engine of similar displacement, and it cannot be started with a hand crank. GMC does make available a hydraulic hand-starting lashup, but it is expensive and prone to deterioration from rust at sea. The Jimmy starts easily, however, if the batteries are not down. Its initial cost is high when compared to the cheap foreign diesels available, but it makes up for that by its easy repairability and by its great life expectancy.

For vessels under thirty feet, provided they are not inherently crab crushers, a good strong British Seagull outboard serves well to move you around the anchorage, but it really won't propel you against much of a seaway. John Guzzwell had one as his only engine on *Trekka* on his circumnavigation, and it never failed to amaze him with its dependability.

An engine requires batteries and some auxiliary generator system, of course, unless it is a hand-starting model. (See the following section on generators.) Usually only the smallest diesels have hand-starting rigs.

The engine, regardless of its type, is usually buried in the bilge or under the cockpit where it takes a professional contortionist even to change the oil. In such a place it is often hard or impossible to start, even if it has a hand starter. Old John Hannah was wise when he specified that a boat should have a large engine room or that the engine should stand in the middle of the cabin. At least then it will be kept clean and oil-free and will have a fighting chance to do its job properly.

Cruising Generators

If you have an engine and some electrical equipment aboard, it will be wise to carry some auxiliary generator. The generator may be of the commercial diesel type, which is heavy and expensive and costs nearly as much as the main engine it services, or it can be one of the Honda gas-burning portable kinds. The portable type must be kept dry or it soon turns into an unserviceable ball of rust at sea. The portable also usually has only minimal battery charging ability but has ample alternating current capability. For quick battery charging get a commercial battery charger and hook it up to the 117-volt AC circuit of the generator.

Another kink I used on *Astrea* was a Briggs and Stratton 4-horsepower air-cooled engine coupled to a 65-watt automotive alternator. The whole business weighed less than 60 pounds—base, tank, and all. It produced only 12 volts DC, but it had current enough to start our diesel engine with all our batteries so flat that the cabin lights would not light. Converters are available to provide all the 117-volt current you need from one of these alternators.

Auxiliary battery charging rigs, as well as the charging set on the main engine, have automatic tapering charge rates. This is good automotive practice, but it increases engine time. It means that for the first few minutes the generator puts out full charge to the battery. As the charge in the battery increases, however, the charging rate decreases. If you happen to have 200-ampere-hour batteries, this could mean that a much longer time is spent running the engine than would be needed if the charge did not taper off, but rather went on at a full rate. This is simple to arrange by bypassing the voltage regulator with a double pole switch so that you can cut in a heavy duty rheostat in the feedback path. Use a voltmeter and ammeter to set up the charging rate to the maximum the generator will put out, or all that the battery will stand. Use a hydrometer or

MANUAL CHARGING SCHEMATIC

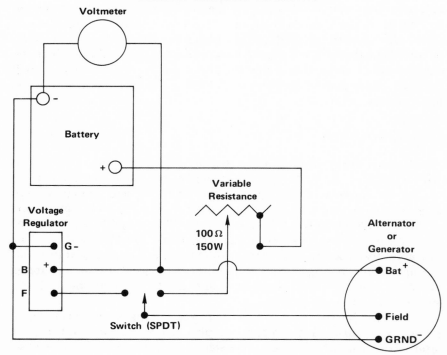

Regulate Charging Voltage to 14.6 to 15.0 Volts

Figure 6

sensitive voltmeter to monitor the state of battery charge, and instead of taking five hours to charge a 100-amp-hour battery, you can do it in two. Any good electrician can make these changes, or you can do them yourself.

Tanks

Fuel tanks should be well secured and located as low as possible in the bilges, as should the water tanks. Be sure, however, that they are all removable without dismantling the yacht. Tanks of any material have a less than infinite life span, and you don't want to replace most of the cabin joinery just to replace the tanks.

Tanks for diesel fuel should not be of stainless steel, because the sulphur in it reacts with the stainless and leaves a white residue that can clog filters and injector systems. Good diesel tanks are made of black iron, well red-leaded on the outside. The tanks should have adequate ventilation space between them and the hull, if it is wood, or rot is likely to develop behind the tank.

Water tanks should be of stainless steel, Monel, or one of the more modern plastics. I would shy away from fiberglass water tanks because of the terrible smell and taste that will be with you for ages. I buy water tanks from trailer suppliers, and, if they have adequate baffles, they work out well.

I prefer also to have a kerosene tank aboard with either gravity or pump delivery to a small spout in the salon. This allows one to fill the lamps without pouring kerosene all over the place from a jerrycan while trying to hit the ridiculously small filler holes with which most lamps are provided.

Stoves

The selection of a galley stove is a more serious matter than most inexperienced cruisers may guess, and the wrong choice can cause no end of grief. The average weekender is provided with an alcohol stove "because it is safe." That may be so, but I have seen more yachts afire from alcohol stoves than from any other cause. The big problem with the "alky" stove is that when you prime it you can hardly see the flame until the heat begins to get high. Consequently, another priming charge is added, thus flooding the stove with burning alcohol. The second problem is that quite often the priming is not sufficient to preheat the burner properly, so a good flareup occurs when a match is touched to the burner. (This latter weakness is also common to the kerosene pressure stove.) Third, alcohol has a most disagreeable odor and produces very little heat for the fuel burned. Last, alcohol is most expensive and often unobtainable in foreign ports. Of course, you could burn tequilla or vodka, but most of us have better uses for those commodities. On a ninety-day cruise with a crew of three we burned eleven gallons of alcohol. At somewhat over three dollars a gallon the cost was nearly forty dollars for stove fuel. That forty dollars would have been much better applied to the food supply! The only saving grace of the alcohol stove is that when it goes ablaze the fire can be put out with water sloshed liberally over it. But have you ever thought of how you would get a bucket or two of water quickly into your galley?

The butane or propane stove is most satisfactory, and I have nothing but good to say about it, provided the installation is done properly. I would have nothing but solid copper piping in the system. This means that the stove cannot be gimbaled, and that's not so bad if the yacht is large and has an easy motion. *Astrea* had her stove set athwart-ships and not gimbaled, and only once did she chuck a pot at the cook. The cakes and bread from her oven bore silent witness to the tack she was on, however! A good shutoff valve should be provided both at the stove and at the tank, and it should be used religiously. The tank will, of course, be mounted on deck, where any leakage or spillage may drain safely overboard and not collect in low places. The heat from gas stoves is much greater than from alcohol, but I don't think it beats the efficiency of kerosene. The drawback to bottled gas is that, although most foreign ports sell butane and propane, their filler apparatus is different from the American variety. To beat this problem, either carry spare tanks enough to finish the cruise, or be prepared to make up adapters for foreign threading systems (having a good brazing torch along helps here). On *Astrea*, which had a three-burner butane stove with oven, we baked all our bread and cooked three meals a day for two of us, and five gallons of fuel would last as long as seventy days.

Perhaps the best bet for a strictly cruising yacht is the time-tested Primus kerosene (paraffin) stove. Kerosene stoves are hotter, boil water faster, and are easier on fuel than any other type. If you watch the priming, they are safe and reliable. If priming is insufficient, a flareup or a cloud of smelly black smoke is your reward! Kerosene is universally available and cheap, and it is also the fuel of choice for cabin lamps. You can substitute number one diesel fuel as well, in an emergency! On *Dawn Treader* I solved the stove problem by buying a three-burner trailer stove for seventy dollars, removing the butane burners, and replacing them with Primus burners at a cost of fifteen dollars each. The pressure tank is a used beer keg that is pressurized by a bicycle tire pump. So, for a reasonable hundred and fifty three dollars and some cents I have the hottest, most economical stove possible. Parts are available anywhere in the world, as is fuel. The "marine" version of such a rig costs well in excess of four hundred dollars if bought from your local marine hardware store.

Every marine stove worth its salt has a good set of "fiddles" on it. I prefer the "Princess" fiddle, which is available from trailer suppliers at a much reduced cost compared to the same thing marketed by marine stores. This fiddle has shaped arms that hold pots securely over the burners, and it is superior to the straight ones that form sort of a bowling alley for the pots to slide up and down. Some skippers use two springs attached to the front and back of the stove to snap over each side of the pot and hold it in place, but I have found that the spring gets weak from the heat of the stove in time and fails.

To gimbal or not to gimbal? I believe that gimbals are necessary if the yacht's motion is quick enough to fling things from the stove. As I mentioned, *Astrea* had no gimbals and she never threw pots and pans around. *Laguna* had gimbals and yet she was greatly celebrated for her ability to chuck a pot the full length of the salon in a seaway. If the stove is mounted longitudinally, perhaps gimbals are best, because they give you a fighting chance of getting the bread out of the oven without its falling on the cook. If the stove is athwartships, however, this danger is less and gimbals are not needed. If gimbals are the thing, they must be near the plane of the pots and pans. The idea is to make a teeter-totter of the burner plate rather than a swing. The swing type (set above the plane of the burners) can set up strange harmonics, which, if they get out of phase with the pot, can cause the famous catapulting effect. The stove should be provided with generous counterweights in the oven or bolted to the bottom of the stove, or the whole thing is likely to turn turtle just when you have four lobsters on the burner.

In the tropics it is wise to have a good extractor vent above the stove. A good old "Charley Noble" is fine if it has a good seal and admits no water below. I have used a six-inch rotating type (like the kind you see on industrial buildings) for years, and it has never admitted any significant amount of water unless that part of the ship happened to be submerged at the time. The rotator is quite cheap and can be bought from Perko Hardware at surprisingly reasonable prices.

Heating stoves are necessary if the voyage is to enter the higher latitudes. I like the vented kerosene type that is popular in Europe, since it doesn't require you to carry still another type of fuel. I used a coal burner for a time but found the fuel too bulky and messy. The smoke smeared the deck paintwork, and the cinders endangered the sails. Larger yachts sometimes are equipped with fireplaces, but they are seldom usable at sea. If you have a kerosene cook stove with a vent above, it will make a great heating stove. The alcohol ones are not so good, since a goodly amount of water is given off. The butane ones are fine, too, but most owners shy away from using them too much because of the difficulty of obtaining fuel.

How grand it is to pop below on a cold, blustery night to a cabin that is warmer than the outside temperature, if only by a few degrees. Morale is reinstated, and that bitter slog to weather becomes almost worth it.

A good deal of thought must be put into finding the proper place to plant any heating stove. It must not make too obvious a handhold, or some crew member clutching in the dark for support may get a most unpleasant surprise. It should clear any flammable structure by at least a foot, and the surroundings should be well insulated by asbestos faced with bright stainless steel so that the heat is reflected away from woodwork.

The venting of heating stoves is critical. The vent must be protected by a water channel iron so that the cabin overhead is not burned up some cheery night, and the vent must have a sprayproof outlet. The sails must be considered, or backdrafts from them may make the heater useless under sail.

Dinghies

Most often the ubiquitous Sabot is chosen as a dinghy for a cruising yacht. The type will carry three or possibly four adults ashore if the landing is to be a dock, but it is miserable and wet in a surf. The Sabot was intended to be, and is, a fascinating training racer for the younger set. It has too much deadrise and too wet a bow to be a serviceable yacht tender.

The nylon-rubber dinghy is far more suitable as a tender in spite of its high cost. It is easy to store below out of the weather, and it will carry a staggering amount of weight through the surf or over moderate-sized rocks without upsetting and dumping the crew and shopping bags in the drink. The rubber boat will not row as easily as will the "hard" dinghy, but it reacts well with a small outboard motor if it has some kind of stiffening for the bottom (usually plywood floorboards).

The rubber dinghy will serve well as a survival boat if you can figure some way to get it inflated and in the water when the yacht is busily foundering. CO_2 inflating kits are available for some, but the problem, as I see it, is keeping the dinghy from simply blowing away before the crew can get in it. One blustery morning beneath the lee of Moana Loa volcano we were struck by a williwaw of better than fifty knots. I looked astern where we had tied a five-by-ten-foot rubber dinghy by a thirty-foot painter. Astern of it we had tied a six-foot plastic shoreboat on another twenty feet of line. The rubber boat was at an altitude of about six feet and was rotating swiftly, chucking coconuts and paddles and the like all over the place. The plastic one was merely jumping up and down about two feet. I realized how hard it would be to use that rubber thing under survival conditions. The answer is to have a few good small drogues attached to the bottom of the beast, so that if you get it down to the water, it will stay there.

The entire matter of lifeboats is perhaps academic as far as small yachts are concerned. The small yacht is more like a lifeboat than anything else in the first place, and if you can't keep the yacht afloat, how in hell are you going to keep a dinghy afloat? In a racing yacht on an organized race there is a good chance of being picked up if you take to the liferaft, since people know where you are, more or less, and will report you overdue. In a cruising vessel, no one usually knows with any certainty where you are, or whether or not you are overdue. Your chances of being picked up are much less, unless you drift to that handy island to leeward.

I am shocked at the prices charged by Avon of England for their survival rafts. When I commented on this to one of their representatives, he asked, "How much is your life worth?" I replied, "Will your company *guarantee* my survival?" Since most cruising accidents happen on reefs rather than at sea in the first place, perhaps a good, seaworthy rubber dinghy is the better bargain. The eight or nine hundred dollars that would have bought a survival raft can best be spent in making sure that the yacht and her crew will never need it.

Perhaps if one spends too much of his time worrying over whether he will survive a passage he should not go to sea in the first place. This is not to say that a skipper should not be prudent and prepared.

But once he has taken the reasonable precautions and has his vessel in shape, he should go ahead and enjoy the voyage and concentrate on driving the boat and making a pleasant passage.

Some so-called cruising boats carry the dinghy over the transom on davits. This is fine in soundings and for harbor-hopping down the coast, but it is less than prudent at sea. A good following sea may break on it, smashing the dinghy or davits or perhaps dumping the whole apparatus on the helmsman. Many a dinghy has been lost from stern davits, and also quite a few from the cabin top. In gale conditions it is not uncommon to hear of dinghies swept away, sometimes carrying a good part of the cabin top with them.

I carried a dinghy on the cabin top with a good stout canvas cover over it and the whole lashup secured to deck ringbolts by half-inch dacron lines. Unfortunately, it interfered with forward visibility and undoubtedly added to wind resistance going to weather. In addition, the dinghy would mysteriously fill up with water every so often, soaking the goods that were stored in it. I always kept a sharp stainless steel knife lashed to the gripes so that in any emergency I could quickly cut them and free the dinghy, which contained a rubber boat, rations, and water. The idea was that the whole package would hit the water and could be sorted out later. Actually, in gale conditions when one would be likely to need it, the whole thing would simply have blown away or have been previously swept away by a sea. Still, I never lost a dinghy carried this way.

I now dispense with the hard dinghy and keep a rubber one below where it cannot be swept away before I need it. It has a CO_2 inflation system, drogues, and survival rations when I am at sea. I pump it up with a hand pump, normally, so that I am always sure it hasn't deteriorated. It is absolutely amazing how much harder you can drive a yacht in a gale if it has a rubber dinghy rather than a hard one.

Pumps

No sea boat can be said to be complete unless she has a pump system that will clear the vessel of water quickly and efficiently. Most production yachts either have no pumps at all, or they have one of those pitiful little electric ones that wouldn't even clear a goldfish bowl efficiently. What you need is a man-sized hand pump that will throw a minimum of twenty-five gallons per minute and that will not clog with the inevitable junk that finds its way into the bilge. The modern diaphragm pump, if it is large enough, serves far better than the old "navy" lift pump. The hose connections should be a minimum of one and a half inches, and the valves should be full bore size and made of neoprene.

The pump must be mounted in such a manner that it can be actually used at sea. I like one at the helmsman's station, so that a man may both pump and handle the yacht, and another one below out of the weather in case sustained pumping should be required. Each pump should have a good "strum" box of half-inch mesh at the intake. It is not sufficient to merely wrap screen around the end of the intake hose, as it will rapidly clog. A box about ten by ten inches, made of mesh, is more resistant to clogging. A kink that few people think of is to put a Y valve in the intake line to the marine head. In case of too much water for the normal pumps to handle, just flip the valve and the head sucks water from the bilge instead of from outside. It's surprising how much water a good marine head will pump. In addition, many a yacht disaster has been averted by having a few stout buckets aboard, and strong backs to man them. *Tzu Hang* was saved from sinking by this method, and Vito Dumas never carried a bilge pump at all!

Galley pumps are a good source of argument and comment, because so many are so bad. They generally are made of plastic and have ball or flapper valves. Many of them are cheaply made and cannot stand the rigors of ocean travel. The actuating shafts usually get leaky, so water gets out and sometimes air gets in, causing the pump to lose its prime. My main complaint is when I wash my hands. First I pump some water to wet my hands, then I soap up. Then I use one soapy hand to pump water to rinse the other. Then I get soap all over the rinsed hand from the pump handle. Also, when you are using one hand to hold a plate with, and one hand to pump with, how do you wash the dishes? The result is a lot of wasted water. Whale Pumps of England makes a fine foot pump that works well. It is easily installed by boring a large hole in the deck (about one and a half inches). I have used such pumps for more than five years for both fresh and salt water with never a failure. The foot pump also leaves the galley less cluttered, since it needs only a small spout at the sink.

Life Lines and Pulpits

In recent years it has become fashionable to rig cruising yachts with rather high life lines and stanchions. In actual fact, an extremely high life line may be more dangerous than a low one because it tears out of the deck more easily due to its greater leverage. Life lines should be double with stanchions about every seven feet or so.

A good attachment to the shrouds can be substituted for the odd stanchion. Double lines make a good corral for downed foresails, and many useful things can be tied to them at sea, handy to get at. But never trust the things to really save you from going overboard.

In heavy weather it is the life line stanchions that most often fail, usually due to a poor job of installation. Stanchions must have a large base, at least four or five inches square, and be through-bolted to the deck. The large base gives a little more advantage to the fasteners when some moose of a crewman lurches into the life line. I have had perfectly good stanchions rip up a section of kingplank because there were not adequate washers or plates under them. Life lines should be of wire, rather than rope, but some skippers still use a rope line for the lower one. The plastic-covered wire makes for a good-looking installation. The plastic has a habit of turning brown every so often, and then it can be cleaned with a good detergent; if cleansed with cleanser or abrasive, however, it becomes porous and then gets dirtier faster and more permanently.

Bow pulpits are seen on nearly every yacht these days, and they are handy things, too, as long as the headstay is out at the end of the boat. Some yachts with more inboard stays do not really need pulpits. Bow pulpits should enclose the crewman who is working the headsails in such a manner that he can work with both hands without coming adrift. Modern pulpits have a double row of tubing to match the double row of life lines. It has become popular to rig the running lights on the pulpit. This allows a clear and unobstructed view of the lights when an overlapping headsail is carried. The problem is that the lamps get wetter there than they would on the cabin side, and there is generally a higher risk of failure in that position. Careful attention to sealing the light and its wiring usually eliminates the trouble (and, of course, the wise sailor has a set of kerosene lights in case of power failure anyway).

The stern pulpit, or pushpit, is the least necessary of all the life line arrangements, but it provides a good place to fish from, and a spot to hang the taffrail log and ensign. Yachts with self-steering wind vanes usually need a pushpit because one often needs to go aft to adjust the mechanism on dark nights and in stormy weather. The greatest value of stern pulpits is as a place to rig weather cloths.

Weather cloths should be made of strong, durable material. I have used surplus navy hammocks, which have good, strong grommets every three or four inches, lashed to the upper life lines and to deck eyes fitted to match the grommet spacing. I have had several moderate seas burst over the quarter without breaking the lashings. It is astonishing how much water a set of weather cloths will keep out of the cockpit, and how pleasant it is to be out of the tearing wind when on watch. One caution, though—the stanchions must be quite strong, or breaking seas may sweep away weather cloths, life lines, and pulpits in one fell swoop!

Mechanical Logs

I have always preferred the good old taffrail log to any other system of measuring distance at sea, mostly because it always works. The rotating type is more accurate than the drag type.

The principle is simple. Tow a threaded object through the water and observe how many times it rotates per mile. Then make a counter that is calibrated in nautical miles, and you have a taffrail log. I use a Columbia log that was built in 1884, and it has served to measure many thousands of miles. I have been told that the "fish" on the end of the log line is great bait for sharks and the like, but I have lost only two in many years of dragging one behind. The problem is that often one forgets that the thing is there at the end of a cruise and backs down on it, causing the line to foul the rudder or propeller. When fishing it is also wise to keep a sharp lookout, because when you get a strike the fish may get your line hopelessly tangled in the log line.

Walker Logs of England makes a modern taffrail log that uses a smaller fish, which is painted black. It supposedly attracts fewer predators, but I have lost more of these fish than I have the large brass rotator of the Columbia. The Walker has an auxiliary speedometer apparatus, but it is electrical and therefore subject to rapid failure at sea.

Lamps

Perhaps a word should be said about lamps for cruising boats. I wouldn't have electric ones except for a neon over the chart table (this because my eyesight is rapidly failing and my arms are not long enough to get that tiny print in focus). Even my neon lamp is powered by its own separate battery and is portable so it can be carried out into the cockpit for tricky piloting with harbor charts.

Like kerosene stoves, kerosene lamps are the ticket for the ocean cruiser, because fuel is readily available and almost anything in the way of diesel fuel can be used in a pinch. Electric ones are fine for the coastal cruiser, because he can always get to port to have the batteries charged. Kerosene lamps add a warmth and coziness to the salon that just can't be matched by chrome-plated electric ones. Besides, the kerosene lamp helps chase a little of the humidity away.

I don't like any American-made lamps too well, because they never seem to have a true gimbal, being gimbaled only one way, and they have to be unscrewed from the bracket to fill them. Simpson and Lawrence of Glasgow makes a fine seamanlike lamp. It has a one-inch wick that really puts out some light, and the whole thing can be lifted out of its four-way gimbal to fill it. You don't even have to remove the chimney to light the wick, because the chimney is hinged on one side. Anyone who has not tried to light the lamps in a fifteen-foot trade wind sea can't really appreciate the S and L lamps!

Aside from cabin lamps, I carry a large pressure kerosene lantern made by Optimus in Sweden. I call it the "steam boat scarer." It serves as a very bright light to make your yacht look like a fishing vessel to predatory steamers. (It seems that a vessel fishing has right of way even over God.) The pressure lamp also serves well as a cabin heater during a cold spell and puts out about as much light as a 100-watt bulb. In the tropics we always set ours on the bridge deck just outside the companionway so that we got some of the light and the mosquitoes got all the heat.

Electrical Equipment

As I've said, I certainly do not advocate too much electrical equipment on a voyaging yacht. Still, it does come in handy when in port, so plans for such equipment and the necessary support systems should be included in the outfitting of a cruising boat.

In selecting the items you decide to include, you must anticipate their inherent lack of efficiency and prepare for it. For example, an electric refrigerator, so handy at home where you simply pay for the current at the end of the month, becomes a fuel-burning ogre at sea if you use it consistently. Consider a small unit that uses 10 amperes at 12 volts when it is running. The manufacturer claims that it needs to run only half the time in order to keep the box cool. He runs his tests where the ambient temperature is as low as the advertising laws allow. When you get into the tropics, where everything seems to be at 85 degrees all the time, the duty cycle goes up to 80 percent or so, depending on how good the insulation happens to be. Thus, in the first case you would take 10 amperes at 50 percent duty cycle, which would equal 5 amps per hour. Multiply that by 24 hours, and you have the battery drain for a day's sailing—120 ampere-hours. To replace this charge, which has been lost from the batteries, you must run the engine. Let's say you have a 50-ampere generator. If it charged at full rate all the time (which it won't unless you have made the feedback alterations described in the section on cruising generators), it would take 2 hours and 20 minutes just to replace the charge lost to the refrigerator. Of course, you must also replace a few ampere-hours lost just because you used the starter motor to start the engine. With a tapering charge rate, the average charge is less than 50 percent of the rated charge, leaving you with 4 hours and 40 minutes of running time just for the privilege of cold beer. If you consider that the 80 percent duty cycle is probably nearer the truth than the 50 percent—and it has been, in my experience—then the sum (with a tapering charge) becomes 8 amp-hours $\times$ 24, or 192 amp-hours. Divide 192 by 25 amps (average rate), and you get $7\frac{7}{10}$ hours per day, plus some for the starter, that some generating equipment must be run!

Since the food in the refrigerator must be backed up by equal rations that do not need refrigeration in case the refrigerator fails, it all seems too high a price to pay on any but the larger voyaging yachts.

Any electrical equipment has a cost, and that cost is expressed in ampere-hours. Since most electrical equipment is rated in watts, one should know the formula for converting watts to ampere-hours. One watt equals one volt at one ampere. Thus, a piece of equipment using 48 watts of power at 12 volts would use $\frac{48}{12}$ or 4 amps. If it were run for one hour, the use would be 4 ampere-hours.

Batteries are rated optimistically in ampere-hours. A 200-ampere-hour battery should provide a flow of 1 ampere at its voltage for 200 hours, or a flow of 4 amps for 50 hours. The great problem is that not all of the flow is usable. Once a battery is about three-quarters exhausted, the voltage is so reduced that much electrical equipment is not able to function. Thus a 200-amp-hour battery may practically provide only 100 amp-hours of useful service. You must also provide reserve current for starting the engine if the yacht has no hand-starting capability. This is usually another battery, which can be switched on just to start the engine. I am never quite sure that I remembered to switch it out of the circuit after running the engine, and often I have not, leaving me with two flat batteries and no way to start the engine.

Depth Sounders

One of the most valuable pieces of electrical equipment is the depth sounder. It is far handier than the lead line, because you don't have to go out and heave the lead each time you are curious about the water depth. You can also navigate in a fog by taking soundings at intervals and comparing the results with lines of soundings on your chart, provided you have a general idea of where you are and that your sounder has enough power to reach the bottom.

The principle of operation is simple. You excite a piezoelectric device with an ultrasonic oscillator pulse, and it in turn vibrates. The vibration travels away from the piezoelectric transducer until it either hits something or dissipates. If it hits something (hopefully the bottom) the echo is picked up by the same transducer, amplified, and displayed on some kind of scale. The flashing kind with the round face shows a "blip" when the pulse is sent out. At this time a rotator starts spinning at a constant rate and another "blip" is given off when the return echo is received. Since the speed of sound in salt water is known, the distance that the rotor travels is directly related to the distance the pulse has traveled. Divide by two and you have the depth. Most makers just calibrate the face in fathoms or feet so you need do no division or calculations.

The location of the transducer must be chosen with care, because it will not work efficiently if there are bubbles or foreign matter on it to any great degree. It should be mounted on the front half of the yacht, because when underway there is separation of the boundary layer on the back half. This produces turbulence and bubbles, which can cause misreading. The transducer should be mounted so that it is square to the bottom when the ship is level, in order to reduce heeling error. Normally heeling up to 20 degrees results in little error, provided the water is less than ten or so fathoms.

In fiberglass yachts it is a good idea to make a "sea chest." In this system the transducer is mounted *inside* the yacht where it cannot be fouled by barnacles or weed. Just glass in a box about six or so inches square, make a watertight lid for it, and mount the transducer in the lid, just as though it were the bottom of the boat. Then drill two small holes through to the outside water (through the hull, not the box). You then have a watertight box full of water inside your boat, in which the transducer is ensconced. Because of the density of fiberglass structures the transducer ignores them and sends its pulse to the ocean bottom and receives the echo just as though it were really in the water. The trick saves a lot of cleaning of the transducer and saves cluttering up the bottom with a lot of parasitic drag. You should secure the lid on the chest with a rubber gasket and some screws, however, so that the transducer can be removed in case of failure, or if algae begin to form.

The recording type of depth sounder is dandy for navigation, because it leaves a record that can be compared easily with lines of soundings on the chart. It uses quite a bit of current, however, and it is much more expensive than the flasher types, which are more than adequate.

Many of the flasher types can be ordered with self-contained batteries so they will be independent of the ship's battery. This is important, because it is at the end of the voyage that the depth sounder is most likely to be necessary, not at the beginning. At the beginning the battery is usually in good shape, but you already know the depths in your home port. At the finish of a passage, if my experience serves me well, you will have batteries that are dead or nearly so and at the same time knowledge of water depth will become crucial. For safety's sake, have a sounder that has its own small batteries. Some models made in England have connections for both ship's batteries and self-contained ones—surely the best of all possible worlds!

Radio Gear

Nothing identifies the novice voyager faster than looking below and finding a ship-to-shore radiotelephone. Such a radio is fine for the coastwise cruiser. He can call in to get reservations at a good restaurant, and he can advise the Coast Guard that he is out of fuel and needs a tow. Current FCC regulations, however, limit him to a very high frequency (VHF) rig that has a range of about twelve miles under good conditions. The ocean voyager may purchase one of the high seas single sideband units, and it will allow him communication with one of several coast stations.

Suppose that you have been in a gale and have sprung an uncontrollable leak that your two pumps can't keep up with. You get on your radiotelephone rig and try to raise some Coast Guard station. Unfortunately, radio propagation in the bands you have aboard are bad today. Suppose conditions get better that night and you get through to Long Beach Coast Guard station. You notify them of your position and advise that you are sinking. They in turn will send out a broadcast the next morning advising ships to be on the lookout for survivors. Or suppose money has become less scarce and they have enough fuel to send out a search plane. How will it find you now that your yacht has sunk and you are floating about in your dinghy in a gale sea? Your chances of being found are, in my opinion, about the same as that proverbial needle in the haystack, if indeed any one even bothers. I have a few friends who were lost on a voyage back from Hawaii. They had a radiotelephone aboard, but no signal was ever heard. I would assume that weather bad enough to do in the yacht would long before have done in the highly vulnerable electrical system on which the radio depends. Unless a more reliable system than present ones can be found, I would rather use the money to strengthen the yacht and equip her so that she need never use a radio at sea. As a matter of fact, have you ever noticed how much nonsense is heard on the "safety" radio if you listen in?

If you must have communication aboard, for peace of mind or whatever, one system, although not perfect, is far better than the official ship radiotelephone system. That is the amateur radio. Amateur or "ham" gear is far superior to anything marketed for yachtsmen to use, for radio amateurs just will not put up with the cheap circuits that afflict marine radio gear. Amateur gear has the capability of changing to a wide variety of frequencies, one of which is almost always in a good propagation condition at any hour of the day. The power of these sets is variable, so you need use only enough to accomplish your ends. I have sat in Los Angeles with a ham set putting out 10 watts of power and had good, audible contact with hams in New Zealand and Japan.

The General Amateur license is not unduly difficult for the average yachtsman to obtain. You must learn some elements of electronics, but you should know those anyway. And you must demonstrate an ability to copy and send Morse code at the rate of thirteen words per minute without error for one straight minute. Since radiobeacons, weather reports, and often communications from passing ships are in Morse, the exercise is well worth the effort.

Many cruising sailors are turning to ham sets, and a worldwide network is now in operation. In case of emergency just call any ham operator in the world, and he will see that your message gets to the proper party. You can even call a ham near a Coast Guard station, and he will "patch" you into the local telephone, so you can tell them your troubles directly.

While you almost never see a transmitter on a real voyaging yacht, you will see a fine collection of receivers. My short wave receiver is the best I can afford. During those long, boring days in a calm, my receiver keeps me in touch with reality, and during the ripping, tearing noise of a gale, it drowns out some of the enervating noise. The short wave bands carry an incredible assortment of information, from the exact time from station WWV, to weather reports, to just plain entertainment from radio Peking. Most receivers will do double duty as radio direction finders, since most of them have a ferrite loopstick antenna. I hook up a piece of wire from a shroud to the auxiliary antenna connector, so my whole rig acts as an antenna.

The modern transistor radio usually has its own batteries, and this saves power from the main batteries. I have found that I could run my Panasonic short wave receiver fifteen hours a day for thirty days in the tropics before the alkaline batteries ran flat. It is wise to have a backup radio aboard, and this one should be small. It's really fine to have a radio that you can tuck into your foul weather gear and listen to with an earphone on a lonely night watch. You can also take it on deck when you take sights and get the accurate time from WWV.

The radio direction finder is a piece of equipment I would never give locker space. First, most of them are nothing more than transistor radios with antennae that will rotate. Why not spend a lot less for a short wave receiver and rotate the whole thing? Second, the null angle on most RDF's is about 8 degrees or so. If you are out of sight of the radio station (really fifty miles or so) that 8-degree error could put you miles from your actual position. Third, a small yacht jumps about so much that it is hard to tell exactly what course you are really on when you take the bearings.

My system is to use celestial navigation until I make landfall, and then to walk up with my short wave receiver, stand over the compass, aim the radio at the station, or stations, and take a rough bearing. "It's over thataway!" is good enough for me. If the weather is thick, I wouldn't trust an RDF as far as I could throw it anyway! I would rather heave to and wait out the fog than trust a very expensive yacht to the accuracy of a five-dollar transistor radio, which is what usually hides inside a three-hundred-dollar RDF!

Autopilots

The electronic autopilot is popular in America these days, so I suppose I should say something about it. First, it really has little place offshore anymore, because wind vane self-steerers are much better if they are well designed and if the yacht is of a proper hull form.

The autopilot uses a sensing compass, usually read by a photo-electric cell, that can be set to any course desired. When the yacht's heading veers from the assigned course, signals are amplified by a solid state amplifier and sent to the right or left rudder motor until the ship is back on the predetermined heading. Some are called "hunting types," and the steering motors of these are always at work, shifting from port to starboard, keeping the heading relatively constant. The hunting type uses more current than does the non-hunting type, but its cost is usually less. The nonhunting type uses less current because its motors are idle until a deviation is sensed by the master compass. Only then does it send power to the steering motors.

The autopilot has become popular mostly in power boats. Since a great number of cruising yachts now fit that classification, they can use the autopilot to advantage. Under power the autopilot is better than a wind vane, and since the engine is running, there is plenty of power available to supply it. Offshore under sail, the wind vane is the only choice for any but the larger yachts, unless you just happen to like the sound of a generator or engine running all the time.

The cost of the autopilot, together with its often complicated installation, can approach two thousand dollars in some cases. When compared to the cost in the United States of a Hasler wind vane system (imported from England, and not even the best for the cruiser) with its complicated and ugly installation, the autopilot is far more expensive. Compared with the two home-built and simple wind vane systems described in a later chapter (two to three hundred dollars, installed) the autopilot is a bigger loser.

On *Astrea* I found that I could motor sail with my wind vane if I had someone on watch just in case of an occasional veer from course. Along the coast these veers could be dangerous if no one happened to be looking. Offshore while motor sailing, the veers would be of little consequence. Under sail, the wind vane automatically compensates for wind changes, while a major shift sometimes overloads the autopilot, requiring sail changes at odd hours.

Refrigerators

Although you already know what I think of refrigerators offshore, I will comment briefly about the various kinds. Refrigerator systems are of three types: electrical compressor, mechanical compressor, and percolator. The electrical compressor is the least reliable and efficient and also the most common. It lacks efficiency because it depends on a less than efficient generating-battery system for its power. The mechanical compressor type is highly efficient since it is connected directly to the main engine. The drawback is that the box insulation must be quite efficient or the engine time gets too high for comfort. The percolator type uses a flame—butane, kerosene, or anything else. The drawback is that the cooling coils must be kept level in order for the system to cool efficiently. Some skippers just gimbal a kerosene burner and put up with the slightly reduced efficiency, and De Ridder, on *Magic Dragon*, gimbals the whole refrigerator.

The primary problem is to reduce the amount of time that the compressor must run or the flame must burn. To accomplish this end, several dodges are in order. First, do not have a box that opens from the front. Front openers spill out cold air when opened, requiring much more compressor time than does a top opener, which saves its charge of cool air in much the same way as meat displays in a supermarket. Second, have the box well insulated. Since cold tends to subside rather than rise, it is the bottom of the box that needs the greatest insulation. I like to build the box of plywood, well glassed over, and then pour in Polyfoam insulation to a thickness of at least six inches. Since the water temperatures in the tropics are in the eighties at times, rather more insulation is needed if the box is close to the hull. Of course, on a wooden yacht, ample ventilation space must also be provided near the hull to help reduce the chances of rot. On *Dawn Treader*, which has only an icebox, the chart table is thirty inches square by twenty-six inches deep. Into this is set a smaller box eighteen by twenty by sixteen inches deep. The space around the box is taken up by blocks of foam and poured foam to leave a minimum of six or so inches of insulation at the thinnest point. The thing will keep a block of ice weighing fifty pounds for twenty days.

The refrigerator system can take advantage of some space age technology, both in terms of insulating materials, and in the way of holding plates. Holding plates or "cold plates" are really eutectic solutions surrounding the expansion coils. They get very cold and tend to hold (or release more slowly) the coolness pumped into them by the compressor. Cold plates can be obtained from refrigeration firms. With a good cold plate system and an engine-driven compressor, I know of a yacht that runs her refrigerator for only five hours a week. When you get to this level of efficiency the refrigerator starts to become worthwhile. The cost of such systems is no higher than that of many of the less efficient ready-made systems, but a good deal of ingenuity and skill are needed to set one up in the first place.

Windlasses

I would say that any yacht requiring more than a hundred pounds of anchor gear should have some sort of windlass to help raise it. I have lived with both electric and mechanical types, and both are good for different reasons. I have never given space to an electric one on my own yachts, mostly because of cost and weight of batteries required.

On *Astrea* I used a small Albina windlass to raise a thirty-five pound Danforth anchor with three hundred feet of five-sixteenths-inch chain. When it was all out, when I was anchoring in deep water, it took about an hour to get it all back in. The windlass was not hard to work, but it brought in only four links per stroke. I used to sweat and groan and say that my epitaph should read "Found dead close by an anchor winch" until I saw someone with a dead battery and an electric anchor winch. In the land of the blind, a one-eyed man is king!

I once used an electric winch on another yacht, on which I was crewing, to lift a plow anchor and three hundred feet of heavy chain. Being not terribly bright, most of the crew were forward watching the operation. Imagine our surprise when we looked aft and found the yacht on fire! The electrical cables had been too small for the current load and had become so hot that they set the engine room on fire! The cables must be as heavy as you can afford. The cost of cables for a fifty-foot yacht can approach the cost of the windlass. The switch must be of robust capability because of great current requirements when you lift heavy gear.

The location of the windlass switch is sometimes critical because of the inherent danger of automatic devices. The foot, or step, switch is dangerous if there is a chop running. The forward section of the yacht is narrow, and having just come in from sea you will be somewhat unsteady in the new motion. It is easy to stumble and accidentally trip the switch. I know of more than one loss of legs from this kind of accident. A hand switch of the solenoid type with a master switch aft is perhaps the best combination for safety. I, for one, will never forget the picture of a man sitting on the foredeck staring incredulously at his leg lying on the opposite side of the yacht after tripping a foot switch and getting tangled in the rapidly moving chain. Modern medical techniques saved his life, and even the use of his leg (after years of surgery and bone grafts), but he has sold his yacht to pay the bills and still pales when anchor windlasses are mentioned.

If all safety precautions are taken, the electric windlass is a good piece of gear. The main engine should always be running when it is used so you won't run the battery flat. In shallow water the load is not excessive, but in deep water you can motor slowly forward to ease the strain on the windlass, thus saving a good deal of battery.

The windlass must be through-bolted to the deck and should have generous additional plates or stiffeners both above and below the deck. When mooring, or lying to a sea anchor or drogue, the windlass can take a great deal of strain, as it can when you accept an occasional tow. Having sheared a few windlass bolts in my time, I would bend an effort to have the strongest possible installation.

Anchors

The first thing to say about anchors is that when cruising you can never have too many. Several good types are available, and the use determines which is best. Manufacturers always have tables that show how heavy an anchor should be for various types of craft. I would always go heavier than the recommendations for my storm anchor and have one of the recommended size for everyday use.

Every yacht should have a minimum of two working anchors, and I add a storm anchor and a "lunch hook" to my collection. There should be two cables forward, one for each of two large anchors. I usually make up one with fifty feet or so of chain and a few hundred feet of nylon line for temporary anchoring and have the other all chain for long-term anchoring in coral waters. The stern anchor should have a very long line and a light chain. You can then run in toward shore, throw out the hook, and motor on until the line has all run out. Then drop the bow hook and haul aft on the stern line, and you are anchored snugly bow and stern even in a crowded anchorage. How much more difficult to drop a bow hook first and then try to back down without hitting everything in the anchorage!

I favor the Danforth anchor over all others in most conditions. It is light and relatively inexpensive and holds like mad if set properly. Europeans seem to like the plow anchor for the usual muddy bottoms in the Thames River. The plow type is awkward to stow unless you carry it in a bow roller hanging beside the headstay. The plow is not as prone to being hauled free when the tide or wind shifts as is the Danforth, but I have never had that problem with the Danforth, either.

The traditional Herreshoff pattern yachtsman anchor is outmoded today, since it is large and clumsy in relation to its holding power.

The folding Northill anchors that were used on our flying boats in World War II are great for stern hooks and light-duty lunch hooks. They are of stainless steel, and a twenty-six pounder has better holding power, especially in gravel and sand, than the yachtsman.

Some skippers like a "messenger weight" on the line when the water is of a depth that does not allow enough scope. The messenger is sent sliding down the anchor cable to set about halfway down the line. This weight, which can either be fixed to the cable or sent down later on a traveler, causes a sag in the cable that makes the pull on the anchor more parallel to the bottom and increases holding power. I believe the things are an unnecessary complication. If you can't anchor in the right place, don't anchor at all, but go and look for a proper spot.

Some sort of an anchor buoy is nice when you want to go off for a short day sail and don't want to haul in all your anchors. A plastic bottle works fine. Just tie it to the anchor cable and drop the whole works in the bay. When you return, just pick up the bottle. But be sure the buoy is large enough so that it doesn't sink if you have a chain all the way out.

Compasses

The selection of a compass for a voyaging yacht should be guided by several considerations. The compass should be rugged (I once broke the globe of one by bouncing a flashlight off it); it should be easily read; and it should be well damped for the type of motion characteristic of the yacht.

Two primary types of instrument are available today—the common boat compass, with a flat glass and jeweled card, and the more popular dome magnifier type. The common boat type is extremely rugged and can be refilled with compass fluid by anyone, while the domed type usually requires special handling because of its rather involved sealing system. The boat compass is more difficult to read under bad lighting conditions than is the modern dome type.

The size of compass you need depends on two main things—the acuity of the helmsman's eyes and the degree of steadiness of the yacht. It is wise to avoid those historical monstrosities with the cards laid out in the old point system with picturesque triangles and arrows corresponding to NNE $\frac{1}{2}$ W and so on and to get a compass laid out in modern 360-degree notation. These usually have black and white numeral systems and show figures every 15 degrees. They are far easier to read than the old-style card and lead to fewer helmsman's course errors. The compass must have damping characteristics that allow it to follow, but not overreact to, the twistings and turnings of the vessel. I have found over the years that a small quick yacht cannot always use a six-inch compass card, because the card just can't keep up with the speed of a small yacht's turning rate.

Before buying a compass, check that its gimbals are adequate to handle a 45-degree heel and 30 degrees of pitch. The full spherical bowl type will do this, while some of the less expensive types will not, as they do not have a true spherical bowl.

Hold the compass in front of you and rotate it 20 degrees or so, with a speed as close as you can guess to the maximum rate of turn that your yacht will develop. The card should follow smoothly and should not markedly move past the stopping point of the movement. It is a delicate job to engineer the baffle system in a compass, and the system is designed to handle as wide a variety of motions as possible within the mass-inertia range of the card itself. Some of the cards are so heavy that they cannot be made to follow very quick motions without sacrificing ability to follow large but rather slow motions.

The lubber line should be on the forward half of the compass, and some modern compasses have several lubber lines in various positions. These are necessary for the racing crew so they can more readily detect wind shifts and determine the favored tack. I have also found them of value while voyaging, both to signal significant wind shifts and to allow me to steer from a position other than directly behind the compass.

Since the lubber line represents the bow of the yacht rather than the stern to most helmsmen, it is perhaps not wise to use the kind of compass that reads from the after edge of the card. The coordination of tiller or wheel movement with a compass card that behaves backward to what you are used to is exasperating at the least. I have seen magnificent helmsmen reduced to absolute idiocy by one of those backward-reading compasses. Have you ever tried to write while viewing the paper through a mirror?

I would not use any compass that was not designed for marine use. Aircraft and automotive compasses have respectively too much and too little damping for marine use. Often they are not made of corrosion-resisting materials and will deteriorate rapidly at sea.

Any cruising yacht worthy of the name will carry at least two good steering compasses. One of these is kept below, safely stowed, against the day when some crewman kicks the glass out of the main compass on his way through the cockpit, or when some shattering block or winch showers it with shrapnel. Yachts with self-steering systems should have a tattletale compass below, mounted in such a manner that it can be easily seen by the watch below. I made the mistake in *Astrea* of mounting the tattletale on a forward bulkhead in the main salon, and then I constantly had to walk down the salon, occupied by the sleepers, to read it adequately. The tattletale is best mounted on or near the chart table, where the watch spend most of their time.

Compasses should if at all possible be mounted on the centerline of the yacht to avoid differential heeling error. In any event the lubber line must parallel the centerline of the yacht or a constant error will be introduced. Such error cannot be corrected but must be compensated for in the reading of the compass. I personally like the covered, or hooded, binnacle mount, provided the cover does not prevent the helmsman from reading the compass in any of the strange positions he is likely to assume on a long watch. Ideally, the compass should be mounted in such a manner that you can stand over it to take rough bearings when doing coastal navigation. The compass must be strongly mounted as well. I have several times been thrown rather violently against the binnacle while at sea, and once I even managed to tear the whole compass right off the binnacle pedestal! You must also protect the compass from whipping sheets and tossed winch handles. Some racing boats now carry a cage made of stainless steel tubing running from the deck over the compass to protect it.

The compass should be lighted with a dim red light, and the wires leading to the bulb must be tightly twisted to cancel out any magnetic field effects due to the electric current. Offshore there is little need to keep the compass constantly lighted, since the primary use of the compass is in the detection of wind shifts. Most of the sailing is done by watching the sails rather than the compass. A quick check of the compass heading every ten minutes or so suffices to advise of wind shifts.

5 Self-Steering Systems

A yacht can be made to self-steer in many ways—by systems of sail trim, self-steering twin headsails for downwind work, and the recently popular wind vane servosystem. Self-steering systems are, of course, the best of all possible worlds for the voyager, since they take no power-operated devices as do autopilots. Using only the forces of wind and water, the little ship finds her way across the seas to her port, while the crew relaxes below in the relative security of the cabin. The catch is that many yachts simply cannot effectively use a self-steering gadget. They are of hull forms and rigs that are so unbalanced that even the most powerful and sensitive system is defeated.

Many a skipper brags about his yacht's ability to self-steer. Perhaps a rather stiff definition of the term would cause him to back off a bit. It is true that many yachts find their ways from port to port without the benefit of a helmsman, but do they self-steer? I would say that almost any old barge will hold roughly to a course if the foresails are sheeted flat or hauled slightly to weather, provided that she is on the wind. Vito Dumas apparently used this principle to advantage when he needed sleep on *Lheg II*. But forereaching along at a reduced speed, even though roughly on course, does not constitute self-steering in my book. I would not say a vessel is self-steering until she holds well to her course with all sails drawing efficiently and with no loss of speed. She should also do this in any but gale conditions.

Astrea would hold within 5 degrees of the apparent wind on any point of sailing and in winds exceeding fifty knots for days at a time. In the final analysis, I would not consider any self-steering system to be good enough unless the skipper felt quite secure putting on his nightshirt and turning in at dusk with all sails set in force seven winds! Using this last criterion, not many systems are good enough.

In self-steering systems as in all else at sea, the simplest system is the best. There are quite a few systems now on the market, some of them quite good, like the Hasler system and the Aries system, both from England. Both suffer from that British tendency to continually add things to a design until it works well but lacks both looks and reliability. Most of the production American systems that I have seen are either copies of the Hasler system or mechanical monstrosities made of aluminum, stainless steel, and phenolic sheet and generously anodized and chrome-plated. Most of the American systems have not been adequately tested at sea. In fact, several that I know of have never been to sea because electrolysis destroyed them before the voyage could begin!

While self-steering is a delight if it works well, it can be truly disastrous if it does not. In choosing any system, ask many questions of men who have made voyages with the system you desire. Do not buy on the basis of advertising.

Aside from the "hove to" system previously described, the oldest system of self-steering is with twin headsails. The system is simple but likely to chafe at sea if plenty of tallow is not used on the rubbing surfaces. Basically, one gets two headsails of the same area and shape and sets them side by side four or five feet forward of the mast, separated by some six to twelve inches at the tacks. Two spinnaker poles pivoted from the spreaders rise with the sails and are attached to the clews. Sheets run from each clew through blocks aft and then to each side of the tiller. Note that unless you have a tiller you cannot profitably use the system. When on a course with a downwind component you adjust the lines from each sail so that the yacht stays on course. Should she veer from the selected course the pressure will be greater in one sail and less in the other. The sheets will then pull unevenly on the tiller, causing it to move and thus bringing the yacht back to the selected course, at which time the pressures are equal again.

Some longer yachts can apparently operate without leading the sheets to the tiller if the clews are allowed to run forward of the luffs, forming a broad V with the arms facing forward. Thus, with a deviation from course, pressure becomes greater on the weather sail and helps force the boat's head back to the proper course.

The main drawback is that twin headsails encourage truly herculean rolling. Rolling on the downwind leg offshore is to be expected, of course, but twins really put on a show! The second drawback is that as soon as you put twins aboard, the wind never seems to come far enough astern to allow you to use them. Hiscock, on his second circumnavigation in *Wanderer III*, used his twins for only a few days during his three-year voyage due to the fact that the winds were seldom truly astern.

The twin system, of course, cannot work well except on a run. And hard on the wind, any well-designed yacht will sail herself with the right combination of sail trim and tiller position. It is on a reach that some other system must be sought. As a matter of fact it seems that a great number of my passages have been made on a reaching wind.

The wind vane self-steering systems, if suitable to the particular yacht, serve well on any point of sailing. The notable advantage of the vane system is that it virtually replaces two crewmen. With an adequate wind vane, man-and-wife cruising becomes not only possible but pleasurable. I would even stick my neck out a bit and say that the wind vane makes obsolete both ketches and yawls as cruising vessels and also retires the various self-steering sail rigs.

The wind vane heeds only the apparent wind, so if there should be a shift in the wind during the night the yacht simply changes course slightly without calling up the crew for a trimming session. When it comes time to heave to, the vane will help hold even a notorious fore-reacher head to wind. When setting or reefing sail, you need only set up the vane and then go forward and do the job, without calling up the watch below.

Unfortunately, not every yacht is capable of self-steering. If a helmsman has a hard time keeping a yacht on course, so will a wind vane. I have designed vanes for many yachts to date, and some of them simply do not self-steer well. Still, the owners, with one exception, say that the vane is better than any helmsman, even though the final result is not perfection.

The shape or pattern profile of the keel seems to matter little, nor does the shape or location of the rudder. I have had fin keel–spade rudder boats steer superbly, and I have had long-keel boats behave disgracefully. I would judge that a vessel with a fairly long waterline in relation to her overall length is the best prospect to self-steer. A vessel with a great beam, or one with a great difference between waterline beam and beam at deck level, tends, in my experience, to be less directionally stable than the "skinny" boat. Multihulls seem to self-steer the best of all. I give these simple guidelines only as a result of my experience; due to the rather mystical nature of the art of wind vane designing, there is as yet no body of expertise on the matter. Indeed, there is little expertise in the matter of yacht stability or speed, either.

Wind vane systems are of three general types: (1) those that are extensions of the ship's own rudder, such as were used on *Buttercup* in 1952 and advanced considerably by "Blondie" Hasler in later years; (2) those that use some servosystem to move the tiller, such as the various pendulum systems and the more recent horizontally pivoted vane systems; and (3) those that use some independent rudder system such as devised by De Ridder (of *Magic Dragon* fame). This last system I have modified somewhat and used successfully for some years.

The types that are extensions of the ship's rudder are the oldest of the successful systems, and they are extremely simple. On any yacht with an outboard rudder and no gearing or wheel mechanism, they are simple to rig and work relatively well under most conditions. To construct one, first find the area of the rudder and then make a trim tab of wood that equals approximately 20 to 25 percent of that area. Mount it on the trailing edge of the rudder, using two rather sloppy gudgeons and pintles. (The reason for the sloppy fit is to allow the ship's motion to pound out the inevitable accumulation of marine fouling growth.) A control shaft should be mounted to the leading edge of the trim tab. It is usually of tubular metal, selected so as not to react with the metals in the rudder construction. This shaft can also form the pin part of the attachment, being then run through fabricated gudgeons. The control shaft is allowed to extend up out of the water to the top of the rudder post, where it is kept from swaying about by a third loose gudgeon attached to the rudder head. The wind vane (its design will be discussed later) then must be coupled efficiently to the control shaft. One may simply make a sleeve that fits over the control shaft and attach the vane shaft to it with a set screw, which will allow adjustment of the vane direction, or make some sort of a clutch arrangement. The control shaft must be vertical, of course, if this system is desired. While simple to build, this system is prone to zigzagging on downwind courses due to the lack of "differential action" between vane and trim tab.

If the vane is mounted on the transom in two bearings, one at the heel of the vane shaft and one at the top of the stern pulpit, then two bell cranks and a connecting rod will provide the desired differential action. The bell crank from the control shaft should reach exactly to the line of the main rudder pintles, and the connecting rod must pivot exactly over the same spot, if you want little differential effect. If the boat oversteers, shorten the bell crank or make another pinhole closer to the tab shaft and more differential effect will be felt.

It has been my experience that a reduction should be made between the vane and the trim tab to stop oversteering in heavy winds. This is accomplished by having the vane bell crank shorter than the one on the control shaft. A reduction of two to one is good for a start, and you can leave the bell cranks long and drill a number of holes at different distances from the center and have the whole thing

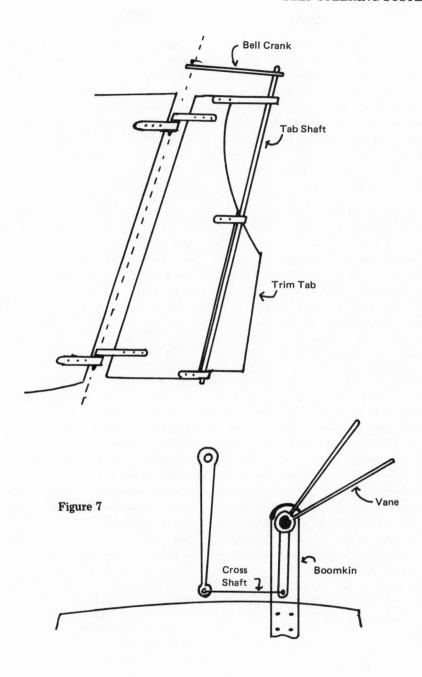

Bell Crank

Tab Shaft

Trim Tab

Figure 7

Vane

Cross
Shaft

Boomkin

adjustable. The vane can be mounted on a short boomkin or on the transom, as long as the connecting rod lines up evenly with the end of the control bell crank. Remember also that the trim tab must move in the same direction as does the wind vane. Otherwise, the yacht veers away from wind changes rather than correcting for them.

Many of these trim tab systems are in use, but they seem to work really well only on outboard rudders. Some skippers have found ways to get a control shaft down through an inboard rudder and report good results, but the engineering is difficult. Most of the trim tab systems also require some tiller lines to prevent oversteering and occasionally a shock cord to help correct weather helm.

As with any system that controls the main rudder, some provision must be made to allow the crew to control the rudder if desired. Chance meetings with steamers and sudden man-overboard drills require that the helmsman be able to take instant control of the yacht. The vane must be capable of quick release, and the trim tab should have some provision for locking it on the centerline, or it may cause the yacht to veer wildly under power.

While the trim tab system is perhaps not the most elegant, it is simple and reliable. Except for the fact that it is attached to the main rudder system, it is perhaps the best of all the systems, and I have installed several of these and had acceptable results.

The "pendulum" systems use a relatively simple principle to steer a yacht, but then complicate it to the point where I would not consider one for cruising purposes. If you have ever held an oar vertically in the water from a moving boat, you will have noticed that if you rotate it even slightly from a steamlined condition, it veers markedly. Consider now that your oar is pivoted in the center and that you rotate it slightly. The top half will move in the direction opposite that of the bottom half. Now attach two lines to the top and lead them through suitable blocks and sheaves to your tiller, and you will note that a slight twist of the oar applies a powerful force to the tiller. Go one step further and connect a wind vane to the oar. When the wind direction changes, a slight twist is put on the oar. The oar veers to one side, causing the top part of it to pull on a tiller line and turn the rudder. The rudder turns the yacht until the wind vane is normal to the wind, and the twist is taken off the oar. The oar then reduces its veer and takes the pressure off the tiller lines and everything sits back and waits until the next time the vane senses a change of course or wind direction. It is obvious that terrific forces can be generated by this servo principle and controlled by only slight vane pressures.

This system is the brain child of "Blondie" Hasler, and I bow to the absolutely remarkable inventiveness of this most unusual man. This system has become the standard for all self-steering rigs in single-handed racing offshore.

While the steering abilities of the Hasler system are second to none in accuracy and power, there are a few drawbacks to the system for strictly cruising. First, the cost is high. Second, hanging the pendulum requires a tangle of stainless tubing and other paraphernalia over the stern of the yacht, which is exposed and vulnerable when one is docked Mediterranean style or swinging at anchor. Third, tiller lines must be run through four blocks on the way to the tiller. These lines are likely to chafe through fairly frequently due to the terrific forces generated by the pendulum. Fourth, the oar itself is long and cantilevered and subject to frequent breakage. Fifth, the system is overly complicated in spite of its obvious efficiency. Last, it is difficult to get control of the yacht in an emergency. The oar may jibe all the way to one side, causing a jam that requires you go to the stern and pull the oar out of the water to correct it. While you may disconnect the vane easily, the oar must be brought out of the water in order for you to steer at all effectively. Try that some dark night with a freighter bearing down on you!

The horizontally pivoted wind vane is said to develop much greater force than the vertically pivoted one. Several systems on the market are based on this assumption and purport to be able to steer the yacht by action of the wind alone. The horizontally pivoted vane, with provisions for aiming it into the wind, is attached to tiller lines that run much like the ones described for pendulum systems. When the wind veers, the upright vane develops a force some seven times greater than would a normal vane of the same area, and this force, instead of turning a trim tab or pendulum, is applied directly to the tiller. It sounds simple and efficient, but in practice it works well only with a hydrodynamically balanced rudder and a light, sensitive yacht. In light airs, which seem to be the most common kind, the system is a loser.

The type of system that utilizes an auxiliary rudder and trim tab works well with either tiller or wheel steering, as long as the rudder is inboard. It is easy to design, and its construction is simple. It has few moving parts to wear out or break, and although it lacks the supreme accuracy of the Hasler system, it always seems to work. In addition, taking over the helm requires only that you grab the wheel and steer, thus easily overpowering the vane, even though it is still in gear. In case of a broken rudder (not unknown with spade rudder yachts), the auxiliary will serve as an emergency steering system that will work almost as well as the original rudder.

I have used two types of auxiliary rudder systems, and they have all worked out extremely well, which is to say that none of the owners has come back and taken a shot at me! For larger yachts, and for those with overhanging transoms, I use a steel shaft with a wooden rudder blade and trim tab. For small yachts with nearly vertical transoms having little overhang, I use an all wooden rudder, pintled to the transom. Both systems use the same principles as does the trim tab system, with minor simplifications.

In order to design one of these devices, you should follow a few general guidelines. First, avoid friction of any kind. Everything must be free almost to the point of being sloppy and rattling. Second, beware of any kind of ball bearings or roller bearings. They gum up at sea and defeat their own purposes. A simple bearing, loosely fitted, is far more reliable. Third, select metals that will not add to the dangers of electrolysis.

A good rule of thumb for determining the area of the auxiliary rudder for a normal vessel is to make it one square foot for each ten feet of overall length, including bowsprits and the like. Yachts that steer clumsily or that have large wetted surface need 10 to 15 percent more rudder area. Spade rudder–fin keel yachts can get by with a reduction in area, but I have found that it is better to err in the direction of too much rather than too little area. Too little area results in poor light-air performance, and too much merely increases the wetted surface.

The trim tab can be mounted directly to the trailing edge of the auxiliary rudder, in which case I like its area to be 20 to 25 percent of the rudder area, or it can be set back on standoffs six inches for each ten feet of waterline length and its area reduced to 20 percent of rudder area. Setting the trim tab back from the auxiliary rudder gives it tremendous mechanical advantage and increases tracking accuracy, but it also makes the trim tab somewhat vulnerable. De Ridder uses the offset system with great success, while I find nothing to complain about with the tab set right up on the rudder. I suppose if the yacht has tendencies to wander under self-steering, a little offset would certainly help.

In designing a rig for a forty-footer, I first measure from the stern toerail to the waterline and add (for a four-square-foot rudder) four more feet and another six inches for slop. This gives me a rudder shaft that reaches from the bottom of a four-foot-deep rudder one foot wide to just above the cap rail. I next measure from cap rail to water

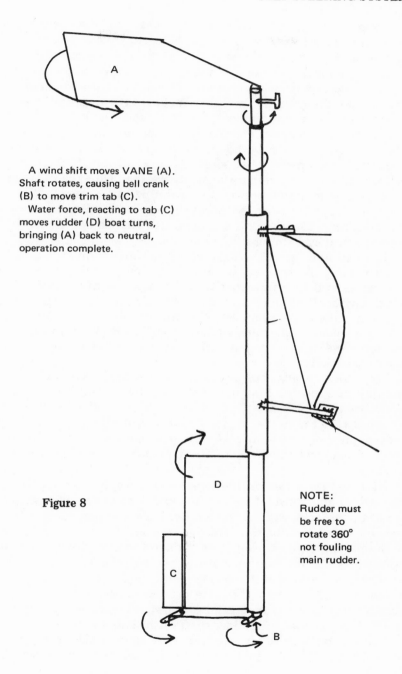

A wind shift moves VANE (A).
Shaft rotates, causing bell crank
(B) to move trim tab (C).

Water force, reacting to tab (C)
moves rudder (D) boat turns,
bringing (A) back to neutral,
operation complete.

Figure 8

NOTE:
Rudder must
be free to
rotate 360°
not fouling
main rudder.

111

for a support tube in which the rudder shaft will turn and which in turn will be attached to the stern of the yacht by a welded bracket at the top and by three pieces of one-inch tubing near the bottom, making a triangulated truss. I make this support tube rather larger than the rudder shaft, which is normally made of one-and-one-quarter-inch schedule forty piping, and then make up bushings for its top and bottom which clear the rudder shaft by at least .03 inch.

The rudder shaft is retained in the support tube by means of a collar, a piece of steel bored to fit snugly on the rudder shaft, to which it is clamped by set screws. It should be of an outside diameter sufficient to overlap the support tube. Thus the rudder shaft merely hangs in the support tube, rotating on a single collar. You may use a Teflon washer in the collar, but I have sailed for five years with nothing in the way of a bearing other than an occasional shot of motor oil, and everything still works fine.

The trim tab for this design would be roughly one square foot in area. I make mine two feet by six inches, believing that a high aspect ratio works well with rudders. To the leading edge of the trim tab I attach a length of half-inch rod about four inches longer than the tab. This unit will be gudgeoned to the trailing edge of the rudder with some homemade gudgeons, which are short pieces of half-inch pipe with tangs welded to them so that they can be bolted to the trailing edge of the rudder.

The rudder is attached to the rudder shaft by four bands of steel that wrap around the shaft and extend about a foot back along the rudder itself. These are rivetted through the rudder and are only tack welded to the rudder shaft, since no great twisting strain is going to be applied by the shaft. All that is needed is to hold the rudder and shaft somewhat together. The trim tab, not a tiller, applies all the force.

We now have a rudder shaft and rudder hanging in a support tube attached to the stern of the yacht, and a free-moving trim tab attached to the back edge of the rudder. Now we must get a wind vane connected to the trim tab. Take a long length of one-inch tubing, which will slip easily through the rudder shaft, poke it through until it protrudes about a half inch below the shaft, and cut it off so that it projects a few inches above the stern pulpit. Another collar must be now made, similar to the one on the rudder shaft, to hold the control shaft in position. Again, it merely floats on its collar in the rudder shaft, as does the rudder shaft in the support tube.

For the bottom of the control shaft make a bell crank that extends one inch (to the center of a hole) from the wall of the shaft.

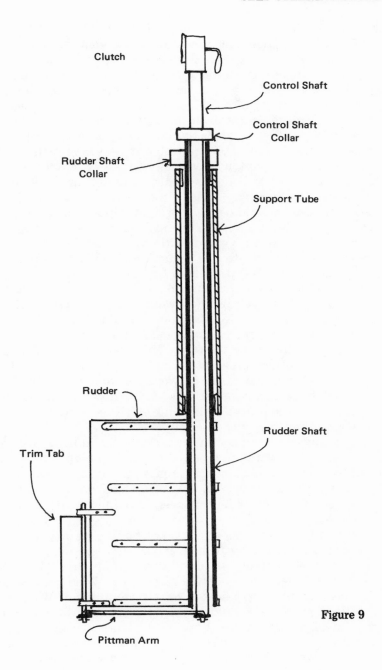

Clutch

Control Shaft

Control Shaft Collar

Rudder Shaft Collar

Support Tube

Rudder

Rudder Shaft

Trim Tab

Pittman Arm

Figure 9

Make another that extends two inches from the shaft on the front of the trim tab. Then bend a piece of one-quarter or five-sixteenths steel rod into a connecting rod between the two bell cranks, and the lower part of the unit is complete. You now can, from the deck, turn the control shaft, which will in turn move the first bell crank, which will move the connecting rod, which will in turn move the second bell crank, which will move the trim tab half the distance you move the control shaft. All that is left is to make some provision for attaching an adjustable wind vane to the control shaft. A sleeve with a clamping nut, a spring-loaded clutch, a V belt and pulley clutch, or another system can be used. The idea is to have a clutch that will allow you to set the vane easily at any angle to the control shaft.

The vane itself should be made as light as possible consistent with the strength needed to weather a good blow. I like a vane made of one-eighth-inch marine plywood, with an area of five times the area of the trim tab, if a two-to-one reduction is used. If less reduction is used, the vane should be up to seven times the tab area.

A vane of an airfoil section looks good, but since boats are not airplanes, and lift is not what you want, it is the least efficient pattern. Rather, look at the old-fashioned windmill. It had a swallow-tail vane made of two plates that spread away from each other in a narrow V with the apex forward. This planform allows a greater generation of turning force with a relatively slight change in wind direction. The optimum angle between the vane blades is about 30 degrees, but since this is rather awkward, I now use about 15. This wedge shape is much more stable and much more powerful in light air than any other shape yet tried.

Be sure that your connecting rods and bell cranks are securely attached. The bell cranks should be welded on and perpendicular to the trim tab, and the connecting rod should have cotter keys to keep it from coming off the cranks. All the underwater rudders and trim tabs should be streamlined for better speed, but they steer just as well if they are left square.

It is wise to attach a good zinc teardrop to a metal piece near the trailing edge of the rudder to help in the battle against electrolysis. If stainless steel is used, be absolutely certain that all the metal, including the fastenings, is of the same type. When completed, the entire unit should be passivated or electropolished. When treated thus, little electrolysis should be apparent. If you do not passivate stainless steel, however, the little bits of nonstainless left in the surfaces by machining operations start an insidious reaction that may turn a shaft here, a bell crank there, into Swiss cheese in about six

114

weeks or less. I learned this the hard way when I broke a tab bell crank halfway to Hawaii and had to *steer* the rest of the way watch and watch. I had welded the crank with the wrong alloy, and the dissimilar metals had been at war ever since.

The wooden rudder for vertical, sawed-off transoms is made up of three pieces of mahogany or apitong glued to make a three-ply rudder. It is attached to the yacht in exactly the same way as is any outboard rudder in normal construction. The dimensions are figured the same way as for the previous unit. It is wise to have a deep rudder so that the pitching encountered offshore does not bring too much rudder surface out of the water.

The trim tab is attached to a control rod on the leading edge just as in the case of the trim tab setup described first. The bell crank is placed at the top of the control rod rather than at the bottom, as in the steel design.

The wind vane can be attached either to the transom, as described earlier, or to a short stub mast on the wooden auxiliary rudder. The same two-to-one reduction gearing can be used, or one-to-one gearing together with slightly larger vane area.

A stub mast can carry the wind vane, and it is here mounted on the rubber itself. Note the "V belt" clutch arrangement with Highfield lever to tension belt.

115

Astrea running in force seven. Note lashed wheel, wind vane, and weather cloths. The following sea is just getting ready to break and soak the photographer.

View of the wind vane installation on *Astrea*.

A few practices I have noticed over the years that usually lead to disaster are putting balance area on the rudder to make it "easier" to steer and machining tolerances too closely. The balance area must react hydrodynamically to assist the rudder in turning, but being a dynamic device it depends on speed through the water for its effect. When the boat is traveling slowly, the balance area does help reduce steering force. When speed increases, the same balance area produces much more force and makes the steering so unstable that the boat fishtails all over the ocean. Close tolerances should be avoided like the plague. Fouling still takes place when you are under sail, and loose tolerances seem to allow the motion to shake out the debris.

The actual use of wind vane systems is not well understood by many sailors who buy them, and they are consequently disappointed in their performance. To adjust the system, first get the yacht trimmed and sailing on the course you select. Next, lash the tiller or wheel so that the yacht tends to maintain the course. Finally, set the vane to stream like a wind flag away from the control shaft and lock it in position. The yacht should then be self-steering. If she tends to creep up or off the wind, you may trim sails slightly, adjust the main rudder slightly, or take a slight additional hitch in the wind vane angle. Be cautious in moving the main rudder, because if wind strength varies, so will weather helm, and frequent readjustments of the vane will be necessary. The more neutral the main rudder, the more compensation is being done by the vane, which does its adjusting automatically.

Although the wind vane will not steer a completely steady compass course, it is just like a skillful helmsman, keeping the yacht at its maximum efficiency by trimming to the apparent wind. Some novice voyagers rebel at the thought of deviating from the rhumb line. But I, for one, seldom look at a compass except in pilot waters anyway.

The winds of the trade belts do not always blow from the same direction nor with the same strength, but the average is remarkably steady. I once sailed for ten days on course for Hawaii with one of the steel vanes mentioned earlier. At times we seemed high of our proper course, and at others low, but I never reset the vane. The line of our noon position plots was a perfectly smooth drawing of the isobar down which we were sailing! On the other hand, I had sailed *Laguna* down the same course by compass, and her track contained many a dogleg.

The greatest drawback to a smoothly operating vane system is that it places a greater load on the navigator. Since no one is at the helm to keep a dead reckoning log, course and distance estimates are seldom accurate. You must do a real day's work in order to keep abreast of the yacht's position. I customarily take a morning fix, a noon fix, and an evening fix, whereas previously I had taken only a noon position. If I had my choice, I would much rather navigate than steer. Even in pilot waters, with the application of prudent seamanship and common sense safeguards, the wind vane is like having a hired crew!

When in use in large swells the wind vane is likely to begin to oscillate due to the accelerations it receives first to port and then to starboard from heeling. It helps to have a counterweight on the vane to reduce heeling error and thus reduce the sideways accelerations. This weight should be only enough to balance the vane at the point of the control shaft collar.

When the vessel is under power, the vane can sometimes be used as long as a good watch is kept. Steering is more sluggish than when under sail, but I have been able to motor sail to an acceptable degree of accuracy with some rigs.

When going astern, some provision must be made that the vane not interfere with steering. The trim tab type can simply be locked in the central position. The steel shaft type is free to rotate 360 degrees, as long as it does not foul the main rudder. The wooden stern-hung type must be fitted with a yoke and bridle lines to hold it in straight alignment with the stern.

6 Preparing the Yacht for Sea

After you have carefully selected the proper vessel, changed her layout, equipped her with all the mechanical devices that you think prudent, and built a good wind vane system, you *may* think you are ready for sea. Much is said in some cruising stories about "chucking the damned paintbrushes over the side and getting underway," but you just can't do that if your cruise is to be successful. It seems that no yacht is ever really ready for sea unless she stays at sea!

Fitting out requires that every possible emergency be prepared for before the voyage begins, since there are no good marine stores yet in the middle of oceans. I might add that there are precious few good ones in most of the places you may wish to visit, either. Before I go on any voyage beyond the trivial, I like to go over the ship in minute detail and satisfy myself that everything is in good order, and then make sure that I have a repair procedure for every possible breakage, both in terms of the hull and rigging and in terms of the bones of the crew!

Preventive Maintenance

A great number of misfortunes could be avoided if owners would just check out their rig and hull before a voyage. I would no more start a voyage without hauling the yacht and inspecting her keel bolts and through-hull fittings than I would take off in an airplane without a preflight inspection.

In detail, my system runs as follows. First, I haul the boat and check each through-hull fitting. It should show none of the reddish gold look of electrolysis; it should have a solid backing block; and it should have a valve or seacock that works easily. In the absence of a valve a good tapered wooden plug should be hung by a string close to the fitting. Be sure, of course, that a good mallet or hammer is aboard to bang the plug into place.

All the hoses that run from through-hull fittings to engines and cockpit drains should be carefully checked for cracks and deterioration. These are readily repaired at home, but fixing them can become a labor of Hercules at sea.

119

Laguna's rudder was taken off and inspected and the whole yacht painted from keel to truck for a voyage to Hawaii.

The rudder should be pulled and the shaft checked for wear or electrolysis. The rudder bearings should be renewed if there is enough wear so that the rudder makes noise. Sternway while lying ahull or when hove to will add a tremendous amount of wear, and the bearing may fail long before it would under coastal cruising conditions. The rudder pins where the steering is attached to the stock should be replaced, regardless of their age. I like both cross pins and clamps here. The man to whom *Astrea* was sold neglected this procedure, and the pin sheared in a gale, leaving him without means to steer. He took to the liferaft when she began to drift onto a lee shore and endured much hardship and exposure before he was picked up off the beach. *Astrea*, in her perverse way, refused to come ashore, but drifted away, to be rescued by the US Navy. How embarrassing!

If the yacht has keel bolts, it is a good idea to give them a hearty thump with a sledge hammer to see if they will move or fall off. If they do, better now than at sea! Since the bilges are a wet and grubby place, it is a good idea to put some protective paint on the keel bolts after first giving them the hammer business and cleaning them with a wire brush.

In wooden yachts, I always pull a few plugs here and there and try the fastenings. If a screw has a reddish, shiny appearance, it could be an indication of electrolysis. Take a hefty, two-handed screwdriver and try to remove a fastening. If it breaks rather than drawing, forget the voyage until you refasten. I have found over the years that fastenings near the ends of the vessel deteriorate first. Whether this is a peculiarity of electrolysis or merely chance I know not.

A wooden vessel should have the caulking attended to, particularly along the garboards and stem. The pressure of the mast will usually start leaks here first. A vessel may not show much in the way of working alongshore, but a twenty-day trade wind passage may make a very flexible raft of her if the caulking is not well driven. Butt blocks should be checked at the same time. They betray themselves by staying wet and showing a line long after the hull has dried out, just as will a loose seam.

The eyebolt for bobstays, or any other bolt that passes through the hull, should be drawn and checked for wear or breakage, or it may work loose and cause a very hard-to-trace leak.

As mentioned in the construction chapter, now is a good time to check the hull-deck joint in fiberglass vessels. Remove that strip of decorative rubber stripping and take a good look at the seam. I like to lay on about three layers of cloth and mat and then put the stripping back on. In other cases, merely caulking with a good epoxy compound may suffice. Fiberglass yachts are so inherently leakproof that it is a shame to have water dribbling through the hull-deck joint into the lockers and bunks.

Pull a few chainplate bolts, if the plates are outboard. They should not show any wear where they bear on the plate itself. Inboard plates seldom show any electrolysis, but they may show signs of working. All chainplate bolts should be checked for tightness. Where the chainplate comes through the deck, as is the case in many modern yachts, it is wise to look at the sealant system. Usually a metal plate is used, made with a slot to accept the chainplate, under which there is some caulking material. The caulking should be replaced with a nonhardening type. The plates will work, particularly when rolling in light weather, and will lead to aggravating deck leaks if not adequately prepared.

The bottom should be painted with the best of paints, because places to haul out are rare once you are away. I prefer hard epoxy racing bottom paints over the soft sloughing types. When the antifouling power is gone from the hard paint, it can still be scrubbed clean with a bit of elbow grease and a snorkel. When the soft paint is gone, it is just gone! I have used hard finishes on both *Laguna* and *Astrea,* and a good two- or three-coat job would last two years before recoating became absolutely necessary. Take the bottom down to

121

the bare hull before a heavy bottom paint job. To do otherwise is to invite paint heaviness and resultant flaking and peeling of your new paint.

I generally have to move the boot top up a few inches after I have loaded the yacht. I also like to have at least two inches of bottom paint showing above the waterline to keep that ugly green line from forming. (It forms because the boat rolls constantly, even when at anchor.) Some skippers just mix antifouling paint in the batch when they paint the boot top. The traditional formula is about half antifouling paint and half varnish.

The standing rigging should be thoroughly inspected. Each pin, from chainplate to masthead, must be removed and inspected. I have found many, on yachts less than two years old, that were deeply grooved and at less than half their strength. The turnbuckles should not have egg-shaped pin holes, for these are caused by allowing the pins to wear too much. The turnbuckles should adjust easily and should be protected with a good coat of grease and a wrapping of boat tape. All the cotter keys should be well covered with tape to keep them from snagging sails, lines, and skin.

The wire, if it is more than five years old, should probably be replaced before attempting a long passage. In any event, discard any wire that shows "pussycats," the little bits of broken wire that stick out and cut your hand as it passes over the wire. Use a bit of cotton waste and the pussycats will be revealed by a telltale tuft rather than by a drop of your blood!

The mast, if it is wood, should have tight seams and glue lines and should be well coated with either paint or varnish to protect it from heat and from the amazing abrasize effects of sea water. After five or six days of a whole gale, *Astrea* lost all nine coats of varnish on the weather side of her masts. They had simply been eroded away by the constant spray. Aluminum masts really need no paint, but I like to paint them anyway to reduce the surface corrosion. I prepare the mast by etching it and then putting on two coats of hard epoxy paint. That makes it nearly bulletproof!

The masthead sheaves should be inspected carefully for wear or electrolysis and replaced if doubtful. All tangs and mast fittings should be checked for looseness and hairline cracks.

The running rigging should be in new condition. I am deathly afraid of going aloft even in port, so you can imagine how I dread the thought at sea! I always replace all halyards before a cruise, feeling that the small extra expense more than compensates in peace of mind. Blocks should be checked for wear in the bushings and for strain on the frames. I have had several of these literally explode at sea, spoiling an otherwise pleasant afternoon.

Each sail should be checked for worn stitching, and the luff hanks and slide shackles checked for wear. The storm jib should be capable of sheeting to a strong pad eye. Most of us generally find out about the storm jib only when it's too late. Set it and find out where the proper lead is. The battens should be of some fiberglass composition, or almost anything other than wood. I have broken every wooden batten I ever went cruising with. Sooner or later the sail will shake, and when it does, it will break wooden battens and tear up the batten pockets as long as there is a good breeze blowing. On the other hand, I have never broken a fiberglass one.

The winches should be broken down and greased with a good, light, waterproof grease. Check the pawls and springs for cracks and wear. A shiny line on the base will tell you if the winch is rubbing under strain. If it is, replace it with a stronger one. Examine the winch handles for wear, particularly the ones with square or hexagonal sockets. If the corners are shiny and worn, they may slip and injure the winchman.

Check all hatches to be sure that they can be adequately dogged down under storm conditions. Gaskets, if any, or water channels should be tested with a high-pressure hose liberally applied.

The companionway ladder should have a good nonskid surface on each step, and you should also check its attachment points for any weakness.

All cupboards and drawers should be checked for good locking systems that will stand the weight of their contents slamming repeatedly against them.

The head should have a new set of valves and gaskets if it is more than a year old, and the through-hull valves should be overhauled and reset.

All the pumps aboard should be thoroughly tested for effectiveness and the absence of leaks. A spare parts kit should be installed in any that are old or doubtful.

The galley stove, if gimbaled, should have a new flexible feed line if the old line is more than two years old. The fuel shutoff valves should work freely, and one should be located at each remote tank as well as at the stove itself.

The engine, if any, should have a good tuneup. Its water pumps should be overhauled or thoroughly checked out; the fuel filters should be renewed; and the generators should be checked by an electrician to see that they maintain full output.

Provision should be made to allow you to service the engine easily yourself, including changing ignition parts and changing oil.

Check the batteries to be sure that a roll to the horizontal will neither dislodge them nor cause them to spill acid all over the place. Batteries, incidentally, should be mounted with their long dimension fore and aft rather than athwartships. I failed to do this once and was rewarded with dead batteries and a bilge full of battery acid after being hove down repeatedly on my beam ends in a spell of bad weather. Battery acid and sea water, by the way, combine to produce chlorine gas. Batteries should be mounted in stout boxes with a bit of baking soda in the bottom. Ideally, the boxes should be vented to the outside atmosphere, because in addition to the danger of chlorine gas the battery will produce highly explosive hydrogen gas when it is charging.

Check the lamps to be sure they have good long wicks. Do not tolerate leaks in the bases, since the smell of kerosene is apparently cumulative. A little Gluvit sloshed around in the dried basin will cure most minor leaks.

Be sure the electrical wiring is free of any worn spots, and either solder or replace the terminals where any wire is not well connected to its binding post or other electrical part. Switches and fuses should show no signs of corrosion or they may suddenly fail.

Blow up the survival raft and check for leaks, and recharge its CO_2 cannister.

Run out all anchors and line on a dock and check for wear or deterioration. I like to paint bands of different colors every twenty-five feet so that I know approximately how much anchor rode is out. The windlass should be worked over and well greased.

It is popular among experienced cruisers to cover over any varnish work with a good coat of enamel before going into tropical waters, thus reducing the maintenance required. Before doing so, however, don't forget to put on two good coats of varnish as an undercoat. To do otherwise will require that you laboriously strip and sand out all traces of the enamel before you can bring back the brightwork when the cruise is finished.

Emergency Repairs

Once at sea, you must be able to repair quickly any damage that is critical to the yacht's operation, so a good deal of thought must be given to the supplies that must go along—hopefully just for the ride.

I am inclined, perhaps, to overdo the contingency planning, but then I am still alive to do so! I am naturally skeptical of the longevity of anything manmade on a yacht, since I have been known to break almost every possible piece of equipment at one time or another. The handle to my head broke off one afternoon, and I found that there wasn't one piece of metal aboard that would serve. My spare bucket was put to good use, of course, but I wondered where the incredible breakage would end. I once had a Merriman deck eye fail even though it was three sizes larger than was recommended. I built a bobstay for *Astrea* of very heavy wire, at least twice the size called for in the rigging charts, and it broke after a two-thousand-mile passage! The piece of ordinary chain with which I replaced it has been there for three years and is doing fine. A halyard winch on *Laguna* broke completely in half, narrowly missing Jim, my mate, as it whizzed off into the Pacific. The shaft log stuffing box on *Astrea* once broke all four studs and came adrift, nearly sinking the boat because the water drowned the batteries before anyone noticed the leak. I learned the value of hand-operated bilge pumps from that one!

Anchored in Todos Santos one afternoon with the auxiliary generator running, I discovered that the load was too great and that all the insulation had melted off my battery cables, thus setting *Astrea* on fire. I did repairs with some barbed wire found ashore, wrapped with sacks, tape, and what have you, and I have since put in two sets of cables.

My system is to decide in advance that everything is going to break and to have at the ready everything I need to repair each piece of essential equipment. Obviously not everything aboard is essential, so a list of priorities should be drawn up. My highest priority is the hull, then the mast, the sails, the galley, and the head, in that order. You can do without everything else at least until you reach port.

For the wooden hull, a number of things will serve to repair punctures and even lost planks. Some skippers carry sheet lead (about 10 gauge), some metal shears to cut it, and a good supply of large galvanized roofing nails. I have always thought, however, that if conditions are bad enough to strain a hull that badly, how are you going to be able to go over the side and nail the stuff on? I always carried some heavy carpeting with lines that could be attached to the corners. This could be tied like a first-aid bandage around the vessel, hopefully slowing the leak to the point where the pumps could keep up with it. My latest system, for fiberglass yachts, is to carry a large, heavy rubber sheet along. In case of a puncture, tie lines to the four corners and allow the sheet to pass under the yacht to the point of damage. Then haul away on the four lines and you have diapered the baby! Does it work? I hope I never have to find out.

Small leaks can be staunched from within the yacht, provided you can get at them. Peter Tangwald lost his boat because she sprang a leak that was inaccessible because (I think) of the ceiling. A large fire axe is helpful in clearing away any joinery that may be in the way of a repair, and it also serves well to cut firewood and so forth when you are ashore.

In case of loss of a cabin side, or the whole cabin for that matter, a spare sail can be lashed over the hole, or nailed down if the decks are of wood. Some spare wood that can be made into shores is often helpful if the cabin trunk should shift.

The mast and rigging are the most vulnerable of all the essential parts. I carry several precut lengths of wire aboard. One is long enough to replace any stay. The other are ten- and fifteen-foot lengths. These wires should be of the 7×19 variety for easy stowage. These, together with about fifty or so "bulldog" cable clamps, will serve to replace almost any breakage of stays that does not result in losing the mast outright. Some parachute cord will replace a turnbuckle and is handy in a number of other ways as well. The racers on the TransPac have taken to carrying a "Bandit" tool for use with metal masts. This device is generally used to put those metal straps around shipping cartons. If a mast breaks, they strap it back together with the "Bandit," and even though it is shortened in the process enough sail can be jury rigged to make port in good time.

Robin Lee Graham used a spare spinnaker pole as a jury mast. The spinnaker pole itself is subject to breakage when it dips into a wave top when you are running at speed. I like to carry two, well lashed to chocks on deck.

A good supply of stout wooden battens about one-half inch thick by three inches wide by five or so feet long will serve to repair a broken boom. Just set up the battens and wrap the whole ensemble with lots of marline or fishing twine. Some long wooden wedges will serve to tighten the whole thing up.

I always carry at least one of each size turnbuckle aboard and lots of spare shackles of every description. A few spare blocks are always handy, both for repairs and for rigging tackles.

You should remember that in case of a dismasting, your sails as well as your mast may be lost, and there must be something aboard which will serve to replace them. I usually carry spare sails, but often this is not possible either because of expense or because of limitations of stowage space. You must have aboard a good sailmaker's kit containing sailcloth and thread to repair any sail in the inventory and some grommets and hanks. In dire emergencies sails can be jury rigged out of awnings, blankets, old trousers, or whatever.

I always carry a spare single-burner kerosene camp stove after my experience with the stoveless yacht mentioned earlier. There are many mishaps that may disable the main stove, and while you can always eat cold food, it is a great boost for the morale to have it hot.

Be particularly sure to carry enough parts to repair the fresh-water pump in the galley regardless of what happens to it. It is most aggravating to have tanks full of fresh water that you cannot get at.

The head seems of little consequence, but in survival conditions you sometimes risk your life going on deck to take care of biological functions. I carry a complete repair kit (and a spare handle) as well as my trusty bucket.

For the engine, it is wise to carry points, condenser, spark plugs, starter, generator, and a spare carburetor. As mentioned earlier, you should also have spare fuel filters in case your type is not available in some ports. For diesels, carry a spare injector and injector pump instead of points and carburetors. Some like to carry a few dry-charged batteries as a guard against the time when all the switches have been left on and the main engine won't start. I am not so certain that they will work, since every time I buy one they have to charge it just the same as any other battery.

Of course, you will carry wrenches to fit everything aboard, including a huge monkey wrench for the packing gland. That large wrench will make you one of the most popular persons in most cruising anchorages!

No yacht should put to sea without a means of rapidly clearing away rigging in the event of a dismasting. A forty-foot mast over the side can take on all the attributes of a battering ram. I prefer a very large set of bolt cutters. Do not fall for the small economy types that claim to be adequate. Bring in a piece of cable equal to the largest on your yacht. Ask the salesman to cut it with his device. If he can't, you probably can't, either. An axe will sometimes cut through the turnbuckles, but usually not through cable.

Beryl Smeeton was renowned as a hoarder of spare wood and other goodies. According to many, *Tzu Hang* never would have survived her ordeal without just that supply of plywood, timber, bolts, nuts, screws, and whatever, that she shoved back into the yacht's stern.

I might add that this kind of preparedness can be carried too far. I knew one fellow who carried along a spare thirty-foot mast and

127

said it was there in case he was ever dismasted. I made him a bet that he couldn't get it up even in the slip, and he was crestfallen when I won. What a waste of money!

In my boats I always have what becomes known to the crew as a "hell box." In it are all manner of wondrous, some say useless, things—spare pins, shackles, pawls for odd winches, rubber bands, gasket material, nuts, bolts, needles, sail hanks from yachts I owned ten years ago, scribers, awls, knife blades, gaskets for water pumps, packing material, waterproof grease, and so on—all in glorious dissarray. Of course, no one else can possibly find anything there, but I can repair a fantastic number of things with the contents of that box. It is strictly the domain of the skipper, and no meddling cleanliness nut should be allowed to see it. I throw into it anything that is left over from any job I do around the yacht, with no thought of order or neatness. It is helpful always to buy one more bolt or screw than you need for any job and to throw the excess in the box. Over a period of time you will have collected almost everything you need for repairing small catastrophes. Besides, it is comforting to know that even if it is hard to find, the proper part is aboard.

Safety Equipment

Of course, you will have aboard the required safety equipment demanded by our boat equipment manufacturers, speaking through the US Coast Guard. If you must have such things as flares, horns, and so on, make sure they will actually work. I have tried to light a few hand-held flares, but most of them will not light with the handy little scratcher provided, since it has become wet or has been rubbed off from years of rattling around in a locker. Flares can be taken below and held over the flame of the stove and they will usually light, much to the delight of the sleepers. I would eschew the use of these and get a good 35 mm. military flare pistol and a supply of parachute flares. The tiny flare pistols sold for coastwise use (12 gauge and 25 mm.) are just about as effective as a firefly in storm conditions at sea.

My horn is simply a conch shell picked up on the Baja California coast with a suitable hole knocked in one end with a hammer. It is louder than blazes, and its reed will never corrode, nor will its freon cannister ever run out. One of those plastic bugles makes a grand horn as well, as long as you don't get too musical in an anchorage at dusk.

One piece of safety equipment never mentioned by the Coast Guard is a means of getting those obnoxious freighters off their collision course with your yacht. A good bright light of the sealed beam variety shone on the sails will sometimes help—if there should happen to be anyone on the bridge, which there usually isn't at sea. The autopilot is on, and the bow watch usually goes forward with a cot and blanket anyway! The bridge watch often will be in the radar shack or may be distracted by other duties. Consider also that on many of the supertankers, one cannot see the water forward for a mile or so from the bridge. I have used the "big bang" technique in a few instances. This consisted of getting out my old service .45 caliber automatic and getting off a few quick rounds. If you get no results, a few rounds into the bridge should bring out the watch. I have never had to fire at the bridge to get results, but I would have no compunction whatsoever against putting a few rounds into the bridge of a vessel, that was at the time trying to kill me and mine by running me down.

Fire extinguishers should, of course, be aboard if you have an engine or a stove. I use the dry chemical type. They make an absolutely incredible mess when you use them, but they are cheaply replaceable and they quickly rust out under sea use. If I had a gasoline engine, I would want a large CO_2 fire extinguisher rigged to discharge directly into the engine room by the pull of a lanyard. To extinguish electrical fires, you should have a large master switch located where it can be used even if the main panel is on fire. All the fire extinguishers in the world will not stop an electrical fire until you turn off the main switch.

A radar reflector is a good piece of safety equipment, I suppose, but I would only put it up when visibility is very poor. I had never owned one of the things until my 1970 voyage on *Astrea* to Hawaii. More freighters came around than I had ever seen on a passage before. The reason is simple. When the radarman gets your "pip" he sees a target moving very slowly. Since most commerce moves at ten or more knots, except for towed barges, he will notify the bridge. Most captains will divert to take a look, on the chance that you are a lifeboat or a vessel in trouble. This is not true of all skippers, judging by the stories often heard of yachtsmen being left sitting there with distress signals flying, while the captain of a freighter just steamed on, keeping to his sacred schedule.

For those good seamen who will change course to take a look I give my eternal thanks. I reciprocate by not flying my radar reflector until there is a good need for it—either the weather is thick, or I am in distress. Consider the case on the California coast. On an average Sunday there are perhaps a thousand yachts traveling around within a few miles of the steamer lanes. Many of them have radar reflectors up. If the captain went to look for every one of these, he would cost his company many unnecessary dollars. I would, in most cases, prefer to stay out of the steamer lanes and to remain invisible to ship's radar. If fog sets in, as it often does on our coastline, then put up the reflector. The radar reflector would be a better safety device if it were used less.

Life jackets are a sore point with me, and I can't imagine what earthly good they do offshore on a yacht. I was forced to wear one twenty-four hours a day once during World War II, so perhaps that's the reason I don't like them. The approved kapok type take up an unusually large amount of space on a small yacht, and in addition, I have seen a few drowned bodies washed ashore wearing kapok life jackets that were soaked and utterly without buoyancy. Some say that wearing a life jacket of some sort is a good idea in stormy weather, and in many cases I have seen small fry wearing them during good weather. I would not take as crew or passenger anyone who had to wear a life jacket to feel secure. The watchword is "Never fall off a yacht!" If a life jacket is preferred, for either psychological or security reasons, I would use one of the excellent foam vests that dinghy sailors wear. These fit well and are not thick and bulky. They will not hamper you as you move around the deck. They also will not soak up water and lose their buoyancy if you must remain in the water for an extended period. I wonder why the Coast Guard is so slow in approving them? (Is it because many of them are foreign-made?) It is said that they will not support the head of an unconscious man out of the water, yet the Coast Guard approves as a life-saving device a square pillow with arm loops!

If one is going into the water deliberately, or taking to the lifeboats, or going to work in some manner that makes it likely that he will go into the water, then a buoyancy device is certainly wise, but I would not wear one as a matter of course.

That recent development, the "float coat," seems a good compromise for everyday protection. These are made of dacron cloth with a filler of foam, much like that in a wet suit used by divers. I like them not so much for their safety, but for their incredible warmth.

The top half of a wet suit, worn under any old shirt or jacket, is my favorite in very heavy weather. It is warm, it does not hamper movement, and it will float you rather well should you be swept overboard. You will be soaked anyway, so why not stay warm? I have been known also to wear my face mask when going to weather in force seven or more. A mask will keep the needles of spray out of your eyes, but unfortunately it will fog up. Another drawback is that you can't smoke very easily, because you tend to blow smoke out your nose and add to the haze inside. I heard about one skipper who wore a motorcycle helmet and plastic face shield that served as a hard hat and a windshield; it even had a built-in radio.

I carry a horseshoe-shaped man-overboard buoy with a strobe light attached, which can be cut loose by anyone in the cockpit should a man go over the side accidentally. This system sounds secure, but it may not work in a cruising yacht, which usually has only one man in the cockpit at a time. And the advent of self-steering has changed the problem of surviving an overboard drill. I often wondered what the drill would be if someone came on deck for his morning watch to find that his mate had gone overside sometime in the night! Obviously, the yacht cannot be turned to her reciprocal course and run back to find him. The twistings and turnings of a self-steering yacht are too unpredictable for that. Again it all boils down to one thing—*never fall off a yacht!*

I have aboard a good supply of safety harnesses, which I would like to say are worn all the time at sea. Unfortunately, they are not, and I am the prime offender. I wear one religiously when I am in the cockpit, since I am prone to catching a little sleep from time to time when on watch (my crews say that when I am steering it makes little difference whether I am asleep or not). When I go forward, I feel that the harness restricts my ability to duck and dodge, and I feel safer without it. I do not leave the cockpit, however, without calling out the watch below to notify them that I may not be back!

Medical Supplies

Being the skipper of a small yacht means that you are the family doctor in addition being the librarian, schoolteacher, minister, psychiatrist, critic, and taskmaster. Most ocean voyagers are a healthy lot, and I have heard of relatively few major medical problems at sea. Accidents will happen, however, and one must be prepared for them. The environment at sea is less populated with disease germs, and it is possible that you will lose some of your resistance to common disorders if you spend extended times at sea. (Blood poisoning seems to occur with more regularity at sea than elsewhere, perhaps because of this lowered resistance.)

It is my custom to divide the medical problems into a few broad categories. Accidents result in broken bones, torn skin, and bruises. Broken bones must be splinted and immobilized. This can be accomplished with strong bandages and some of the wooden battens that you carry along for fishing spars and whatnot. Badly torn skin must be sewn up, using either prepared sutures from the medicine kit or a sail needle and sewing thread that have been boiled for a few minutes. Bruises I consider to be a badge of courage to be left alone and shown to admiring docksiders when you arrive. Sometimes a little Vaseline on a bruise seems to help, but for what reason I know not. I strongly recommend that someone in the crew take a good semiprofessional first aid course.

Disease at sea can be perplexing and dangerous. It is wise to get a good medical checkup before leaving, to reveal any possible disorder. Once at sea, as a preventive measure, I like to use a good disinfectant once a week or so to wash down the eating and cooking areas of the cabin.

Most disorders that will occur at sea do not require precipitous action unless the victim is bleeding severely or his respiration is obstructed. In these cases you must act fast, but before attempting treatment of any other type of disorder it is best to look into your Red Cross first aid handbook, your family medical manual, or any of the other excellent books available.

A man can lose an astonishing quantity of blood before he dies. Most men can lose a quart before the consequences become disastrous! I once lost about a pint on the dock after jabbing a chisel through my arm, and it looked more or less like a slaughterhouse. Pressure applied over the cut will usually stop any but severe arterial bleeding. In the case of arterial bleeding, use a tourniquet or apply pressure over the appropriate pressure point. Remember that the use of a tourniquet is a temporary expedient. Gangrene and other complications may arise if the tourniquet is not released often.

Your doctor can advise you in the use of a hemostat and show you how to ligate an artery. Basically, you must open up the wound and wipe away the blood with a sterile piece of gauze. Find the artery and clamp the bleeding end with the hemostat. Run a loop of silk suture material around the hemostat, push it down over the artery, and draw it tight, making a square knot. Be sure that you ligate the artery, not the end of the hemostat! You can tie off the other end of the artery next and close the wound either with sutures or with a good butterfly bandage. If this procedure is done in a doctor's office it is simple. In the cabin of a small cruising yacht it can become a nightmare, for both the stitcher and the stitchee! Sterility is perhaps less of a consideration here than in a doctor's office. Just get the bleeding stopped! Better to take a chance with an infection, which can be treated, than a death, which cannot. You can reduce the risk of infection by having your doctor supply you with sterile packaged kits for bleeding control and suturing before you leave. Note that cigarette ashes, bits of sandwich, and other foreign matter in the wound are not considered good form. Have the other members of the crew stand back while you perform surgery. They will all, it seems, have seen a better job done on some other yacht, but I have noticed that few of them ever want to try their hand at the game. I would always dose my patient with a good general antibiotic to reduce the chance of infection, and put him to bed to help overcome the shock resulting from lack of anesthetic and crummy technique! (I do not doubt that portions of this procedure will arouse the ire of some worthy AMA member, but then he will not be sailing with you unless he happens to be on vacation.)

Obstructions to breathing require fast action, because the brain begins to deteriorate in a very short time without oxygen. If the patient is unconscious, make sure that his head is not hanging forward so as to block his air passages. Make sure he has not swallowed his tongue by retrieving it with your finger, and search for any physical obstructions with the finger as well. Chest massage and the use of breathing tubes are best explained by a physician.

Burns are common at sea, and the cook is the crew member most likely to suffer them. In heavy weather, it is wise for the cook to work in his oilskins. Severe burns require treatment for pain, shock, and infection. Some believe in covering burns with a Vaseline bandage, others in leaving them more or less open. Consult your doctor concerning the latest thinking here. You should encourage the patient to drink a lot of fluids, because of the toxicity of most burns. Give him a strong pain killer and a general antibiotic. Get medical help as soon as possible.

In case of a head injury that produces unconsciousness, keep the patient quiet and lying down until all symptoms disappear. This can be several days in severe cases, and you should be making tracks for medical help.

Appendicitis can be better avoided than treated. If you have had any inkling of trouble, get rid of your appendix before the voyage! Do not give a patient with suspected appendicitis a laxative or a stimulant. Give a general antibiotic, keep the man down, and get medical help as soon as possible.

Simple fractures may be splinted by pulling lengthwise on the limb, laying a good, well-padded splint on both sides, and bandaging. Keep the patient in his bunk. Compound fractures, in which the bone protrudes through the skin, are dangerous, and antibiotics should be administered immediately. Broken fingers are a mark of the seaman,

133

and I seldom give them much thought. Wrap the hand around a roll of gauze so that the fingers fall in a natural curve, and wrap the whole thing with bandage. In a week or two they should be in good shape.

Heart attacks are extremely dangerous at sea due to the lack of any good intensive care facilities. Persons from a highly stressed walk of life, and those over forty years of age, should have a good cardiac examination before leaving. Those with a history of cardiac trouble had best leave the sea alone or be prepared to die in it. (Incidentally, I know of many sailors whose hearts were considerably improved by sailing.)

Seasickness may not sound like a medical emergency unless *you* happen to be the victim. I have worked in the scientific investigation of motion sickness in regard to space flight for the last ten years, yet I know precious little that will help the voyager, and I suffer from the malady myself to a remarkable degree. Almost every animal, too, will suffer at least some symptoms of seasickness at one time or another if he is on a vessel at sea. Even fish in tanks set on the deck of a ship have been known to vomit!

There are several ways of relieving the symptoms. The most obvious is to get off the boat. If this is impossible, there are several good drugs on the market that work at least for some of the people some of the time. I favor Bucladin. It lacks some of the side effects of the dimenhydrinates (like Dramamine), and it can be taken when you begin to feel woozy, not some hours before. It contains an antihistamine and a drug that partially blocks the vomiting reflex.

A few tricks can help delay or reduce symptoms. Reading below in the early stages of a trip does *not* help. Sitting on deck, keeping dry and warm, keeping busy, keeping moving, and lying down will all help to some degree. Having the head tilted backward about 20 degrees also helps, considerably, but you look a bit ridiculous.

Adaptation to the motion of the sea takes about two or three days for the average person, and he will stay adapted unless there is a major change in the motion, as in a storm. He will remain immune until he has been ashore for about two weeks. After that, it's back to square one.

Preliminary preparations may help reduce the severity of motion sickness symptoms. The Russian cosmonauts were required to swing in swings and fly severe aerobatic maneuvers in preparation for their space flights. I have been doing research with a simple motion picture film that one views for ten minutes a day for a week or so before going to sea. It is merely a picture of the road taken from a fast-moving car driving through mountains. So far viewing the film has markedly reduced the symptoms of even highly susceptible individuals. Apparently one can learn to cope with visual disorientation, thus leaving himself less susceptible to motion sickness.

Needless to say, wild drinking bouts the night before departure do not discourage seasickness. In fact, I often recommend that my racing rivals participate in these bacchanals the night before ocean races, thus giving me and my crew a little added advantage on race day!

In all things medical on a small yacht keep the following in mind. A human being is on top of the evolutionary heap because he is the hardest to kill, the toughest, and the most adaptable animal of them all. Get him breathing, stop his bleeding, and make him lie down. Nature will take care of much of the rest. Beryl Smeeton often remarked that the tendency in nature was toward cure, and I suspect she was right. You can aid the process, but you may in ignorance hurt your patient more than you help him. Give him pain-killers to stop pain, paregoric to relieve diarrhea, a laxative to relieve constipation, and an antibiotic to reduce infections. If any of these symptoms is uncontrollable, find a doctor fast.

Your medicine chest should contain the following items in order to be minimally effective. Your doctor must prescribe many of these and may suggest alternatives.

> 2 hemostats or kelly clamps
> 1 needle holder for suturing
> 1 pair surgical scissors
> 1 pair forceps
> 1 pair splinter forceps
> 1 clinical thermometer
> 1 container sterile Vaseline
> Bandages, ace and gauze, 1- and 2-inch
> Bandaids in all sizes
> Surgical sponges (gauze pads)
> Adhesive tape (wide roll for taping broken ribs)
> 3 tubes prepared sutures, silk, catgut
> Iodine or Merthiolate
> General-purpose antibiotic (injection or oral)
> Strong pain-killer, such as Demerol
> Sedative or tranquilizer
> First-aid compound for scrapes and such
> Aspirin
> Eye ointment
> Sunburn remedy
> Skin lotion for immersion sores
> Bucladin or other seasick remedy

135

Amphetamines for long nights without sleep
Laxative
Paregoric or other remedy for diarrhea
Tourniquet
Breathing tube
Eye cup and eyewash
Vitamin complex to ward off scurvy
Antacids
Book describing poisonous fishes
Survival manual
First-class handbook of first aid

In the final analysis, there is no substitute for sound medical advice, so use the transmitter if you have one. As in all else at sea, prepare for the emergency well, and then forget about it until it actually happens.

Food and Supplies

While food may not seem to belong in a chapter on fitting out, it is probably one of the most important items in the planning of a successful cruise. Emergencies happen rarely, but you must eat every day. Provisioners usually take one of two major approaches to the subject. Members of one group plan each meal for each day and then figure out the required amounts of supplies. Members of the second set up a grocery store aboard and let the planning fall where it may.

The menu plan works well for a passage of, say, thirty days or less. My system is to set up a calendar covering two weeks and work out a menu for breakfast, lunch, and dinner for each day. At the end of the two weeks I simply go back to the beginning and start over. This system is not too monotonous, since no one seems to be able to remember meals for that long. The great advantage of this system is that you can plan right down to the last egg the supplies required. On a protracted voyage, say for six months or more, the system begins to fail. Most yachts do not have enough storage to carry all those supplies. When you get to Kapingi Maringi-Maringi, you often cannot replace the item that has become short, and the menu must be revised, often to the disgust of the cook.

The technique of ordering supplies is simple for the first system. Let's take a breakfast menu as an example:

fruit juice   biscuits or toast
fried eggs   coffee
bacon

Allowing for the number to be fed, determine whether any single can size available will just fit the need for juice. Often you must drink more than you want when the crew is small, say man and wife, even when you get the smallest can available. You can carry single-portion cans, but they are much more expensive per drink. Let's say our crew is two. A one-pint can of juice is needed each time juice comes up on the menu. Count up on your calendar the number of juice meals and multiply by the number of times the calendar is to be repeated.

Eggs are easy. Count the number of eggs needed for each item that requires them, multiply by the number of crewmen, and multiply again by the number of repetitions of your two-week menu.

Bacon is a special case, since it comes either in one-pound cans or in very large institutional containers. You eat all the bacon there is, or you throw the remainder away. Thus you need a can for each time the item appears on the menu.

Biscuits and toast require counting slices and estimating the amount of butter or margarine and jam or marmalade needed. And have you ever tried to find out how many cups of coffee there are in a jar of instant coffee?

Provisioning is an art that comes with practice. After my first cruise on *Laguna* I found that there were still some cans left in the larder a full year after the voyage was over. It helps to keep a running tally in your own kitchen of just how much you really eat. Count the number of cups you get from a given jar of coffee, how many biscuits you can get out of a box of Bisquick, how much sugar is used in a week, and so on, and you are realistically on your way to becoming a provisioning expert.

Once you know how much the various containers hold in the way of meals, you can readily work out the number of containers that you need. To proceed willy-nilly, buying everything that looks good in the market, may result in eating a lot of canned boysenberries in place of something you like more.

For extended cruises my system is as follows. I decide how many days are to be prepared for, or how many weeks. I decide how often I can afford to eat eggs, for example, in a week. I buy enough to cover those days, and cross breakfasts off for that number of days. I then think of pancakes, cold cereal, and so on, and cross off days until all the breakfasts are gone. I now have a shopping list that contains everything needed for all my breakfasts. Lunches on my ships are usually cold—canned kippers, cheeses, pilot biscuit (contains no salt and doesn't become soggy), or ship's breads. Don't forget to account for the generous use of butter when eating cold meals. Dinners are usually rice or curry dishes with generous use of canned ham, shrimp, and so forth. I have come to detest canned stew, chile con carne, and canned spaghetti, since they always seem to have the texture and taste of library paste, although they serve well in heavy weather. Canned beef, chickens, pork loins, and so on can always be used together with canned vegetables for good hot dinners at sea. Again, count up the number of vegetable cans, the number of meat cans, and so forth, and you now have a complete shopping list. I start with three or four pages, one labeled "Meat," one "Vegetables," one "Fruit and juices," and one, "Staples." As I go through the various meals, I add my tallies to the separate lists. I put each category in a different bin on board, and I sometimes mark off the list each item as it is removed from the bin. This gives me a running inventory if I should happen to be in a place where I can replace something.

I have found that for the first few days at sea I eat a great deal, but that as time goes by I require much less. Sugary desserts are readily replaced by freshly baked bread with a little margarine and some brown sugar on it.

(My old friend Bill Horton could never understand my concern over shopping and provisioning. A few bags of rice, some canned tomatoes, some potatoes, plenty of rum, and a fishhook are all he needs to go voyaging. He also detests self-steering systems, claiming that one goes to sea precisely to stand watches, get wet, and drink rum! As I think of it sometimes, he may be right.)

I have found that eggs will keep for about thirty days or so in the tropics without any treatment. Be sure to break them in a dish, not the pan, however, in case there is a bad one in the lot. I have heard that eggs that have never been refrigerated will last longer, but I don't know if that is true. Mine always came out of cold storage, and they did quite well. For extended voyages, eggs can be greased with Vaseline, or they can be dropped in boiling water for ten seconds or so, and this is said to extend their life considerably. Powdered eggs can be used in other dishes, but they are strange in texture when you try to cook them up alone.

I no longer carry baker's bread except on very short passages. The mildew gets out of hand so rapidly in the tropics that it sometimes looks like an invasion from a moldy planet. Any voyaging yacht worth the name has an oven and bakes her own bread. A lot of recipes work well at sea, and every cook has favorites.

Oranges, apples, potatoes, and onions keep well at sea, if you do not put them into some dank, airless cupboard. Bill Taylor used to put onions, carrots, and potatoes in a gunny sack and tie them to the boomkin, where they would be wetted down occasionally, and they lasted well. Some say that even lettuce, if it is not trimmed first, will last a few weeks this way.

I am indebted to my old cruising buddy Danny Johnson, for the following idea. Take along a pressure cooker and plenty of Mason jars. When you are able to find fresh meat, eat some and can the remainder. In that way you constantly replenish the larder without constant dependence on supermarkets.

I usually try to have good eating aboard for as long as the passage should normally last. I plan poor eating for half again as much time (fifteen days on a thirty-day passage), and I have survival rations for at least thirty days always aboard. I avoid the more modern freeze-dried foods, because they all require water—always in short supply—to reconstitute them, and they are extraordinarily expensive.

Some skippers, or their wives, insist on taking along quantities of paper napkins and paper towels. I have never seen the need. I find that plain old toilet paper is a dandy napkin, and in fact it is customary to see a roll of it on any cruiser's table in the Pacific area. The fancy foibles of American civilization don't survive too long on an extended cruise. I remember one yacht that had to limit its cruises because the crew used a roll of paper towels each day, and they just couldn't carry enough to stay away more than a month or so!

Fishing is a great way to augment the larger. My mouth still waters when I think of those first days in the trade winds when the Mahi-Mahi first begin to show up. I have been known to eat half of a fifteen-pound Mahi-Mahi in a single afternoon.

My fishing tackle is rudimentary, consisting of about a hundred feet of nylon parachute cord (that stuff again?). I attach about ten feet of braided stainless steel leader and tow a lead head blue and white feather. Spinners, spoons, or almost anything will attract ocean fish, but I have found the Mahi-Mahi will go mostly for things that look like the flying fish, its natural food. I sometimes carry a trolling rod and reel, but this is mostly for sport, not for serious fishing.

Hunting is less valuable than fishing as a source of food. Some uninformed, or totally mannerless, yachtsmen still believe that any animal on foreign soil is fair game, but a goat or a pig may comprise some islander's total worth. Assume that everything you see while cruising belongs to someone, and treat it accordingly.

If you carry a weapon, and I do, you must declare it with customs and be prepared to surrender it at times or be able to lock it in a sealed compartment for the duration of your stay in some countries. I believe that the best firearm to take along is a heavy-gauge shotgun. You can use it to blow up sharks, to hunt for your dinner should the opportunity arise, or to signal for help. In any event, do not take along any fine or high-class weapon. It will ultimately rust or be confiscated by a Central American port captain.

Sails

I have often wondered whether sails were part of the design, the equipment, or the fitting out of a yacht. I have put them in the section on fitting out, because most cruisers seldom look at their sails until one blows out. A yacht can never, it seems, have too many sails, but many yachts do not have the space to carry them.

Since most offshore work is done under working sails, it is best to consider them first. You must carry a working jib, and it is wise to have the clew very high-cut so as not to catch too many wave tops when going to weather. I also carry a storm jib, designed for at least sixty knots of wind. I carry a 150 percent genoa, a 150 percent reacher, which is very fully cut and serves as sort of a spinnaker, and a 180 percent genoa for light airs. I would have a light nylon drifter or ghoster also if I could find the locker space. The main should be heavier than that usually used for racing. Storm trysails are mostly a thing of the past. Dacron mainsails, with their tremendous strength, are just as strong when properly reefed. The trysail, of course, makes a good jury sail should the main blow away.

The working sails should be of dacron, of course, and, as mentioned before, I like mine triple-stitched. The design of cruising sails used to be different from that of racing sails, but since the vessels do not differ much today, the sails do not either. Select the best sailmaker you can find. Some of the biggest advertisers are not necessarily the best sailmakers. Go to the man who will give you good personal service, who will take the time to discuss your needs and your vessel. Shy away from the one who wants to know what great yachts you have owned or raced on; he is seeking to enhance his fortune, not yours. One sailmaker I know about sends out the work for relatively unknown skippers to one of the cheaper sailmakers, while he fawns and scrapes over the owners of the local superyachts. Others, like Saint Cicero of Baxter and Cicero, for example, do the same job for you or me as they would for Mosbacher. As a matter of fact, I have won a lot more races using Saint's sails than I have using those made by the aforementioned superstar.

I look for good, strong sails that will not change shape too much if you hang onto them too long. If you are of the "hang on and blow 'em away" school of thought, like me, please tell your sailmaker so. I hate to waste wind, and I love to see lots of white water in the wake. I pay for that propensity by buying lots of sails. Your sailmaker should know if you favor high pointing over footing off, and he should be given a realistic evaluation of your yacht's relative pointing ability.

A good sailmaker can tell you for what weight of wind the sail is designed. Take his word for it. If he tells you that a given genoa, for example, should be downed when the wind gets up to twenty knots, don't stand around crying if it blows out of the tapes or goes out of shape because you left it up in a force eight squall.

Beware of gimmicks on cruising sails. "New" ideas are usually old ideas that were discarded long ago and are being tried again.

I am somewhat confused by all the claims over sailcloth. One East Coast sailmaker claims that his cloth is superior to the cloth used by some West Coast sailmaker. The arguments rage in the advertising columns, but when the East Coast skippers come out west they place last in our regattas. Could their sails have been less than perfect? The down easter claims that no America's Cup was ever taken by a boat with West Coast sails. It is also true that no contender ever *used* West Coast sails! It is true that the uncalendered cloth is more flexible, softer, and easier to stow. It has one fatal drawback as far as cruising sails go—it blows out of shape easily. When you can go to the sailmaker for recutting every three or four races, soft cloth is OK, but where are the sailmakers on Tonga?

The truth of the matter is that most sailmakers, coast to coast, use sailcloth made by the same mills. A few make great advertising hay out of the fact that they weave their own cloth. But who do you want making your sails—a sailmaker or a weaver?

You can send abroad for sails at good discounts, and I once made that mistake. They were of English manufacture and were strong as blazes. Unfortunately, they were all shaped like sacks, and I spent more than they were worth to have them all recut. The British have traditionally misunderstood the shaping of sails, and this is thought to be at the bottom of their inability to retrieve the America's Cup. I once saw some Japanese-made sails that had been in use for a time, and the owner had washed them in a mild detergent. The cloth had not been hot set, or calendered, and the result was that his sails looked and felt like soft silken handkerchiefs. They were made to look like dacron sailcloth by putting on sizing. These experiences have only confirmed my belief that American sailmakers are the best in the world. Why take chances?

Most cruisers are aghast at the idea of using the parachute spinnaker as a cruising sail. As I've said, I happen to like them, provided they are sensibly handled. For strictly cruising I would like one with a width of 150 percent of "J," and it should not be quite as full-cut as a racing spinnaker. You can set it on two spinnaker poles, or on the boom and a single pole. The sail should be fairly heavy, say one-and-a-half-ounce material instead of the usual one-half- or three-quarter-ounce racing stuff.

Mizzen staysails belong on ketches in boat parades. A mizzen spinnaker, however, pulls like the very devil. If cut properly, it can serve under a wider variety of wind conditions than the mizzen staysail, picturesque though the latter may be.

A chat with the designer or a competent sailmaker will allow you to make an informed decision as to what sails to take on your cruise.

7   Planning

How pleasant it is to dream of simply getting on your boat and sailing away, without timetables, schedules, or everyday cares and worries! True, some sailors have made (or survived) cruises made utterly without planning, but those lucky souls must have had the protection of deities yet unknown to me! The prudent voyager does not endanger his yacht or his crew by deliberately sailing into dangerous conditions. On the other hand, I believe a voyage can be overplanned as well. I have known people to leave harbor on the appointed day even though gale warnings were flying. There is obviously a happy medium, here as in most other things pertaining to the sea.

The primary consideration in planning the cruise is to be where the winds are and where the hurricanes, typhoons, willie-willies, and so on are not. The next consideration is to take in as many ports of interest as possible while sailing the fewest doglegs in your course.

Weather Planning

In order to become versed in wind systems, I believe that every prospective ocean voyager should take an introductory course in oceanography. Such courses are offered by many junior colleges and university extension systems. Reading cruising stories and journals may help somewhat, but such accounts require a lot of cross-indexing and correlation in order to contribute solid planning data.

Most successful passages are made by running down the trade winds, so named because they pushed the ships that were the basis of world trade for centuries. In the Northern Hemisphere they are northeasterly, while in part of the Southern Hemisphere they rise from the southeast. Note that in the South Pacific the southeast trades are only relatively constant in the winter months—June, July, and August.

Winds in the trade belts do not usually blow with gale force, but average about force four on the Beaufort scale. The weather is usually clear and fine, and the nights are not uncomfortably cold. There may be line squalls in the evening hours, and the winds may pipe up again around sunrise, but the sailing is usually everything a sailor could ask.

How pleasant it is to run down the trades with the main hatch open, the sun awning up, and the miles ticking off steady progression.

The trade wind belts are usually limited to the areas more than 5 and less than 30 degrees from the equator. The seasonal variations in the locations of these belts can best be found by looking at the pilot charts. The equatorial areas are typically called doldrum belts. These areas, usually about two to four hundred miles wide, are regions of light airs, squalls, lightning storms, and generally devilish weather.

On the higher latitude sides of the trade belts are the variables of Cancer in the north and Capricorn in the south. These were called the horse latitudes in days gone by when men in ships caught there were sometimes forced to use their horses for food or throw them over the side to conserve water. The winds in these belts are from light to nonexistent, though their direction is more or less in the direction of the associated trade wind belt.

As one approaches 40 degrees north or south he reaches the zone of the westerlies. Winds of these regions, not depending so much on thermal heating, sweep around the world in endless procession. In the northern latitudes large land masses break them and reduce their force. In the southern hemisphere they are known as the "roaring forties," for no major land masses slow their progression, and they sweep on in a frightening show of the strength of nature. It is these same westerlies that must squeeze between Antarctica and Cape Horn. The tremendous winds recorded in the area are said by some to be due to the venturi effect of the squeezing process.

There are seasonal winds such as the monsoon winds of Asia and the pamperos off the South American coast. These are due to local climatic conditions, and they are quite predictable. The occurrence of seasonal winds is important in planning, as they may run counter to the prevailing trades in some cases. To find out when such seasonal winds may be encountered, consult the pilot charts of the areas.

Tropical cyclones, be they called willie-willies, cyclones, hurricanes, or typhoons, are the children of summer. They are found in the trade wind belts, for the most part, which makes them a danger to the voyager. Winds of two hundred miles an hour have been recorded in some of these revolving storms, and the sea conditions can be absolutely unbelievable. A tropical storm of the cyclonic type forms as a local area becomes hot. Hot air rises, setting up a marked low pressure area. Cooler air must rush in to fill the void, but because of the Coriolis effect, due to the earth's rotation, it does not go in a straight line toward the center of the low pressure area. Instead, it spirals in a counterclockwise flow in the Northern Hemisphere and in a clockwise spiral in the Southern.

The speeds of the winds increase toward the center of the depression. In the actual center, or eye, of the hurricane, the sky is fair and the winds insignificant. As the eye passes over, however, the wind begins again with a bang, and from the opposite direction.

The approach of a tropical storm is heralded by several signs. The barometer starts a slow, steady decline sometimes days before the actual approach of the storm. Large swells start to arrive, pushed by the tremendous force of the winds. Mackerel sky develops—high cirrus clouds in well-defined rolls. These clouds, together with the other signs, indicate that the storm is from three to six hundred miles away. Mares' tails are said by some to converge toward the center of the storm. The cirrus clouds will become more dense as the storm approaches, and stratocumulus and altostratus formations will appear below the veil. A misty rain will develop, followed by winds of from twenty to forty knots. At that time the wall, or bar, of the storm should be visible. It is a literal wall of dark cumulonimbus clouds. As the bar approaches, heavy squalls develop, the sea becomes mountainous and confused, and heavy rain may fall. I have seen the bar of a tropical storm twice, and the portents can be described only as awesome. Luckily, neither one was a fully developed hurricane, one being a Mexican "chubasco" and the other merely being called a tropical storm by the weather folks. Both, I might add, nearly blew my hair off nonetheless.

As the bar passes, the weight of the wind increases markedly, reaching hurricane force in a well-developed storm. The barometer falls sharply, as much as a full inch. The sound of the wind, even at a mere sixty knots or so, is beyond description. I would go below, after battening everything down and setting the little storm jib, and turn on my receiver as loud as I could get it to try and drown out the incredible sound. I have thought that nothing made by man could possibly stand up to the fury of a tropical hurricane, and many man-made things cannot. But many good yachts have encountered and, surprisingly, most have survived hurricanes. Notice that I said *good* yachts. Many bad ones have been lost. After the Gulfport Hurricane of 1947 I saw fishing boats a good quarter-mile from the shoreline, resting securely on football fields and in front yards!

If one is both lucky and fast, he can locate the center of the depression and steer clear. Tropical storms have two sides, one of which is called the dangerous semicircle, the other the navigable semicircle. (Navigable for a battleship, maybe.) The part of the storm on the *right* side of the storm's track is called the dangerous semicircle in the Northern Hemisphere. It would be the part on the *left* side in the Southern. These directions apply if you face where the storm is heading. Winds in this area are stronger than in the opposite, or navigable semicircle. They are said also to tend to blow one more and more into the path of the storm center. Winds in the navigable semicircle are said to take the ship away from the center.

The storm can be tracked by listening to radio WWV. This station, besides broadcasting the correct Greenwich Mean Time (now called Coordinated Universal Time), gives the positions of major depressions in both the Atlantic and Pacific Oceans at fifteen minutes before and fifteen minutes after the hour.

You can use the old standby, Buys Ballot's Law, to find the approximate center of a depression. If you face directly into the wind (any wind caused by cyclonic activity), the low-pressure area is to your right and slightly behind you. It would be to your left in the Southern Hemisphere.

Tropical disturbances of the hurricane variety occur in five rather well-delineated areas of the world:

1. The Caribbean and adjacent Atlantic waters. Storms in summer and autumn with a peak of activity in September. Stay away from July through November for maximum safety.

2. The coast of Mexico and Central America. Peak activity in September.

3. Japan, China coast, Philippines. Peak in August. Never free from typhoons, but February has the fewest.

4. The South Indian Ocean, east of Madagascar. September and October are the peak months.

5. The area bounded by Tahiti on the east and Australia on the west. December, January, February, and March are the danger months.

You can see that in the Northern Hemisphere one should stay away from hurricane areas in general during August, September, and October, at the least. According to the U.S. Naval Oceanographic Office, there is an average of forty-three cyclonic storms per year strong enough to be called hurricanes in the Northern Hemisphere. In the Southern, the average is thirteen.

Pilot Charts

Pilot charts, issued by any good Oceanographic Office agent, are probably the most valuable of all planning aids. These publications cover the conditions of wind and current to be expected on the oceans, give average weather conditions for ocean areas, give the percentage chances of gales, average temperatures, percentage chances of fog, the limits of drift ice, and other valuable information. For the North Pacific area, for example, a chart is issued for each month of the year. For the South Pacific and Indian Oceans each chart covers a three-month period.

Winds are noted for each 5-degree square of the ocean involved. A wind rose appears in the middle of each square with arms extending in the directions from which the winds may blow. The relative length of each arm depicts the percentage of time during which the winds may be expected to blow from each direction during the period covered by the chart. "Feathers" on the extreme ends of each wind arm give the average force, expressed in Beaufort numbers, that can be expected. Four "feathers" indicate force four, for example.

Arrows show the drift of the currents, and a small number printed in the corner of each square represents the average set, in nautical miles, to be expected per day. The observations that make up the averages printed on the charts have been taken since the early nineteenth century at noon by various vessels. Lieutenant Matthew Maury, USN, started the collection of these noon observations of weather and current, and the result is the compiled average of observations taken by a vast number of ships over a period of at least one hundred and fifty years.

An important piece of information in the pilot chart is the location of steamer lanes. The wise yachtsman would do well to steer clear of them unless he just happens to like a lot of company! If any steamer lanes are in the area of my track, I usually plot them on my navigation plotting sheet so that I may keep sharp watch. I get out of them as fast as possible so that I can again sleep all night.

As is the case with all averaged data, there will be times when the pilot chart will say you should be getting force four trade winds from the northeast, and you will be caught in a northerly gale. At other times no calms will ever have been observed in the section, and you will have been becalmed for three days. I once sailed for six days in a tropical storm in an area that showed less than 1 percent gale conditions. It showed no storm tracks of tropical storms, either. Remember, a force five average can be obtained by winds that are zero half the time and force ten the other.

Faulty though averages may be in predicting the weather exactly, the pilot chart is the best way to find the most probable route from one place to another. You may find that the direct course to some point, although shorter, brings you afoul of contrary winds, whereas a dogleg will bring more favorable winds, thus shortening the passage time. Besides, the backs of the pilot charts contain entertaining reading about marine collisions, meteorology, sea monsters, and the like.

Route Planning

To follow my system of planning, you should first obtain a hemisphere chart that covers all the areas you would like to visit. Mark your route line after consulting the pilot charts. Then take a bunch of drafting pins, and glue a little name flag on each for each month of the time you have available. Put the first flag at your home port—for example, June, 1974. Consider your first passage, say for the Marquesas Islands. Measure off the time required by the following process. Calculate a reasonable day's run (about $.9 \times \sqrt{\text{waterline length}} \times 24$). Let's say it works out to about 100 miles a day, a reasonable figure for thirty-footers or larger boats. Pick off with your dividers 100 miles on the latitude scale halfway between home port and the Marquesas. Using this setting, mark off hundred-mile increments all along the route line you have drawn. Count the increments, and you have the expected passage time. My route would take 30 days at 100 miles a day, so I place my next pin, marked July, 1974, on the Marquesas. It is wise to plan a somewhat longer stay than you would like at any major port, because the passage could be a slow one, and you want to be sure to have enough time to rest before taking off to chase the next flag.

Let's say you want to go on and see Tahiti, Moorea, Isles Sur Le Vent, Rarotonga, and Fiji. You will know that December through March are the danger months once you are west of Tahiti, so you will want to put all those flags in a good hurricane hole. Only Tahiti and Fiji are good possibilities. Most of the others may not serve well as anchorages in very dirty weather, and four months on some of the smaller islands may seriously strain the local hospitality. You would not select Tahiti for the hurricane season because you are already at the Marquesas in July, and you would not wish to stay until March in expensive Tahiti, with its tourist traps. Besides, the French require that you move along after six months. Fiji it is then, unless you postpone the start of the trip for a few months.

Now you must divide the time from July to December among the islands you wish to visit. It is obvious that a good deal of juggling must be done to accommodate weather, desire to visit as many places as possible, and the available time span allotted to the voyage.

If you are uncertain as to the right harbors in which to lie doggo during the hurricane season, read the Pacific Islands Pilot Books. These, while really written for the masters of larger vessels, still describe well the anchorages and harbors.

I would advise reading voraciously everything you can about an area before you sail there. Every bit of information is valuable to a man who knows nothing. *Pacific Islands Monthly*, an Australian publication, is the business and commerce newspaper of the Pacific. It is a mighty good indicator of the conditions you can expect all over the Pacific. It tells how many new American or Japanese hotels and airstrips went in during the last few months on islands you and I never heard of. It indicates where the latest fish cannery is going up, and it tells which group of islands most recently obtained independence from some "protector." It indicates the latest spirals in the price of eggs in Papeete and catalogues the latest beefs against the Americans.

By the time you have shifted your pins from island to island, found the best routes, read about the various harbors, and finalized the planning, you will find that a great deal of the anxiety over the voyage is replaced by great expectancy.

You must plan well so that the inevitable depletion of supplies coincides with a port where supplies are easy to obtain. With a very small yacht this is more of a problem than many realize. Most small islands do not cater to American tastes, so if you shop there you will have to revise your eating habits somewhat. Any American-administered island will have a good store, but its use may be limited to American military personnel and dependents.

You will find that such staples as flour, salt, and sugar can be obtained in most places. If you want much else beyond canned tomatoes and the like, you had better bring plenty along, or get someone to send them to you.

Major ports like Papeete are good places to replenish stores, but the prices are very high. Peanut butter, a favorite of most cruising families, is relatively scarce in the South Pacific. A friend of mine regularly sends home for a supply. In the more primitive areas you will just have to make do with native food (which is excellent once you get over your squeamish American tastes) and save the sea stores for when you are at sea. Whangerei, New Zealand, is a favorite hurricane hole, and plentiful stores are available at low prices. American Samoa has a good supply status, but the administration there does not in any way encourage yachtsmen to visit. Harbor dues and anchorage charges were the order of the day the last I heard.

In addition to the availability of stores, you should consider

149

where to haul out, paint, and refit. The day is rapidly drawing to a close when you can just run her up on a convenient beach and do the repairs. Most modern yachts are not of hull forms that allow such treatment. Some sages say that therefore you must have a yacht with a long, straight keel. Consider that the modern yacht, having less wetted surface and usually being built of fiberglass, can simply be cleaned with mask and snorkel, and then hauled out for painting anyplace that has a good crane, thus eliminating the need to look for a place with a slipway or marine railway.

Most yachtsmen will want to put in at some major port at least once a year for refitting, rest, and resupply. It is perhaps wise to make these ports coincide with the hurricane seasons in your planning.

Formalities

Some yachtsmen contrive to sail around the world in a rather haphazard manner, not paying much attention to customs regulations, but they usually suffer fines and penalties for doing so. You will save a lot of aggravation by clearing properly for the next port.

Before setting sail for any foreign port, first get a passport. Some will tell you that if you have a documented vessel you have no need for a passport. This is true but often not practical. Only a United States citizen can document a vessel under the US flag, and if you can prove that you are indeed the owner, you may get away with it. The customs official that you run into may not be familiar with that little fact, but he *will* know what a passport is. Often you must leave your document with the harbormaster or port captain, and if you have no passport as identification, you may not be able to travel very far.

Once you have your passport, go to a customhouse agent or to the consulate of the country that controls the port to which you are going and ask for a yacht clearance. After the customary declarations a clearance will be issued in the language of the host country saying roughly the following: On January the fifteenth the American yacht *Laguna* sails (ed) for Guadalupe Island on a pleasure voyage. The yacht was of 7.5 gross tons, and carried document number such and such (or was numbered under California law such and such). The crew consists of

David Parker, Captain   U.S. Citizen
Raymond Dugas, Navigator   U.S. Citizen
Doris Dugas, Mariner   U.S. Citizen

When you reach the port, a copy of the crew list is given to the representative of the port captain and signed, and the vessel may be inspected by the port doctor, agriculture officials, immigration officials, police, or any other functionary. When they are all satisfied that nothing is amiss, the crew is cleared to go ashore. Until then, only the skipper rates shore time. You will, of course, fly International Code Signal "Q" as you come into port. Fly your national flag at the stern flagstaff and the flag of the country you are visiting on the starboard spreader. The "Q" flag signifies that your ship is healthy and that you require "pratique."

Once you are cleared into a country, you are usually allowed to go from port to port without further clearance. You may be required to give a copy of your clearance and your crew list to each port captain along the way, or in rare instances be required to clear each port formally. Note, for example, that the port of entry for French Polynesia is Papeete. If you land first at the Marquesas, the port captain is not required to allow you to go ashore. He may insist that you first go to Tahiti to clear into the territory. This does not often happen, but it is perfectly proper procedure if the port captain does not like your looks!

On leaving the jurisdiction of one country you should again go to the port captain and request clearance to depart. He will check that none of the crew is left behind, that you leave no outstanding debts, and that no escaping citizens of his own country are aboard. Usually, these formalities are done right in the port captain's office. At other times, perhaps if the ire of some official has been aroused, the whole formal business must be carried out. This can be quite expensive, since much of it is done on "overtime," and you must pay in cash.

In terms of red tape and aggravation, American customs men run a close second to the Australian in the number of forms and the amount of hassle required to clear. I was once clearing in from a short cruise to Baja California, where none of the port captains cared a damn whether I cleared or not. I made the great mistake of arriving at the customs dock in San Diego after 5 P.M. on a Friday. Now, everyone knows that the United States government cannot afford to pay customs inspectors for weekends. I was told by a very sympathetic harbor captain that I must either pay "overtime" for a senior man to drive fifty miles or so from home or wait until Monday morning after 8 A.M. The overtime would have amounted to over seventy dollars, an amount I refused even to consider. We waited until Monday morning, and still the customs men did not show up. My crew was close to rebellion and was by that time bumming cigarettes

151

from passing yachtsmen, who must have thought that we were being held for smuggling at the least. I called the customs office and asked politely where the hell the gentlemen were that were not able to work weekends due to the poverty of my government. They replied that the men were tied up at the airport, due to heavy influxes of people who were wise enough not to enter the country on the weekend. I inquired whether, since we had been waiting nearly three days, we shouldn't therefore gain some small priority. He said no. He admonished me by saying essentially that those people on airplanes were in a hurry and that we would have to wait our turn. Finally, at noon, a harassed-looking official from the Department of Agriculture dropped by and asked if we were carrying any fruit from Mexico. We replied that we had indeed brought some, but we had eaten it while waiting for him to arrive. He never even stepped aboard the boat, which by that time resembled the Black Hole of Calcutta and smelled equally bad! I asked if he were not afraid that we had smuggled in some alien or contraband. He replied that his business was fruits and vegetables, not wetbacks, and disappeared, dropping my clearance as he left.

The use of the magic word "overtime" has spread to the Central American countries also, and it is wise to enter port only during normal working hours. These are between 9 A.M. and noon and between 2 and 4 P.M. To do otherwise is to lay yourself open to substantial charges for "overtime."

Failure to fly the flag of the country you are visiting is discourteous and may lead to your being fined by some patriotic port captain. Many cruisers carry colored cloth and make up their own as they go along. Others buy cheap printed ones and keep a good supply on hand.

You may enter a port without having cleared the last country you visited, but the practice may raise questions in the mind of the harbor authorities.

In cases of emergency you may enter a port under "protest." Fly code flag "Peter" as you come in. The use of this flag signifies that you are entering not of your own choice. Damage to the vessel, severe weather, injury to the crew, and other emergencies are good cause to force you to enter a port that you otherwise would pass up. Some yachtsmen use this dodge to enter when no clearance has been made to the port, but this is an abuse of a very valuable rule.

Notice that you can enter most ports without a clearance, but only the captain can go ashore, and then only on ship's business.

Code flag "Peter" is also hoisted twenty-four hours before you plan to weigh anchor. It used to be a signal for all the local tradesmen to hustle down to the ship or to the port captain's office to present their bills. If they did not, flying the flag was considered to be fair warning!

Even though clearance may not be required at some ports, it is considered courteous to pay a call on the port captain nonetheless. Quite often he will give you good advice as to the best anchorages and sources of supplies and repairs. In many American ports he will not even talk to you.

Finances

In this day of inflation and the diminishing dollar it is difficult to make any statement about how much it costs to cruise. Some have sailed around the world without a penny to their names. Others have thought that a thousand dollars a month was too little.

The great interest in cruising shown by the unwashed generation has caused a somewhat lessened welcome in many foreign ports. At one time a visiting yachtsman was hailed as a sort of hero. Now he is often viewed with distrust. It has been mentioned more and more frequently that one should leave his long-haired children and acquaintances at home if he wants to be well treated in foreign ports. On occasion, a yachtsman pulling innocently into a port just ravaged by hippies is practically lynched by the irate populace.

The wonderful hospitality that used to go so far in reducing the cost of a voyage has gone in most places and is replaced by a not too gentle anti-Americanism. The change has been mostly our own fault, to be sure, but it is there nonetheless.

When the unwashed scion of an American yachtsman has just stolen all the fruit off the local trees, stolen his lunch from the local store, and planted marijuana seeds in the local taro plantation, we can hardly scream when the prices go up. Of course, no American that I have seen cruising would ever admit that *his* child is a hippie. He is just "finding himself." Most foreign ports would be a lot more hospitable and somewhat cheaper if he found himself in San Francisco, however.

The good old American dollar used to be the prime currency in cruising territory, but it has lost its stability and value of late. As a consequence, one can no longer live out of the country much more cheaply than at home. You should consider that the cost of food, other than what you can catch, will cost as much as, or more than, at home. You will have your living quarters, of course, along with you,

153

so at least you don't have to pay rent. You will have to maintain the yacht, however, and that may prove expensive if you have too many mechanical contrivances aboard that require parts shipped in from the States.

It is sometimes a problem getting money transferred to banks in foreign ports, particularly the small ones. Traveler's checks are probably the best way to carry money, since the tourist trade is well established everywhere. Carrying personal checks is usually a waste of time, since a number of telegrams or phone calls are usually necessary in order to cash them. Letters of credit can be arranged with some banks. See your own bank regarding the best arrangements to make.

There are a few ways to reduce the cost of voyaging. The first is to forget about insurance. The policies, if you can get them, are quite costly and often very hard to collect on if there should be any problem. The second is to find a way to reduce taxes on the yacht. Many would-be voyagers are unaware that if a yacht is documented in California, for example, it will be taxed even if you are out of the country for ten years. The bill will be waiting when you return. The state of California believes that as long as a yacht is *documented* in the state, it is *in* the state, and so, therefore, are you. You can beat this little larceny by one of your own. Before setting out on a cruise, move to a state that does not tax yachts, like Hawaii, or to the Virgin Islands. You must be a bona fide resident with a mailing address in order to change the document, however. If your yacht is numbered with a state numbering system, surrender the number and renumber in some other place, or refuse to number at all.

Mail

Most people will want to receive mail while cruising, and it isn't as easy as you might think. In a place like Tubuai communication with the outlying islands is still often by boat, and the schedules are just not up to American mail standards.

It is wise to select a few major ports where you want your mail to wait for you. Some address all mail to the yacht, in care of the harbormaster. This sometimes works out all right, but often the mail will be lost or misplaced. The harbormaster is not a mailman. Mail addressed to General Delivery usually is received all right. A friend, or a bank with which you have set up a letter of credit, serves well as a mail drop. Some skippers wait until they hit a major port and then send home for the mail, which has been collecting at a friend's house, at his bank, or with his attorney.

Hospitality

In spite of the hippie transgressions, there are still times when you will be greeted by the old familiar cruising greeting: Hi, there. How about coming up for a shower and some dinner?" The greeter seldom means that you look unsanitary or underfed. There is just no better way to greet a voyager. Such greeters are usually yachtsmen or ex-yachtsmen themselves. There is a comaraderie among cruising yachtsmen that would ordinarily not be expected except among astronauts, old soldiers, or survivers of great natural disasters.

The local yachtsmen of Hilo, Hawaii, take great pleasure in making the stay of cruising yachtsmen pleasant, and, unfortunately, they often have been cheated by yachtsmen passing rubber checks. Still, they haven't lost all their faith yet. One of my fondest memories of Hawaiian cruising is the constant round of parties, car trips around the island, and general good fellowship, which are truly astounding to the man geared to Marina Del Rey, where everyone has his hand out and gives absolutely nothing without a demand for double repayment.

I have been rather embarrassed by the hospitality that I have been shown while cruising, because I have been able to do little in return, aside from trying to give the same hand to others who may cruise by my way. Most cruisers will avoid my harbor, Marina Del Rey, like the plague, and right they are. Its notoriety has spread afar, and few people stop by anymore.

A good supply of white or red table wine, California variety, is always appreciated by visiting folks, and, incidentally, by harbor pilots and port captains as well. Some visitors like a picture of the yacht and its crew, but I have always felt that offering one would be a bit presumptuous of me. Almost any sailor or ex-sailor will appreciate a tour of the yacht. By all means have each visitor sign the guest log.

One of the greatest joys of cruising is just gamming with the other yachtsmen. No sooner does a new yacht arrive in an anchorage than someone comes over in his dinghy to inquire if he can be of any help. You say no, of course, even if you're sinking, and ask him aboard. A few glasses of your house wine, and the stories and friendship start.

It seems that no matter what kind of a vessel you have, visiting yachtsmen will be free in their compliments. I have had the owners of vastly superior yachts pay rather strong compliments to old *Laguna*, and I knew that it was out of a sense of courtesy rather than strict truth.

There are times when visiting should be curtailed, and that is during the late evening and early morning hours. Unless I have some business, I do not approach a yacht unless there is someone on deck. I likewise refrain from playing loud music or running any engine after dusk. At parties, however, anything goes, and I will sing as loudly as the next guy!

The hospitality given by the local populace is genuine and spontaneous, and the behavior of the yachtsman will largely determine whether the next visitor will be welcomed or rejected. The ugly American is just not appreciated anywhere. My friend Earl Schenk perhaps put it best when he observed that many cruisers just cannot get the idea through their heads that when they are visiting a country they are *visitors*. The laws and customs of the host country are not fit subjects for critical commentary. You just cannot be a special case, bringing your own laws with you and obeying only the local laws and customs you approve. If you don't like the way they run their country, please stay home.

8   Navigation

Small boat navigation, simply defined, is the art of knowing almost where you are. It is an ancient art, to be sure. I always tell novices to forget their fears of the mathematics involved, to concentrate on the general principles, and to take the results of their calculations with a liberal grain or two of salt. In this chapter I will try to give a brief synopsis of the rather casual method I have developed over the past years. I do not hope to replace a good course in navigation, which all but the mathematically adroit should have, but I hope I can allay some of the fears that beset many novice navigators. Pilotage, the art of navigation by noncelestial means, really does not apply to ocean voyaging except at the end, so I will not discuss it.

All you really need in order to fix your position are a knowledge of the geographical position of some heavenly body (that is, the place on earth directly under it), and some means to measure the altitude of that body above the visible horizon.

Imagine that you are standing in a field that contains a flagpole. You are aware of the actual position of the flagpole, (its geographical position), and you know how tall it is (how high its top is above the horizon at its geographical position). Knowing these things, you can observe the angle that the top of the pole makes from where you are standing and know exactly how far you are from the pole. Obviously, around the pole there is a circle from every point on which the same angle will be measured. Suppose now that there is a second flagpole of known position and height. You again measure the angle to its top and draw out the circle from which such an angle can be obtained. In order to get each of the angles you measured, you must have been on the circles you computed. Since you are on both of the circles, you can only be at the point where they cross.

It is by exactly this process (a lot of technical mumbo jumbo notwithstanding) that a navigator "fixes" the position of his ship. It is a "line of position" that the navigator seeks. Most modern methods of sight reduction give only a line of position (an arc of the circle of equal altitudes) rather than the longitude or the latitude. There are methods of solving sextant sights for each, but they are tedious and have fallen out of favor in recent years. Since the vessel is actually

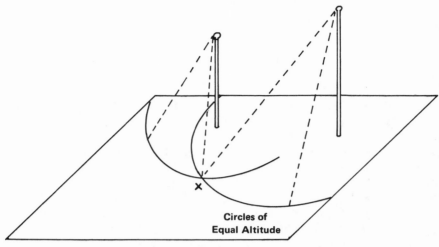

Figure 10

somewhere on each line of position that is observed, it becomes obvious that if two lines of position are observed at one time, then the
vessel must be at the point where the two lines cross.

It is not always possible to get two lines of position at the same
time, for only one heavenly body may be visible at any one time. The
navigator may retrieve an old sight, even of the same body, that he
took earlier, move it along the course line the distance he has come
since taking the sight, and see where it crosses the line he has most
recently obtained. The result is called a "running fix."

Obviously, to use such methods, you must know the geographical
positions of the heavenly bodies that you wish to observe. The efforts
of astronomers over the years have led to astoundingly accurate pre-
dictions of the movements of celestial bodies, and these movements
are recorded in almanacs published in various parts of the world. I use
exclusively the *American Nautical Almanac*, although several others
do just as well.

The almanac gives the longitude and latitude of the point on
earth that each body is directly over for each second of every day of
any given year. So a very precise knowledge of time also is essential
to the navigator. If you know the precise time that you observed the
sun, for example, you can look into the almanac and find out precisely
where it actually was at the time. Solving for the line of position then
becomes very much like finding your position in a field by using a
flagpole.

Time

The almanac uses the time at the zero meridian (Greenwich meridian) as a reference, so you must have the correct Greenwich time in order to get lines of position. Note that you can solve for your noon latitude without it, however. My system is to carry a small chronometer that is set to Greenwich mean time. When I take a sight, I call out "mark," and someone writes down the correct time, or I set a stopwatch from the chronometer and stop it when I make the sight. Another good source of the correct Greenwich Mean Time (GMT) is the radio station WWV, or its counterpart WWVH. These stations are continuously broadcasting the GMT at one-minute intervals, and they can be heard in most parts of the Atlantic and Pacific Oceans on 2.5 MHz and 5, 10, 15, and 20 MHz.

Consider the following possibility. You look up and notice that the sun is directly overhead when the clock reads exactly 1400 hours, GMT. (You would not be able to do this with sufficient accuracy to work it in practical navigation, but it serves well as an example.) Relying on only a few facts, you would know your longitude immediately. Consider that the earth is rotating eastward and that it goes through one complete rotation in twenty-four hours. The apparent movement of the sun is therefore 15 degrees each hour ($360° \div 24 = 15°$). The sun was directly over Greenwich, England, at 12 noon (1200 hours). If the sun is directly over you at 1400 hours, Greenwich time, then the sun has apparently moved 30 degrees to the west, and your longitude is 30 degrees west!

Longitude and time are intimately related. You cannot know your longitude unless you know the exact GMT, to all practical intents. I keep the following little table in mind to help me visualize the relationship between distance and time.

Distance (ARC)	Time
15°	1 hour
1°	4 minutes
15′ (miles)	1 minute
1′	4 seconds

Obviously, if your time is off by four seconds, your calculated line of position will be off by one nautical mile (measured at the equator).

Great care must be taken that the timepiece, does not start to vary in its rate. The chronometer should be wound at the same time each day, and its box should be kept below the waterline and shielded from rays of the sun in order to have the chronometer stay at as nearly the same temperature as possible at all times. It matters not if the timepiece gains or loses time, so long as it gains or loses the same amount each day. You simply tune in WWV or some other time signal each day and check the rate of the chronometer. Once it has been set, you mark the date. Multiply the rate amount (the number of seconds lost or gained per day) by the number of days that have passed since the piece was set and add or subtract the amount.

If you have aboard a good receiver or two, it is no longer absolutely necessary to carry a chronometer. A very good wrist watch, well rated, will serve for those rare times when you cannot get a radio time "tick." I have tried many kinds of wrist watches, and none of them could be trusted for more than a day or so, because their rates varied with changes in temperature. I am told that the new quartz crystal controlled ones are better, but I would have to see it to believe it.

My chronometer man tells me that a good pocket watch, kept under your pillow, is the best compromise.

The Almanac

The almanac is set up three days to a page. When you open it you will see that the information concerning the sun and moon are on the right-hand page, while data on the stars and planets are on the left.

The information you are seeking is the Greenwich hour angle (GHA) and the declination (Dec.) of the body at the instant of observation. Let's imagine that you took a sight of the sun (lower limb) at 16 hr. 25 min. 38 sec. GMT on 24 June 1973. You would open the almanac to the proper day, and, looking down the first column of the right-hand page, you would take out the following values:

1600 hrs.   GHA 59° 24.8'   Dec. 23° 24.6'

You would then look at the bottom of the daily page and find d, which represents the rate of change of declination, and it equals 0.1.

You still have 25 minutes and 38 seconds to account for, and the GHA and Declination both will have changed, or progressed, in that fraction of an hour. Since the almanac only gives even hours, not minutes and seconds, you must go to the yellow "increments and corrections" tables at the back of the almanac. You would seek the page with "25 minutes" at the heading and look down the sun-planets column until you find 38 seconds, and then take out the increment in GHA, 06° 24.5'. Look under v or d corrections (on the same page) and take out the correction for declination that agrees with the *d* that you looked up earlier (0.1), which would equal 0.0, or no correction needed for declination.

Add the 06° 24.5' to the original GHA, giving 65° 49.3' as the actual Greenwich Hour Angle for the sun. The declination remains 23° 24.6'.

Stars are listed in the almanac by Sidereal Hour Angle (SHA). In order to get a GHA, which you will need in order to reduce the sight, look in the far left-hand column of the daily pages and take out first the GHA of Aries. Aries is a point of reference for all stars. To get the GHA of a star, add the GHA of Aries and the SHA of the star together. Use the appropriate increments and corrections column for Aries, not the one for sun. Notice that the SHA and declination for a star remain constant over a three-day period, so no increments and corrections for the passage of fractions of an hour are needed. Remember that a circle contains only 360 degrees, so if the summed GHA of Aries and SHA of the star equal more than 360, you should subtract 360 degrees from your total.

Sight Reduction

Once you have obtained the geographical positions of the celestial bodies you have observed, you must obtain lines of position to plot on a chart so you can fix or closely estimate your position. This process is called sight reduction. The last time I looked, there were literally hundreds of methods available. Some, of the Haversine-cosine variety, are too tedious for the yachtsman. The modern "inspection table" is just the ticket. It comes as close as anything yet devised to the process of looking up an address in a phone book.

The job to be done by the reduction method is simple. Once you know where the body is in relation to the earth, you must calculate how high the body will appear above the horizon and at what true bearing you will see it. This is simple for a computer. In actuality, a computer figures out the sun's altitude and bearing (azimuth) for every possible spot on earth, for every possible time of observation! The results are then simplified, tabulated, and printed in a set of tables. You enter the tables with an assumed position (somewhere close to your dead reckoning position), the body's declination (labeled north or south) obtained from the Almanac, and the angular distance of the body measured westward of the observer (Local Hour Angle) calculated from GHA. Take out two quantities, the calculated altitude and the azimuth (body's true bearing from the assumed position).

Compare the calculated altitude with the altitude you have actually observed, and this will allow you to plot an "intercept" and a line of position.

I use exclusively H.O. 249, sight reduction tables for air navigation. They are easy to use and do not contain enough error to be of any consequence to the small boat navigator. In order to enter the H.O. 249 table, you must know your dead reckoning latitude to the nearest degree. Use the next degree less than your actual latitude if it is not an even degree. For example, if your DR latitude were 21° 35', you would enter the table with 21°. It makes no difference to the line of position you will ultimately plot where you assume your position to be. You will actually be on the line of position, not the assumed position.

You must know the exact declination of the body, taken from the almanac, in order to locate the proper column. Finally, you must know the Local Hour Angle of the body so that you are on the proper line of the table. LHA is, again, the angular distance from your meridian to the meridian of the body, measured westward from your meridian. Due to the rather crazy fact that someone divided the earth into two hemispheres with similar longitudes numbered up to 180° east or west, a rule is needed in order to find LHA. GHA is noted on a 360° scale, while the earth is numbered 0–180° east or west. To resolve the conflict, you get LHA by taking GHA and subtracting your longitude if you are in the Western Hemisphere, or by adding your longitude if you are in the Eastern.

Imagine that you are in the Western Hemisphere, on your way to Hawaii, in west longitude 135° 15.5'. Use the GHA for the sun that you looked up earlier (65° 49.3'). (Note that since your longitude is greater than GHA, you must add 360° to GHA, to avoid a negative number.) The sum would be as follows:

$$425° \ 49.3'$$
$$- \ 135° \ 15.5' \ W$$
$$\text{L.H.A.} = 290° \ 33.8'$$

In the Eastern Hemisphere you would *add* your longitude to GHA, and if the sum were more than 360°, you would subtract 360° from it.

If you look into H.O. 249, you will immediately see that LHA is available only in even degrees with no minutes or seconds. How do you get into the table with your fractional parts of a degree? Answer: cheat!

Change your dead reckoning longitude slightly so that when subtracted from GHA or added to it, it comes out a whole degree.

$$425° \ 49.3'$$
$$- \ 134° \ 49.3' \ W$$
$$\overline{291° \ 00.0'}$$

$$425° \ 49.3'$$
$$+ \ 25° \ 10.7' \ E$$
$$\overline{451° \ 00.0'}$$

It is wise to pick the closest assumed position (longitude) to your actual dead reckoning that you can for ease of plotting. In terms of accuracy, you can assume a single position and work any sight anywhere in the world. You might, for example, choose your home port as an assumed position and use only that throughout the voyage. Except for the fact that the intercept lines would become tiresome to plot, being overly long, your lines of position would be quite all right.

Armed now with a LHA, in whole degrees, the declination of the body, and your even dead reckoning latitude, go to H.O. 249 and select the proper page, which is identified by latitude. This number should agree with the dead reckoning latitude. Next look across the top of the page for the number closest to your declination and follow that column down until you come across your LHA in either the left or right margin. Note that the declinations are labeled "same name" or "contrary name." This notation concerns your dead reckoning latitude and the declination of the body, north or south. If your latitude and declination are both north, for example, you would use the "same name" page. If they differ, you would of course use "contrary name."

You will now take out a calculated altitude, a correction to be applied for odd parts of the declination, noting its sign, and an azimuth of the body. Inserted in the book you will find a loose-leaf sheet of corrections. Find the number that matches the one you just looked up between H_c and *Azimuth* at the top of the page. Follow that column down until you reach the number that matches the remainder of declination (any overage beyond the even degree). This remainder number will be both in the right and left margins. Either add it to, or subtract it from, the tabulated altitude. Assume that your declination was 15° 25'. You would use the 15° column in H.O. 249. When looking up the correction, you would go down the correction column until you saw *25'* in the side margin.

On the left-hand side of the tabulated pages you will find rules for getting the proper bearing of the body. The quantity you take out of the table (Z) is only the azimuth in northern latitudes if LHA is greater than 180°. If LHA is less than 180° you must subtract Z from 360°. In southern latitudes, if LHA is less than 180°, you add 180° to Z, and if it is greater, you subtract 180°.

You now have a calculated altitude (H_c) of the body, as well as a calculated bearing (azimuth). These calculations apply to the assumed position only. You may now compare a corrected sextant altitude, taken at the time for which you calculated the altitude, with the calculated altitude. If by chance you were exactly at the assumed position, the calculated and observed altitudes would be identical.

If you are not at the assumed position, your observed (sextant) altitude will differ from the calculated altitude. The way it differs and the amount it differs will give you what is called an "intercept."

Let's go back to the flagpole example. Assume that you are standing in the field, and you think you are on a circle one hundred yards from the pole. You could easily calculate the angle to the top of the pole at that distance, since you know the height of the pole. Now you actually measure the angle between the horizon and the top of the pole. Let's say the angle you measure is less than the angle you calculated. It is obvious that you are farther from the pole than you thought. (Mountains look lower from farther away.) If the angle you shot is greater than calculated, you are closer to the pole. The difference, in minutes of arc, between what you calculate and what you observe (shoot) is exactly the distance, in nautical miles, that the line of position is from the assumed position, measured along the azimuth line.

Now move to a plotting sheet, which is merely a grid laid out in longitude and latitude (I use the government's universal plotting sheets VP-OS). Plot in your previously assumed position, which you used in reducing the sight. From that point, lay off a line corresponding to the computed azimuth either toward the body's geographical position or away from it according to the following rule: If the observed altitude is *less* than the computed altitude, plot *away from* the geographical position; if the observed altitude is *more* than the computed altitude, plot *toward* the geographical position. Make your plotted line the same length, measured in nautical miles, as the difference (expressed in minutes of arc) between your observed altitude and your computed altitude. At the end of the line erect a line perpendicular to it. That is the line of position. Note that it is not necessary to make the line of position an actual arc, except when the sun is at or near its zenith.

The line of position that you have thus obtained can be advanced or retired so that it crosses another line of position by merely establishing a true course line and distance and moving the line, while keeping its angle constant, the appropriate distance.

Some problems can occur when lines of position are advanced or retired for the purpose of making running fixes. First, remember that

164

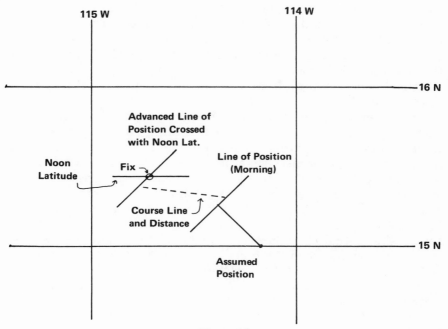

115 W 114 W

16 N

Advanced Line of
Position Crossed
with Noon Lat.

Noon
Latitude

Fix

Line of Position
(Morning)

Course Line
and Distance

15 N

Assumed
Position

Figure 11

a good fix is obtained when the lines of position cross at nearly right
angles. When you consider it, a line of position is at right angles to
the body you have observed. When, for example, you are at latitude
20° north and the sun's declination is 20° north, your line of position
is actually also a line of longitude. When the sun bears due south or
north, your line of position represents a latitude line.

Consider a yacht sailing for Hawaii in the summer months. The
lines of position that are obtained morning and evening, being at right
angles to the sun, will not cross at anything near right angles to each
other. When the morning line is advanced for purposes of making a
running fix, any error in draftmanship may result in a large error in
latitude.

Suppose that some systematic error is being made in the reduction of the sights. If the lines of position that make up a running fix
are both in error, the actual fix will also be in error.

I solve the dilemma by using sights that are independent of each
other in making my fixes, so that if I make an error in working up a
sight it shows up instantly when I try to cross the two sights. I use
two methods other than the time-honored line of position as a cross

165

check—the noon altitude and the latitude by Polaris. Both of these sights are simple to reduce, and they also lessen the chances of letting a systematic error creep in and get you totally lost.

My system is to take a line of position at about 1000 hours and then cross it, suitably advanced, with a meridian altitude (noon sight) to establish my noon position. I take another line of position some-time before dark and cross it with an observation of latitude by Polaris taken just after dusk for an evening position fix. I work up a star sight and Polaris altitude just before sunup, too, for yet another fix if I am in proximity to land, or am unsure of an earlier fix.

The noon sight or meridian altitude is quite simple to get and was the only sight generally available to seamen for centuries. As mentioned before, when the sun or any other body bears either north or south the line of position resulting from an observation is a latitude line. The noon sight is just a simplified way of reducing the sight and getting the latitude directly rather than a line of position. How does one know exactly when the body is due north or south? In the case of the sun, it will be only at noon. Noon is defined as that time (at the observer's meridian) when the sun is at its zenith. In olden times, the mate and the captain would appear on deck in their frock coats and make a series of observations starting sometime before noon, and they would record only the observation that showed the highest altitude before the sun started to descend.

It is possible today to do the same thing, hopefully without the frock coat. You simply go up on deck sometime before the sun reaches its zenith and begin to take observations at intervals of a minute or so. As the sun nears its zenith, its apparent rate of rise will diminish. At the zenith, the sun will appear to "hang" for a few seconds, showing no apparent further rise. Then it will begin a slow, ever-increasing rate of descent. You record the observation showing the greatest altitude. If it were possible to record the exact time of zenith (meridian passage) you would know at once your longitude as well as your latitude. Unfortunately, you cannot time the meridian passage with sufficient accuracy to get a practical longitude, due to the fact that the sun "hangs."

Reduction of the meridian altitude, or noon sight, is relatively simple. Basically you "shoot" the sun and correct the sight. (This process will be discussed later after the principles are clear.) You subtract the altitude from 90° to get a quantity called the zenith distance. You subtract the declination of the sun at the time the sight was taken from the zenith distance and the result is the latitude of the observer. There is one catch, however. You do not always subtract declination from zenith distance to get latitude; sometimes you add. Most texts on celestial navigation go into a great to-do trying to clear up this ambiguity. However, a simple rule is all you need remember. To solve for noon latitude, *always subtract the sun's declination from zenith distance unless your dead reckoning latitude is of the same name and greater than the sun's declination; then add.*

For example, you are in dead reckoning latitude 55° 14.5' N, and you observe the meridian passage at 1800 GMT. You look in the almanac and find that the sun's declination is 21° 12.2' N. Your DR latitude and the declination are both north, hence of the *same name*, and your DR latitude is *greater than* the declination, so you would have to *add* declination to zenith distance to get latitude. On the other hand, if you were in the Northern Hemisphere and the sun's declination were south, you would have *contrary names* and would have to *subtract* declination from zenith distance to get latitude. If you were in latitude 10° 36.1' N and the sun's declination were 16° 10.0' N you would have *same names*, but your DR latitude is *not* greater than declination so you would *subtract*.

The advantage of the noon sight is that it does not require a precise knowledge of time to give the latitude. In the absence (or disrepair) of any timepiece you can estimate the declination by figuring a dead reckoning longitude and simply converting arc to time (remember, the sun moves 15 degrees westward each hour) and looking up the declination in the almanac.

In the case of disaster, if the noon altitude is all the celestial capability you have left, you can still make port by "latitude sailing." Simply find the latitude of the port you wish to make and sail either north or south until your noon sights tell you that you are on it, and then sail east or west until the port hoves into view. Not terribly efficient, but certain!

The figures involved in getting a noon sight look like this:

True altitude (H.O.) 34° 23.5'

DR latitude 69° 23.1' N

Zenith distance = 90° – true altitude

	90° or 89° 59' 10"
H.O.	– 34 23 05
Z.D.	55° 36' 05"
Declination	13 39 00 N
(from almanac)	69° 15' 05" = Latitude

The DR latitude was of the same name and greater than the declination, so by the rule we had to add declination to zenith distance to get latitude. You could advance an earlier line of position to cross with the noon latitude and thus make a fix with sights worked by independent methods, reducing your chances of systematic error. The drawback to the noon altitude is that the sun may be obscured just at meridian passage, leaving you with no good latitude that day. You can get one the next evening, however, by observing the pole star, Polaris.

Polaris, or the North Star, is one of my favorite stars, because it stays put. Polaris can always be found in the close vicinity of the North Celestial Pole. Since that is true, you need only observe the altitude of Polaris directly and you have your latitude. What you read on your sextant is your rough latitude. In many cases no further reduction of the sight is needed beyond the normal corrections made to any sextant observation. If you were to proceed without correcting the Polaris altitude, your probable error in latitude would be less than half a degree in most cases. This is too large an error for practical navigation, but in emergencies it gives a rough latitude as quickly as anything I know, without the use of any tables or mathematics.

In the back of the almanac is a set of tables that allow the navigator to obtain a precise latitude by the observation of Polaris. The process is simple and quick. All that are required are the approximate Greenwich Mean Time, a knowledge of the date, a dead reckoning latitude (from the rough observation of Polaris), and a corrected sextant observation.

To reduce the sight, first determine the Local Hour Angle of Aries by finding GHA Aries in the almanac and adding or subtracting DR longitude (add east, subtract west). Next find the column in the Polaris tables that corresponds with your LHA Aries, and take out correction a_0. Looking farther down that same column, take out correction a_1 that corresponds with the DR latitude. Follow still farther down the same column and take out correction a_2 corresponding to the month of the year. Add the three corrections together and add them to the corrected sextant altitude that you observed. Finally, subtract one whole degree from the result, and you have your latitude. The sight is most convenient to use, since the whole business together with the rules for the reduction are found entirely in the almanac. This is a good sight to teach every crewman aboard. In case the navigator is disabled, the Polaris sight will enable the crew to do latitude sailing and bring the vessel home from any point in the Northern Hemisphere.

The Sextant

The sextant is the device with which seamen measure the angle between the visible horizon and the celestial body of interest. Sextants are made in many forms and types — some good, some fair, some practically impossible for small boat navigation.

I treasure my old Plath sextant as if it were made of gold. It is heavy, to be sure, but you can practically drive nails with it and it won't get out of adjustment. It has superb optics and large mirrors so that with the often violent motion of a small yacht at sea the body being observed doesn't get out of range so often. My Plath is equipped with a micrometer drum for reading out the angles, and with my eyesight I would not even consider a vernier type, which requires a small microscope to read under the best conditions. There are other sextants on the market that are just as good as Plath, I am sure, but you would have to go a long way to convince me. Most of the others available in the United States are cheap Japanese copies of the Plath, sold at a tremendous profit. There are cheap plastic sextants on the market that are fine for practice and for emergency backup, but they seem to warp and fall apart regularly in the tropics.

My mate Jim swears by an old war surplus aircraft sextant that he bought for five dollars or so some years ago. It is a bubble type, but he removed the bubble device and uses it just like an ordinary marine sextant. He was never off by more than six miles from any of my observations with the Plath. The problem with the aircraft types is that they are somewhat delicate and don't take well to seawater baths.

Bubble type sextants belong on aircraft, not on the sea. In spite of a lot of hot air put out by surplus dealers, the inertia of the bubble causes it never to be in the right place for very long on a pitching, rolling yacht. The result is that the sight may be in error by more than a degree due to the movements of the bubble, which may lag behind the motion that caused them by a considerable time period. And some of the weird derivative motions of the bubble could only be explained by a doctoral level physicist. In aircraft navigation the platform is more stable and the need for accuracy is less than in yacht navigation, believe it or not.

My motto in selecting navigation equipment is as follows: Get the best equipment available, so that you are certain that any error is due to your own mistakes, not those of the equipment. You can easily rectify your own mistakes, but when the error is caused by inadequate equipment it is almost impossible to correct.

Taking Sights

I have left the taking of sights until last because I have always found that until you know why you are taking a sight it doesn't matter much whether you can take one or not.

Taking sights resolves into two main parts or tasks. First, you must measure accurately the angle between the body and the horizon; and second, you must correct the sight so that it reflects the true altitude of the body, free from any aberration caused by defects in the sextant, changes in the relationship of the horizon and the body due to your not being exactly level with the horizon, refraction, temperature or pressure variations, or the apparent size of the body.

The novice should practice first with observations of the sun, and then progress to the moon and stars. My system is as follows. Grasp the sextant firmly by the handle with the right hand, holding the index clamp with the left. This means that you must find a position from which to take sights that allows both hands to be free, yet one that will not allow you to be chucked precipitously into the drink. I like to stand in the companionway where I can duck the odd dollop of spray and where I can move the top half of my body freely to keep the sun in view as the yacht crashes along over the chop.

Aim the sextant in the general direction of the sun and move the index arm back and forth slowly until you "catch the sun." Keep the general aim of the sextant at the horizon, and catch the sun with the index arm. Some writers advocate setting the index arm to zero and aiming at the sun until it is "caught," and then moving the index arm until the horizon comes into view. I have found, however, that I invariably have to start looking for the horizon and lose the sun! Once the sun is caught, use the micrometer drum to bring the sun down until its lower border (lower limb) just comes tangent to the horizon. Once the sun has been "brought down," the sextant must be rocked through an arc with the right hand so that the sun seems to rise and fall slightly in relationship to the horizon. Keep adjusting the index arm by use of the micrometer drum until the sun is just "kissing" the horizon at the very bottom of its apparent arc. This point is the only one at which the true altitude can be discovered. And the sextant must be exactly vertical. To measure at any other than the vertical position would result in a greater altitude than actually exists.

To shoot a star, I usually turn the sextant upside down and bring the horizon down to the star, rather than bringing the star down to the horizon. Stars are faint, and there are a lot of them to confuse you.

By focusing on the star and bringing the horizon to it, you reduce the chance of losing the star you want and measuring some other one.

A little practice goes a long way in learning to make a good observation of a celestial body. Most textbooks speak very glibly about taking the observation. Remember that most texts were written by men who took their observations from the bridge of a large vessel. There is a world of difference between the sight taken from a dry, steady flying bridge some forty feet above the sea and one taken from the often desperately unsteady cockpit of a small yacht leaping alternately off one swell and through the next! The first is a wonder of accuracy, the second a prayerful close approximation. Take all your observations, reduce your sights, add a liberal grain of salt, and you will be all right.

The sight must be corrected for the normal errors that occur for physical reasons, but it cannot be corrected for errors made because you brought the sun tangent to a large swell instead of the horizon.

Any sextant error should be avoided through good construction and proper care of the instrument. You can, however, measure some of the error that exists and thus eliminate or account for it. This is called *index error*, and it is caused by a lack of parallel alignment between the index and horizon glasses. It causes the sextant to measure a larger or smaller angle than actually exists. You can determine index error by aiming the sextant at the horizon and bringing the direct and reflected images into coincidence. The horizon should make a continuous line. Now read the sextant. It should read zero. If it does not, there is index error. The rule for correcting for index error is: *If it's on, it's off; if it's off, it's on.* This rather cryptic little rule means that if the sextant reads off the scale, or less than zero, the amount that it lacks must be added to the sextant altitude. Conversely, if the sextant reads more than zero (if it's *on* the scale) that amount must be subtracted.

All the altitudes that you read out of the sight reduction tables are true altitudes, measured from the true horizon. Since you are usually located above the surface of the sea when taking an observation, the position of the horizon will seem to have moved. You must correct each sight for the height of your eye above the true horizon. This correction is called "dip" and will be found inside the front cover of the almanac. The quantity corresponding to your height of eye above sea level should always be subtracted from your corrected sextant altitude.

When you shoot the sun, you usually use the lower edge, or

lower limb, as a point of tangency. It is the precise center of the sun however, that is of interest to the navigator. The correction for finding the center is called semidiameter. It is also inside the front cover of the almanac. Follow down the column, taking regard of the month of the year, and take out the correction that lies between the two values closest above and below your partially corrected sextant altitude. Take note of the sign of the correction. Lower limb observations correct by adding; upper limb shots (used when the lower part of the sun is obscured, for example) are subtracted.

The stars and planets, since they are really only points of light, need no correction for semidiameter, but they *will* require correction for refraction and so on. Tables for the correction of star and planet sights also appear inside the front cover of the almanac.

Both sun and planets tables are thus fully corrected for all the common aberrations, and no further corrections are needed except at very low angles of observation and under extreme temperatures and barometric pressures. These further corrections are found in the pages following the normal corrections. Once these three corrections have been made, you have the true altitude of your body, or H_o (height observed). It is this altitude that you compare with the calculated altitude (H_c) to get an intercept for a line of position, or use to get a latitude by meridian altitude or observation of Polaris.

Navigating a Small Boat

I would say that most of my travels have not been overnavigated. My crews might agree, adding that perhaps they were not navigated at all! I have missed only one landfall in my life, however, and that was precisely in the middle of writing this chapter! I set off in a strange yacht from San Diego bound for Avalon, on the island of Catalina. The distance was seventy miles, and the wind was, of course, directly on the nose, making me tack for the mark. The weather was fair all day, and as dusk approached it got hazy. The stars were bright overhead, lulling me into a false security. When our reckoning had run out, we could see no light, nor was there any usual sign of approaching land. The mate said she saw a red and white light off to port, and I hastily checked the charts to see if any such light existed in Avalon. It did not. "Hallucinations!" I snorted, getting a dark look in return. So saying, I hove to and got an hour or so of badly needed sleep.

With dawn's first light I saw the problem immediately. We were surrounded by a very thick ground fog that reached up to about five hundred feet or so, not enough to obscure the stars overhead, but enough to cover up the island, which now appeared about a half mile away. The mysterious red and white light of the night before was the brake lights and headlights of automobiles traveling in the mountainous highlands of Catalina island! Even though the breakwater lights were obscured by fog, the auto lights, being higher, could be seen once in a while.

The important point is to trust in your navigation if you are going to navigate. If you are going by intuition alone, then chase strange lights and play your hunches. Imprecise though small craft navigation is, it is still better than outright guessing!

At sea, I am usually somewhat lax about navigation until I am within three hundred miles or so of my landfall. Then the chartroom becomes a beehive of activity. I like to take several sets of sights in close succession and plot them all up. If they all cross or converge on a very small area, I am secure about my position and, hence, the proper course to the point of landfall. I usually fix my position only at noon if I am in open sea. If there are islands or reefs about, I make the three daily fixes that I mentioned earlier.

It is important to remember that even the best fix you can obtain from a small yacht is likely to contain a goodly amount of error. You are likely to get a wave top instead of the horizon; your plotting may not be too exact due to the motion of the yacht; you may be taking your own time rather than calling out "mark" to an efficient assistant; you may not use all the possible corrections to every sight. or at times motion sickness may impair your mathematical abilities! Thus you should consider your fixes as only the best possible estimates of your position. I always consider that my positions are really circles with diameters of ten miles. I then set my next course taking into account that possible error, and I have not been fooled too many times.

If an error is discovered in the reduction of a sight, I always feel it is better to go up and get a totally new sight rather than try to repair the erroneous one. If you try to "fix" a sight, you will, to all intents and purposes, be reinforcing the error that you made. Better to start all over and do it right.

In conclusion, I would say that the practice of navigation in small yachts is still the most satisfying aspect of ocean cruising, in the intellectual sense. Taking a small vessel out on the open sea, without signposts, without electronic aids, without traffic reporting helicopters and the like, and then at last seeing your island develop out of the mist is a thrill reserved only for the navigator. It is one of the few thrills allowed to "old computer head," but it is of the very highest caliber.

9   Seamanship

Seamanship is a very tough term to define, because it means so many different things to different people. To some it implies the the management of a vessel in heavy weather; to others it implies safety at sea; and to others it means the ability to have every part of the voyage go well and without mishap.

I like to think that seamanship is primarily excellence, or perhaps confidence, in every aspect of handling a yacht under any condition. Needless to say, safety of the yacht and its passengers plays a large part in making up the goals of good seamanship.

Seamanship cannot be learned from any book, because the sea is never exactly the way it was in some recounted episode. Likewise, no two yachts behave in the same way. Seamanship comes from two sources, in my opinion. The first is the attitudes and skills of the sailor, and the second is the widest possible experience. Reading may help develop the first, since man can supposedly learn from books. Having spent the last ten years as a college professor, however, I have my doubts as to whether most men can effectively apply what they have learned from books without having tested that knowledge in practical situations. It seems to me that one becomes truly confident in his abilities as a seaman only after his abilities have been tested at sea under the actual circumstances of sea life.

I do not mean to imply that there is no value in reading the accounts of seamen and learning what they did in certain circumstances. One can, through reasoning, try to choose viable alternatives from among those about which he has read. He is not yet a seaman, however, until he is confident that his choice of alternatives is the right one.

I, like many other sailors, have often worried and fretted that some condition will arise that I will be unable to meet adequately. Survival storms, capsizing at sea, and other disasters always lurk in the back of my mind. I have gone over in my head many possible courses of action I might take in such cases, but there remains that lingering uncertainty as to whether I would do the right thing. Too much worrying can spoil a voyage by taking away the pleasure of your successes. If one shies away from voyaging because of lingering doubts and fears, how is he ever to become a seaman? Two people in particular helped me in this regard.

I had made several ocean voyages in yachts before I had any suitable yacht of my own. I was, I thought, at least an adequate seaman. I could hand, reef, and steer. I could endure wet bunks and living in foul weather gear and still laugh and smile. I could throw a reasonable splice, repair almost anything on the yacht, and tell sea stories with the best of them (no true seaman is expected to stay too close to the truth when telling sea stories). Nothing the sea had thrown at me in some twenty years of crashing about had done me down. When I became the skipper, however, I was suddenly assailed with doubts. Now it was *my* decision that would decide the issue. I must say whether to go on into a port at night or to heave to until dawn. I must say whether it is time to reef. I must now take the responsibility for the lives of my crew and the safety of the yacht. Up until that time it was someone else's worry. Someone else supplied the judgment; I supplied the steam. I began to wonder if I had been kidding myself, if I really knew when to reef or if I really was able to select the best course of action in a dangerous circumstance.

I had arrived in Hawaii with my own yacht. I had crossed the infamous Alenuihaha Channel, being knocked down eleven times in the process. I had not got on a reef, nor sunk the yacht, but I was full of anxiety about the approaching trip home beating against the trade winds. I had done the passage before, but somehow I feared that some dragon or other was lying out there waiting to see if I would be equal to some fearful but nebulous trial.

Bill Horton, whom I know to be a consummate seaman, took me out for a bash in his new yacht. As we sailed out the Ala Wai Channel, he walked casually to the fantail and announced that she would sail herself from here on. We began to slip ever closer to the flanking reef, and I watched with some apprehension, knowing that Bill had lost his previous yacht on that same reef. Just as the grounding seemed inevitable, I reached for the tiller and headed her up, crying out to Bill, "We almost hit the reef!"

He allowed as how it wouldn't be the first time or something like that and went back to his can of beer. I opined that it was marvelous that he could be so detached. Said he, "Why worry? It's only water!"

That simple statement, from a man who had crossed many a sea, showed me how ridiculous it was to sit around worrying about dire possibilities. We didn't actually hit the reef, did we? I had somehow gotten over here, hadn't I? Why worry about going back? From that moment on, when doubts and worries began to assail my peace of mind I would tell myself, "It's only water."

I talked at length with John Guzzwell about heavy weather sailing. He gave me another truth that finally settled most of my fears of the unknown. He said that basically he never really saw any heavy weather anymore (since *Tzu Hang* pitchpoled in the roaring forties). It struck me as a great truth that until you experience your first heavy squall you wonder if you can handle it. Once it has occurred, and you have survived, anything up to that force of wind becomes inconsequential. The first gale produces many a lump in the throat, but the second one is met with more disgust than fear, and so it goes. Our experience becomes ever greater, our unknowns become fewer, and our confidence grows apace.

Attitudes

The basic attitude of the successful seaman is of prudent self-confidence. Any individual who lacks confidence in his own abilities or judgments does not belong on the sea. His time will be spent worrying whether he made the proper preparations, whether he has the right gear, whether his crew is adequate. He may make a few passages, but he will not really enjoy them.

The seagoing yacht is the epitome of the totally self-dependent system. Whatever happens, it is the crew and the yacht that must master any situation. No outside help can be hoped for in most cases.

How does one build self-confidence and self-reliance? They come basically through experience and through knowing that you have thought through every possible emergency and prepared for it. If you find yourself lacking in any personal way, or find that your yacht or equipment is lacking, don't go. You must decide rationally, of course, whether any self-doubts are realistic assessments of self and yacht or are merely the anxieties that any traveler into the unknown must face.

I always get a lump in my stomach before setting out on an open water passage, and I suspect that it grows less each time I leave. I have many fewer unknowns now than before, and the lump is due more to excitement and eagerness to be off than to any other cause. The excitement or anxiety usually fades after a few days at sea and is replaced by a rather more pleasant feeling, one of happy anticipation of ports to be made, people to be met, and sunsets to be seen.

It is because the best builder of confidence is experience that I feel a season or two of serious ocean racing is a must for any skipper contemplating long-range cruising. It is absolutely amazing how many unknowns will disappear after a season or two of racing.

In the final analysis, confidence is built of experience and good rational preparation. So most of it is developed before the cruise ever starts.

Prudence is to be strictly separated from fear. I define prudence as the art of never letting the yacht get ahead of you. By this I mean never letting a situation be a surprise. Anticipate things to come so so that you have enough time to cope with them before they become emergencies. You should plan your short passages so that you arrive at strange harbors during daylight hours, for example. Thus prudently prepared, you neither take the risk of a reef passage by night, nor do you have to slop around all night in strange waters and then enter tired and unthinking at first light.

When you see a strong wind line behind an island, slow down and take in a good reef. Take down the jib and sail out into the wind line and see how strong it is. If you have too little sail up, it is a lot easier to set more than it is to rebuild one that has blown out of the tapes.

If the weather reports show a significant depression just on the rhumb line for your next port, stay over a few days and save the wear and tear. You will be caught out soon enough without asking for it.

On the other hand, do not make the mistake of being too timid, or you will never make any progress. Prudence allows you to develop experience without experiencing disaster. As you develop confidence your actions may seem imprudent to others with less experience, but if you have made your judgments thoughtfully, you have no worries at all.

A classic example of lack of prudence may illustrate the point. Some years back I was sailing from Oahu to Kauai, bound for Nawiliwili Harbor. We had partaken of a bit too much Island hospitality before departing at dusk, six hours past our intended sailing time. I had neglected to look in the chart locker to see if I had a chart of Nawiliwili, and indeed it was missing. I had a large chart of Kauai, however, and I knew that there was a light on the south breakwater there. We had a fast passage, for the trades were whooping it up that night, and we made landfall on Kauai early in the morning—in a heavy haze.

The seas on the weather side of Kauai are huge when the trades are up, and I was totally miserable with mal de mer. We sailed up and down the coast, looking for the harbor. Feeling sick and weak, I noticed a light stanchion on a south breakwater and immediately

177

drove off for it. Because of the strong breezes we were under only a double-reefed main, the jib being downed. We ran straight for the entrance in great glee until Jim called out that he could see a sand bottom just under the next swell. We hastily jibed to get the hell out of there, and in so doing the topping lift wrapped around the boom, holding it firmly just above our reach. The engine! The engine! A quick push on the starter button revealed that we had forgotten to charge batteries after using the electric lights during our stay in Honolulu. The generator! A quick pull on the starting cord revealed that the whole thing had rusted solid. Set the jib! We did so and found that with the main stuck up in the air and not drawing, we could only make a few feet on each desperate tack to weather. The cliffs surrounding the tiny abandoned harbor of Honaunau were precipitous and afforded no safe landing. We tacked back and forth for some six hours or so before we had sufficient searoom to attempt any repair of the main boom. Once it was set right, we sailed two miles farther south and entered Nawiliwili without further incident. I have never come so close to losing a yacht before or since. It was a supreme exhibition of nonprudent seamanship.

The prudent skipper does not go to sea before everything, both equipment and crew, is in readiness.

Heavy Weather

Heavy weather is no longer the bugaboo it used to be before we had so much knowledge of the survival abilities of small yachts. More and more small yachts are making long passages and surviving them in spite of heavy weather.

It has been said that the small yacht, being light, is better able to survive heavy weather than was the old clipper ship, which was over-canvassed and prone to foundering if seas flooded into her open hatches. This may be so, but remember, too, that what constitutes heavy weather for a small yacht would be only a wholesail breeze for a clipper.

It is not the wind that constitutes the danger to a well-found yacht in heavy weather; it is the seas developed by that wind. Almost any yacht can be hove down by a good blow, but if the seas are not extreme she may lose only a sail or two and her loose deck gear before her crew can get her straightened up. The seas, however, are capable of smashing cabins, crushing decks, and generally destroying structural components.

It is not size alone that may make a sea dangerous; it is the shape and speed. Unusually shaped seas can flip a yacht into remarkable positions. I have sailed in seas that were close to twenty feet high with never a twinge of apprehension, for they were large, trade wind swells, hundreds of yards from crest to crest. There was no breaking top nor any steep side to them, and they contained no malice at all. I have seen seas no more than ten feet high that were dangerous because their length from crest to crest was less than twice the length of the yacht. I would come over one and crash smack into the next just like crashing into brick walls! The differing directions of apparent water movement at the bottom and top of the swells produced very strong turning moments on the vessel, making a broach an imminent possibility.

There are several ways of contending with huge seas that may become dangerous. I am not a great believer in heaving to. In most cases, if you can stand to lie doggo with any sail drawing, you can stand to be underway. This is not to say that I might not heave to so that the cook can work more effectively, or for a little rest, but if conditions are so bad that I must stop, I would prefer to reduce the chances of sail damage by lying ahull or running before. I would say that in better than a hundred thousand miles of sailing I have never found it proper to heave to because of press of weather. In order to qualify that statement let me say that I have always had a yacht of a hull form to allow such tactics. A less refined hull form, such as designed by the traditional "cruising boat" designers, might well have had to heave to in order to keep from having the deck swept by seas, causing damage to her structure or loss of her crew. Obviously, it is the sailing characteristics of the yacht, her length, her freeboard, the determination of her crew, and the judgment of her skipper, that will decide just when some measures must be taken to insure survival or comfort.

As the weather becomes heavier, the yacht will become first uncomfortable, then very wet, then unmanageable. It is this last that must be avoided. I believe that as long as the ship can be readily maneuvered, can be pointed in the right direction, and takes no dangerously solid water, she can be kept going. Any practice that seriously curtails the maneuverability of the yacht should be viewed with caution, in my opinion, except under survival conditions when anything that works is little enough!

Let us first consider shortening sail. When you are going to weather, it is not very difficult to decide when to reduce sail. The lee rail becomes buried, water courses down the high side and washes through the cockpit, the watch below begin to complain about falling out of bunks, and the cook announces his imminent resignation. You may elect to merely scandilize the main (make a fisherman's reef) by easing out the main sheet until a very large luff is carried in the main. Do not, however, ease it out until it shakes, or your battens may fly off to leeward taking most of the batten pockets with them. I have endured squalls of thirty or forty knots this way, but I would be leery of using the technique for a protracted period.

You may also down a jib, reef the main, or, using any means of shortening sail, slow down the yacht and reduce her heeling moment so that the rail rises out of the sea, the cockpit again becomes habitable, and incipient mutiny below is avoided.

When running, you must use good judgment in deciding when to reduce canvas. The apparent wind is less, and the amount of water on deck is less than in the same weight of wind going to weather. I usually carry on too long, not wanting to waste wind, until the yacht screams off the top of a wave and does a wild broach, tossing crewmen from their bunks, the stew from the stove, and me from my pedestal. I usually announce, at that point, that I might just require a reef in the main. (Frankly, I have just never been able to judge well when to reef when running. The result has been some rather magnificent day's runs, as well as considerable wear and tear on nerves among the crew.) It is absolutely astonishing how hard it seems to be blowing when you round up in the trades after running in steadily increasing winds for a few days. The gentle breeze that has been rustling in the collar of your foul weather gear becomes a roaring, slapping, gale when that broach occurs and you find that you are really in a thirty-five knot blow!

As I said earlier, perhaps the best rule for shortening sail is to do so when the thought first occurs to you. If you wind up undercanvassed you can always shake out the reef, and next time you will be that much more experienced.

When you have reduced sail to the point where the yacht will carry no canvas at all without becoming unmanageable, you face the great maritime dilemma. Do you lie to a sea anchor? Lie ahull? Run before the wind under bare poles? Drag warps? Up the storm jib and roar off downwind?

It seems to me that if the seas are not dangerous and if there is no lee shore or other danger you can take your choice of these methods. Two philosophies are involved, and they are somewhat contrary. One school of thought requires that you stop the yacht, supposedly so that she will cause less interference to the seas and thus not increase the chances of having them break on her. The thinking seems

180

to be that a glass fishing ball or a whisky bottle just drifts, and it survives, doesn't it? Unfortunately, the yacht is neither a glass fishing ball nor a whisky bottle, and, furthermore, neither of those most seaworthy objects cares a rap whether it is right side up or not!

Some yachts will doubtless do better under some conditions if they are left to their own devices or stopped. If there is a lee shore or other obstructions you *must* stop. There are several ways to stop or slow down a yacht. You may simply take down all sail and lie ahull. Unfortunately, many a yacht will not lie square to the wind and drift almost imperceptibly to leeward, the ideal position when lying ahull. She may point first her bow and then her stern to the wind. This will reduce the slick to weather left by the drift, and seas may again break aboard. You should try lying ahull sometime and find out how the yacht behaves before you try it in earnest some howling night.

If the yacht is small, under twenty-five feet or so, you may elect to lie to a sea anchor, either by bow or stern. The idea is to reduce drift to leeward and to get the yacht end-on to the seas, giving them the smallest possible target. The tackle should be quite robust, for the strain on a sea anchor is tremendous, as is the strain on the rudder, unless you have remembered to rig relieving tackles beforehand. I am scared to death of sea anchors! They hold the yacht far too rigidly in place, leaving her prone to being swept by breaking seas that may damage her superstructure. If I feel I must stand still, I would prefer lying ahull to using a sea anchor. In a yacht larger than twenty-five feet, the argument is largely academic. You just cannot carry a big enough sea anchor and tackle to do the job.

Partly of the "buoy" school of thought are the systems of running before the gale, dragging warps to slow down the yacht until she has just steerage way, and taking the seas dead astern. If you are running under bare poles and the decks are still scooping up solid water and the yacht is hard to steer, you may elect to drag a small sea anchor as a drogue, or to stream aft all manner of cordage to reduce way. This system has been used successfully by the vast majority of voyagers. One should remember, though, that *Tzu Hang, Vertue* XXXV, and others have met disaster while dragging warps or sea anchors.

I personally believe that this is the favored alternative only in the first days of a gale, when the seas are short and steep.

The final alternative was first suggested by Vito Dumas, I believe, when he simply sailed along without even having a reef point on the boat through weather that would make permanent landlubbers out of most of us. He found that he could handle hurricane force winds by keeping the yacht under a good press of sail and surfing down the faces of the seas at about a 15- or 20-degree angle to the crest. Several other skippers have tried this trick, and all are still around to tell the tale. The philosophy here is to keep the yacht sailing as fast as she can and not fall into the habit of letting a sea get dead behind you. How successful would a surfer be if he persisted in going straight down a wave? Sooner or later he would catch the nose of his board and pitchpole, or pearl. Dumas vastly understates when he calls the first few episodes of the technique "exhilarating."

Taking the seas at a good angle rather than directly from astern reduces the speed with which the descent down the face of a wave begins. The angle of descent is less, as well, and this can go a long way toward keeping the bow from plunging into the next wave and pitchpoling the yacht.

Ocean racers and multihull sailors have come to use the Dumas technique as a matter of course. Most of these dauntless souls would have the average cruising sailor crying for mercy long before they even considered shortening sail!

I believe that in the mature stages of a gale, when the seas have lengthened out, the "give 'em hell" technique has a lot to recommend it. Each skipper must try all these techniques with his own yacht under less than survival conditions in order to satisfy himself as to which one he will try first should the necessity arise.

The primary idea in heavy weather is first to keep the yacht afloat, second, to keep the crew safe, and last, to either make progress toward your destination or at least not be blown away from it.

Some skippers will reduce sail and then use the engine to keep just enough way and control on the yacht to adjust her to the conditions, and this has worked well on occasion. Offshore, however, I believe it wise to conserve fuel and use one of the other techniques if they are workable.

Management Close to Land

An important aspect of seamanship, and one that apparently is often disregarded, is keeping the yacht off the beach.

I am land-shy in the extreme, and for that reason, I have the highest regard for the courage of those who choose to do coastwise cruising. I will take the relative security of the open sea where there are no reefs, unlighted capes, ambiguous lights, foul currents, tidal bores, and the like. I have not researched the matter, but I would bet that a hundred yachts are lost alongshore for every one lost offshore.

Alongshore, perfect navigation and eternal vigilance are the price of sailing. Dangers like reefs and outlying rocks can often be identified by the surf breaking on them during daylight hours. I would not even consider a passage down an unknown coast at night unless I had at least twenty to thirty miles of sea room outside the most seaward danger.

Outside the United States the passes through reefs usually are not lit or the light has gone out and has not been replaced. In the Tuamotus, many of the passes can be recognized by the hulks of fishing vessels and yachts stranded on both sides!

Passages through reef country and lagoons with coral heads are best attempted under visual pilotage from aloft. The observer should be some fifteen to twenty feet up on ratlines or perched on a spreader. The sun should be high and preferably behind the observer. He should wear Polaroid glasses, as these kill some of the random glare.

Coral heads and reefs with little water (three to five feet) show up brown or yellowish in hue. The sandy bottom in a fathom or so is a transparent blue-green, with emphasis on the green. The deeper parts of a lagoon will be more and more deep ocean blue.

I have found that when approaching a strange harbor it is wise to arrive around sunup, when local fishermen often are bringing their catch in to market. You can usually follow one of them in without incident. I would under no circumstances head into a coral harbor if visibility is poor. If you heave to off the pass, someone sooner or later will come to see what's up, or a fisherman will happen by.

Currents around coral-fringed islands may reach almost tidal bore proportions at the peak of the tide flow. Currents of twelve knots or more have been recorded in some of the passes in the Tuamotus. You may have to wait until slack water to attempt many of these passes, unless you are blessed with a yacht that will make twelve or so knots against a good chop.

Because of the currents along many shores, and because of their unpredictability in many cases, it is wise to take every opportunity to fix your position by celestial means or by cross bearings on mountain peaks or other landmarks.

Anchoring

When in a strange port, it seems that your anchor is always too small. You should seek local advice as to the best place to anchor, and then follow that advice! Remember that the calm anchorage you

183

sail into in the afternoon may be visited by williwaws in the nighttime hours.

Anchoring should be done by a reliable member of the crew, not just anyone. I like to veer out a hundred feet or so of chain and let the yacht drift back on it till the slack is taken up. Then I back down gently to set the hook. A second time I back down a little less gently, and a third time I come back for all she's worth. If she stays set under this treatment, she should stay set under a good breeze. I have seen too many yachtsmen just come in, have a crew member throw an anchor and some chain overside, and depart for shore. I have seen most of these same yachts at one time or another zipping around the anchorage with the owners in dinghies in hot pursuit.

Harbor charts are quite good in telling you the characteristics of the bottom in regard to holding ground, as are the sailing directions. Anchoring in a pile of seaweed usually won't hold the boat in a blow. Shale, soft mud, and hard rock are not good holding ground, either. Look for good, sandy bottoms and about five fathoms or so of water. Let out all the scope that you think you can pull back aboard, and keep a good anchor watch for the first two days before letting the yacht stay unattended at anchor. There is nothing much more embarrassing than having someone come up to the bar and tell you that your home and kingdom are now three miles out to sea and heading west!

I like to use all chain rodes on all anchors when in coral waters. Anywhere else, the chain makes for a good catenary but is not needed for chafe protection. I might add that in coral waters you should be prepared either to lose your anchor at times or to go down with scuba gear and free it from its entanglement with some coral head.

Waves

Since waves are the primary danger to the voyaging yacht, some discussion of their properties is in order. The yachtsman can safely disregard the tsunami, or tidal wave, unless he happens to be in port at the time when one strikes the coast. These great destroyers of coastlines are merely long, barely perceptible swells on the open sea. It is only when the bottom begins to shoal that they gain height and develop their dangerous shape.

Waves are caused by the reaction of the surface of the sea to the wind that interfaces with that surface. The height, speed, and distance between crests of seas, (as waves are called if they are caused by wind) are due to three primary factors. The first is the strength or speed of the wind; the second is the amount of time that the water has been exposed to the wind; and the third is "fetch," or the distance of water over which the wind has blown.

The question of how high a wave can get is the subject of many fascinating sea stories. The following figures were gleaned from the U.S. Naval Oceanographic Office's researches into wave properties.

Wind Speed	Maximum Height Obtainable at Sea
Force 3 (7–10 knots)	2.0 feet
Force 4 (11–16 knots)	4.4 feet
Force 5 (17–21 knots)	8.0 feet
Force 6 (22–27 knots)	13.8 feet
Force 7 (28–33 knots)	19.8 feet
Force 8 (34–40 knots)	27.5 feet
Force 9 (41–47 knots)	40.0 feet
Force 10 (48–55 knots)	52.0 feet

Note that these figures are given for the *maximum* heights obtainable. The wind must blow for a steady 50 hours at these speeds, and the fetch must be at least 900 miles for force 10 to produce its 52-foot wave!

I can recall a woman at a yacht club meeting whose hair had all fallen out due to the fact that she had gone out for a sail in her husband's yacht one afternoon, and had encountered a fifty foot wave just a few yards outside the breakwater at Marina Del Rey! The deck was swept by the sea and everything was in a most frightful state, and her hair all promptly fell out! I inquired somewhat maliciously as to what had become of the harbor, the surrounding beach community and that sort of thing, since none of the buildings reached fifty feet above sea level? I looked quickly outside to see if perhaps I had missed the fun, and decided that perhaps there is little hope of convincing a frightened person that what she saw was a five foot shore breaker!

There is a considerable tendency among inexperienced sailors to greatly overestimate the height of seas. You can climb up the ratlines until you can just see the horizon over the tops of the seas, and then measure how high you had to climb, but when the seas are big enough to be really interesting I wouldn't want to be climbing about in the rigging! My system is to judge how high the seas are, cut that estimate in half, sleep on it, and then write it down!

In my mind, the most dangerous seas are the so-called "freak" seas. These seas are not actually freaky but are the product of harmonic interrelationships among waves traveling on the same ocean at different speeds and from different directions. You can see the effects in miniature if you perform the following experiment with a washtub or a swimming pool.

Drop a pebble into the water and observe the pattern of ripples. Now drop two pebbles in close succession in the same spot. You will notice that the ripples from the second pebble will overtake those from the first pebble in some cases and interfere with the pattern. If you look closely, you will see that some of the ripples are attenuated or made smaller. Some are amplified or augmented, becoming higher. If you have winds from the same direction that vary markedly in strength, you have a similar situation in the sea. The speed of a wave group is related to the force that generates it, and thus waves from one weight of wind overtake the waves of other group, augmenting and diminishing them. The result is an occasional sea or two that is much higher or lower than that given in the table of heights.

Granting that the maximum height of seas in force 10 theoretically, may reach 52 feet (if the fetch is at least 900 miles and the wind blows for at least 50 hours) and that there is a random fluctuation of wind force and direction, then the statistics of random stochastic processes predict that about one wave out of 200,000 may reach a height of over 100 feet! This theory may account for the more commonly encountered freak wave in the roaring forties, where wind direction and strength vary widely, as compared to the trades, where the wind blows more steadily and from a more consistent direction.

Since the seaman can do nothing about the shape or height of the sea, he must contend with what is thrown at him. As mentioned earlier, waves twice the length of the boat from crest to crest seem to be the most dangerous. They lead to broaching or falling off the crest into the trough, particularly if the wind is abeam or slightly aft of abeam.

I refer to this condition as having the ship "out of tune with the wave system." It can often be relieved by simply slowing down, or in some cases speeding up. If navigational considerations allow, you can often reduce the wild antics by changing course slightly. Often only a few degrees is enough. As the wave system matures, the seas become lower and lengthen out, and you can probably resume course and speed.

I noticed quite often at sea that when beam reaching in force six or seven the seas would "strike" at the yacht from time to time. The breaking crest would literally explode against the exposed weather bottom and the result was like being hit by an express train. There was an incredibly loud bang, and the boat would shift sideways about three or four feet and then fall into the trough. Very exciting! When we made contact with the bottom of the trough, we were usually nearly horizontal, and there was danger of bursting a cabin window or something. I have never found a canvas weather cloth that would survive that kind of treatment. When my nerves had taken about all of that madness that they could stand, I would don my battle dress and go out and change course just a few degrees, and the smashing and crashing would resume their normal tempo.

Waves in shoal waters (inside the hundred-fathom curve) have different characteristics from those in the open sea. They seem not nearly so high, but they have a steeper shape and are closer together for a given weight of wind.

The Alenuihaha Channel between the islands of Hawaii and Maui, which I have mentioned several times is a prime example. The channel is only about fifteen miles wide at the narrows, and has a volcano nearly 14,000 feet high on each side. When the trades are up, the wind touches force ten easily in parts of the afternoon, due to the venturi effect of the mountains. The seas give the channel its name, which, roughly translated, means "the rolling road." The seas are described by local yachtsmen as "twelve feet high and twelve feet across." It is difficult to go to windward in these waters, because the yacht always seems "out of tune." There seems to be no speed or course that will keep her nose out of the next sea, other than turning and running.

And even running in such seas can become exciting, I was running down the channel one night in a good forty-footer when a sea burst over the quarter and filled the cockpit. Now, that's not so unusual, but the same sea spun the yacht through 180 degrees and left me gasping and spitting out salt water in a yacht that was totally aback in a breeze of about forty-five knots! There had been no warning, no sudden increase in wind. Probably the wave that did the trick was a freak harmonic or riprap from the fringing bluffs. You wouldn't even sneeze at the presence of a twelve-foot wave offshore, but in shoal waters they are likely to break at odd times, causing a good deal of bad language from the helmsman.

Some say that there are certain lengths of vessels that are just better "tuned" to the average length of the seas, and a lot of nonsense is carried on in this vein. Some say that a twenty-five footer is the ticket for the Pacific Ocean, while others say that forty feet is the magic number. What they are trying to say is that you should try not to get into a wave system that is twice or less the length of the yacht. Let's take the average trade wind condition. Wind is force four or five; the fetch is greater than a thousand miles; and the wind blows constantly. What would the average characteristic of the seas be? The height would be between four and eight feet. What would the wave length be? Wave length is related to the speed of the wave, which increases, as does period and wave length, as the wave proceeds away from the area that generated it. The length of a wave in feet is related to its period by the following relationship.

$$L = 5 \times P^2$$

Thus if waves tops were arriving at 10-second intervals the length of the wave would be 500 feet.

Researching the Hydrographic Office's reports again, our average trade wind sea would have a period of between 6.3 and 8.2 seconds. Applying the theoretical formula, we would come up with a wave length of between 198.45 and 336 feet. This would constitute the dangerous sea for vessels between 99 and 168 ft.

If the wind were to blow very hard, we might get a forty-footer in trouble for the first hours. Let's consider force 11. After two hours of force 11 we would expect a sea to be 10 feet high and to have a period of 5 seconds. The wave length would thus be 125 feet, and a forty-footer would still be less than half the wave length. A sixty-footer or over would perhaps be threatened.

Obviously, the length of the yacht is of importance only during the early stages of a very heavy blow, because only then are the periods short enough to create the dangerous short wave lengths. As the wind continues to blow, say for two or more hours longer, the period, and thus the wave length, becomes longer. Our force 11 sea would now have a period of 6.3 seconds, which would give us a wave length of 198 feet, safe enough for a hundred-footer! Its height will have increased to 20 feet, however, and it will probably be breaking heavily.

With all the harmonics and augmented waves, and the varying directions from which the wind may blow, thus generating random patterns of wave activity, it is absolutely impossible to say that one given length of boat is the optimum!

Seamanship Under Self-Steering

Having a self-steering rig requires a few additional comments in the seamanship department. Just having a self-steerer often brings such a feeling of security that crews do not stand adequate watches. Remember, the apparatus may steer better than you can, but it cannot see a freighter, nor can it reduce sail if a squall hoves into view, nor can it detect the presence of a reef or a harbor entrance. What it *can* do is tell you when it's time to reef, once the time comes. Most self-steerers will begin to lose their ability to control the boat when she is noticeably overcanvassed. The "tattletale" compass below will begin to show course shifts and attempts to head up when the wind becomes too strong for the sails and vane to control for. You, as a helmsman, could probably still keep the yacht heading in approximately the right direction long after the vane has given up in disgust, but in all likelihood you would be needlessly lugging sail.

10   Oh!
For a Life on the Rolling Sea!

Perhaps the most difficult job a writer ever has to do is try to communicate to others just exactly what something is "all about." He is certain of his own feelings, emotions, and motivations, but he finds it most aggravating to try to communicate these to anyone else. For a sailor, it may be almost impossible. The relationship between the sea and the sailor is largely a private one that makes the man one with all sailors since time immemorial. It matters not whether the sailor is Lord Nelson or the skipper of a fishing boat; there is an indefinable kinship among men of the sea that knows no ready description.

How does one describe the persistent longing that assails every true sailor when he is "on the beach," when he has no ready prospect for a voyage, when he is immersed in mortgage payments and a proper but enervating "career"? How can you describe the lump that starts in the throat when a tall ship passes, standing out to sea on some venture? You need not explain this to a sailor. He knows full well what you are trying to say, though he may cover up his true feelings by snorting out some epithet like "I go to sea because I'm too damn stupid to do anything else!" But he knows.

I do not speak here of the dilettante. I do not speak of the man who goes to sea because it is the "in" thing to do in the Newport social set. I speak not of the man trying to escape from a life dulled by bureaucracy and politics, nor do I refer to the man who is out to prove his manhood to others. I speak, rather, of men to whom the sea *is* life, of men who have made that happy decision to let the sea be the taskmaster, to glory in it, to be happy in it, and, in the final reckoning, to die in it.

It is at sea that the greatness as well as the weakness of man is made fully evident. More than one thinker has observed that there are no artifices, no rationalizations, no bucks to pass, and no excuses at sea in a small boat. It is at sea that a man must come to grips with his true self. All the accolades, degrees, honors, and bank accounts are dross when the sea is up and it's time to turn to and shorten sail or to bail for twenty hours or so.

It is this process of measuring oneself against that impersonal standard of the sea that perhaps motivated so many voyagers. It is a search for the personal truths, which matter little to most twentieth century men, that sends men again and again to sea, knowing that no one other than themselves really gives a damn.

I recall an acquaintance of mine who came into Hilo Bay one afternoon but did not seem terribly interested in going ashore. He had been at sea for some thirty days, but he turned to and began painting the topsides and doing various odd jobs around the yacht.

His wife, after the third day, asked with some heat, "Aren't you going ashore?"

His reply was classic: "I've been ashore." He had, indeed. Ten years before, when he had last visited Hawaii!

He had sailed better than fifteen thousand miles in the first five months of the year, and going ashore had just not yet entered his mind.

I am in no way trying to make heroes of sailors, for that would embarass most of them to tears. But I will say that the true sailor is a most extraordinary breed, one that is rare in this day and age. He is a man who does not necessarily like hardship, but he will endure a good deal of it to be again on the open ocean, where a man's spirit and thoughts are as free as the Tropic Bird that visits at sunrise.

Perhaps the best way to attempt the description of the lure of the sea would be simply to try to describe a voyage to some place or other. Perhaps then in the sometimes bemused recollections of events past some grains of truth and light may appear.

When the day of departure had dawned, when all the supplies and stores had been put aboard, when all the last-minute preparations had been made, and when I was in a high state of excitement over the prospect of the voyage, the press put in an appearance. They had been called, it seemed, by the manager of the marina, looking for a little free publicity. I was totally nonplussed by that appearance, for I always detest having anyone know just when I am leaving or where I am bound. Supposing I funked it and had to turn back after a few days? What in hell would I tell them then? It is not that I don't want the good wishes of friends; it is just that everyone seems to make such an untoward fuss! Besides, I know I have the good wishes of my friends, or they wouldn't be my friends.

The representatives of the press, being landsmen, knew nothing of the sea, of yachts, or of good manners. They insisted on taking pictures of us raising the anchor! I pointed out that we were in a slip and that it would look ridiculous to see people about to brave the open sea doing a stupid thing like that! They said that no one would notice; it was traditional to have such pictures. They settled for a shot of us hanging on a halyard, apparently raising the jib, while grinning foolishly with our heads all turned toward the camera, looking in the opposite direction from the sail. They asked the usual questions: Will you anchor at night? How will you occupy your time? What will you do if you get into trouble? What if she sinks? How long will the voyage take? The answers were: No; I'll sleep a lot; I'll pray a lot; I shall drown; and I have no idea! Thus satisfied, they departed, no doubt making mental notes to stay away from sailors hereafter.

By now our neighbors at the marina were wise that something was up beyond an ordinary trip to Mexico, so they formed an escort to see us off.

As we stood out into the stream, one of the local harbor police noticed that we did not have any state registration numbers on the bow. Where are your numbers? "We don't have any!" This last disconcerted that worthy, who had never heard of a documented vessel, which carries no external number. After explaining the law to him, we finally stood out for sea. I noticed that my heart was going like a trip hammer, and I felt like shouting with glee.

When the last members of the escort had tossed the last bottle of gin aboard and had said their last goodbyes, we were suddenly alone and off on an adventure the outcome of which was clearly up to us.

We set the 180 percent genoa and cracked on sail, trailed the taffrail log, and generally picked up everything in the cabin and restowed it for the final time. We were almost in a manic state, grinning and laughing and joking. In order to forestall instant insanity, I set the watches and sent the off watch below.

As the hours passed, the excitement began to be replaced with little nagging questions. Is this ship really equal to those huge trade winds seas? Did I forget to put aboard any navigation gear? As the evening went by and suppertime came and went successfully, the old steady routine of sea life began and the familiar feeling of sunset at sea exerted its soporific influence.

I went below at 8 P.M. for my first watch below. I found that my mind was bedeviled by myriad unrelated thoughts and images, making sleep a fitful process, gathered like bits of cotton from a blue serge suit.

At about eleven or so, I heard an anxious, but quiet, call from Jim. He had seen some lights that he could not figure out and wanted some company, besides. Once on deck I saw that the wind had dropped, and that we were just ghosting along, making perhaps a knot or two. The night was overcast, and there was a trace of low haze. No star or other celestial body was visible, but there was a double row of dim red lights off ahead, low above the horizon. We were by that time well clear of Catalina Island and should have been well into the open sea. Could they be fishing boats, all going in the same direction? Why could we not hear their engines?

We puzzled and fretted for a time, and I suggested a slight change of course in order to pass them by. I went back below for a few more minutes' sack time and was promptly called back on deck by a now completely baffled mate who announced that the damned lights still bore dead ahead!

We noticed that whenever we changed course the lights would seemingly shift until they were dead ahead. Were we in the middle of a bombing target with intermittent lights? Were we being invaded by Martians? Why was there no sound?

Suddenly there were four blinding flashes of light from the direction of the mysterious red lights, totally dazzling our dark-adapted eyes. Bombs! But still there was no sound other than the whisper of the bow wave. We began to speculate about hallucinations. Both of us? The first night out? Ridiculous! Shall we heave to?

"Sail on!" said I, but not without a peculiar feeling in the pit of my stomach.

We continued on our course with deep puzzlement, and increasingly fearful of what we might find when we finally came among those lights, but we never could seem to shorten the distance between ourselves and them, even after some three hours. The four flashes of dazzling light still appeared at random intervals.

Suddenly Jim shouted, "Fall off! Fall off!"

In the weak beam of his red deck flashlight, we could make out the plates and rivets of a heavy cruiser slipping by, running blacked out, with only the muffled sound of her turbines to announce her ghostly presence. As suddenly as she was there, she had completely disappeared. We began to notice a difference in the sounds of our own yacht, a vibration, an unexpected pressure on the tiller, little yaws from course.

Suddenly the realization dawned. We had sailed smack into the middle of naval maneuvers! The moving lights were a fleet of heli-

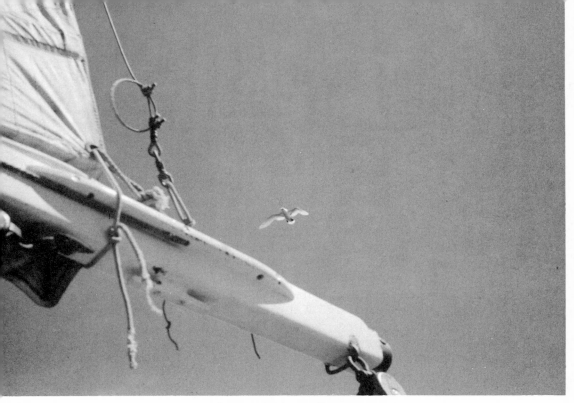

A tropic bird visits *Laguna*.

Fishing for Mahi-Mahi is great sport when becalmed.

copters hovering with their sonar gear extended below to the surface of the sea. The flashes were their condenser discharge lamps, with which they could look deep into the calm sea. The cruiser was investigating various things that they had heard, one of which was us! But why did they seem to be so interested in us? We were a sailing yacht; we had lit our running lights at the first show of a light from them; and we were obviously not a submarine.

Then we remembered. A favorite trick of submarine skippers is to sneak through the fleet while hiding *under* some yacht or fishing vessel. That was the reason for the strange noises, the eddy currents, the little yaws from course.

How incredibly stupid of us not to have realized it sooner. We all had a good laugh at our own expense, but we kept a good watch for dark cruisers all the rest of the night.

The log for that date reads: "June 10. Day's run 125 miles. Weather, fine. Wind NW 8–15. Getting settled into sea routine."

Things continued uneventfully, with the winds shifting gradually northward as we reached the zone of the "nasty northers" between the outer channel islands off California and the zone of the trade winds. These northerly winds can become quite strong. They are caused, I believe, when the Pacific high-pressure zone drifts eastward, causing the isobars on its eastern border to become closer together. That increased pressure gradient causes a strong northerly flow, which can blow with moderate gale force for days at a time. I always figure that the stronger the nasty northers blow, the closer are the trade winds.

By the afternoon of the third day we had reduced sail to the working jib and the whole main and were on a roaring beam reach. About three in the afternoon the sun came out, and up on a spare halyard went Jim's sleeping bag. We had inadvertently left a hatch open for a second or so and a goodly dollop flew through and soaked the bag. With the appearance of the sun, the wind increased further, and old *Laguna* simply flew along. The lee rail would bury for a while, and the cockpit became pretty wet, so we decided to reef the main. That was the last time we were to see a full main for many a week.

Jim, being younger and more athletic than I, jumped up to reef. All went well until it came to tying in the last points, near the clew. We took a good roll, and the main sheet slipped off the cleat. There was poor Jim swinging from the boom by his fingernails, about eight feet out from the side of the yacht! His name became "Tarzan of the Apes" for about three hours, until we noticed that in the flurry

195

of reefing someone had hauled on the wrong halyard and there was his sleeping bag, flapping at about the level of the spreaders. He had not bothered to rig any downhaul, so there it was. He rigged the most incredible looking lashup I ever saw, made of a fishing pole, a boathook, and the flagstaff, and after doing everything but dismasting the yacht, managed to snag the bag and claw it down. This last act led to all sorts of fun, mostly at poor Jim's expense. "Hey Jim! We're going to set a different genoa; does your bag need airing?" or "No, no, Jim; set the spinnaker, not the sleeping bag!" The log reads: "Day's run 185 miles. Wind N 20–25 kt. Rough today."

As the days slipped by we settled down into the old familiar sailor's routine—too little sleep, wet clothes, enough food, and too much motion to read comfortably. The northers held and we made great progress, but the motion of beam reaching and the constant wash of seas over the weather side and into the cockpit began to make itself felt. I was sleeping in my foul weather gear because of a persistent deck leak just over my feet. Everything was soaked through, and we had not seen the sun since the episode with the sleeping bag. We were at times under reefed main and smallest jib, sometimes under just the double-reefed main, and at times we would put up the lapper, when the wind fell below twenty-five knots.

The yacht was crashing along, making a tremendous racket and happily throwing water all over the place as she surged forward. We were averaging close to 160 miles per day!

I would go on watch and ask the traditional questions of Jim: What's the course? How's she doing? The answer would be 230 degrees, and she's wetter'n hell, but the wind is down now. I would reply that I thought the wind was up a bit and would usually get no answer. We would sit together for a few moments, talking quietly, and Jim would depart below to his "burrow" in the forward cabin. He had rigged a canopy of plastic over his bunk, so that the deck leaks would not again spoil his precious sleeping bag. The burrow was his country, and I never went there.

Fatigue was catching up with us, and little tensions began to show. The delicate fabric that constitutes the comradeship among the crew of the oceangoing vessel had begun to ravel a bit at the corners. Jim's use of ketchup on everything he ate began to seem almost criminal to me, and my maddening habit of never putting anything back where it belonged was beginning to strain his nerves. The dishes were not clean enough; the watches were wearying; and "God dammit! When is the goddamned sun ever going to show?" And the litany of minor complaints began to swell and grow.

We had been unable to get any sights for ten days, and we were unsure of our position. The trades had not yet become evident, and to our water-soaked bodies and fatigued minds, the whole voyage had become tiresome drudgery.

We would sit for hours during the day, our backs to the cabin doors, looking aft at the angry cresting seas. We would say little, not wishing to provoke arguments. Once in a while we would both suddenly stand up, as if the next one was really going to poop us and wash through the cockpit. We would look at each other foolishly and sit down, each thinking how absolutely absurd it was for intelligent people to subject themselves willingly to such misery.

I felt secretly that if a freighter or a helicopter came along, I would gladly leave the yacht to the mercy of the sea and accept rescue! Then suddenly Jim said that it was strange that we had spent all our time looking back from whence we came, rather than looking forward to where we were going. We both turned and faced forward, and the change was miraculous! The seas no longer looked menacing, and our separation from land was complete. We had at last cut our ties with the last port and were at once as one with the sea. I knew then the wisdom of the old clipper ship skippers who cautioned the helmsman never to look astern.

The sun came out, and I was able to get a good fix, which showed our dead reckoning to be off by only sixteen miles after ten days of hard sailing. The wind dropped, and the first catspaws of the northeast trades came stealing in. The log reads: "125 miles' run. Sun out. Think we may have finally found the trades."

We left the first reef in the main and adjusted our speed by changing headsails, which were now wing and wing. We rigged a double preventer guy forward to the windlass against any accidental jibe. We broke our spinnaker pole when it dipped into a sea during one of *Laguna*'s demonstrations of the rhythmic roll, but it mattered little. We were on our way in earnest now, with all manner of junk spread out on the cabin top, including Jim's sleeping bag, with the main hatch open for the first time in weeks.

We were content to jog along making 120 to 130 miles per day. We were finally enjoying ourselves!

Jim rigged his fishing line and was rewarded by a twenty-pound Mahi-Mahi. We fell to and devoured it, half cooked, half raw. And so the voyage went, as all trade wind voyages should, watch and watch with a warm wind and pleasant going. Plenty of fish to eat if we bothered to fish at all, yarns and stories in the cockpit with our evening drink, and the inevitable designing of the perfect yacht.

Foul weather gear was put away, and we turned out resplendent in bright-colored swimming shorts. When the squalls came along, we would rush below and get out the soap. We would wash with fresh water and laugh with exhilaration as the needles of rain pummeled our bodies. No thoughts now of reefing; we had seen a lot more wind than that before.

On the eighteenth day, I predicted a landfall about dark on the island of Hawaii. Now the excitement ran through the ship at fever pitch. I surely hope I really know how to navigate! Just to be sure I took another longitude line, as the sun was bearing nearly due west. To my surprise the line of position showed us to be 600 miles east— of Tokyo Bay!

Jim practically fell off the boat laughing. I went below to correct the mathematics, and came up with a position somewhere near Cincinnati. Jim by that time was nearly helpless with laughter.

I now began to be worried in earnest, so I got a new observation and worked it from scratch. It proved beyond doubt that I knew nothing of navigation, because it was equally improbable. At that point, when I had lost all the credibility that I had worked so hard to gain, I spotted the hazy outline of a headland. Land ho! Jim eyed me with some suspicion, for he was looking for the pointed top of a volcano. What we actually saw was Kamukahi Point, some five miles south of Hilo, which was our intended point of landfall. The island was totally obscured in a rain squall and covered the whole horizon before we could see it!

We were only about fifteen miles off when we made the landfall. It was becoming dark, and the breeze had fallen light so we jilled around all night waiting for a good glimpse for the almost indistinguishable breakwater at Hilo.

We cleaned up the ship and ourselves, stowed our preventers, and generally put the yacht in condition to go into harbor. We got out the anchors and shackled on the chains, and we talked excitedly about the steaks, lettuce, and ice cream that would be waiting for us in Hilo. Before first light we spied a few fishermen going into the harbor, so we got underway and followed, savoring the scents of the Pacific islands. The heady smells of flowers, cane fields, sugar refineries, and wet earth drifted out and brought back a flood of memories of my boyhood on another island much farther away. As we approached the breakwater the wind became lighter and lighter, until we were forced at last to turn on the engine to keep up with the fishermen.

We brought out the portable generator, put it in the cockpit, and set it going to charge up the batteries. It chattered away noisily as we took in the sights of awakening Hilo Bay. Suddenly I caught the smell of gasoline! I quickly shut off the generator and the main engine, which we had just started. My feet felt strange, so I looked down and saw, to my horror, that I was standing in a pool of gasoline! I hastily threw my eternal cigarette overside and after it all the matches I had in my pocket. We bailed bucket after bucket of water into the cockpit until all the offending liquid was gone.

The generator, it seems, had jiggled its way over to the corner of the cockpit where the gas supply lived in plastic jerrycans. The hot exhaust had simply burned a hole in one of the cans without igniting any of the gas therein! How lucky can you get? To sail a voyage of 2,200 or so miles and then nearly get blown up by a generator!

After a pleasant week in Hilo, where we were royally entertained by the local yachtsmen in their usual style, we departed for a sail around the back side of the island. We set off under a reefed main and the working jib, for the trades were back at it again, and arrived at the north point of the island in the dawn hours. We had heard about the Alenuihaha Channel and wanted to pass through it in the early hours, before the famous venturi effect made itself felt. We passed without incident and made for a cove on the Kona side of Hawaii, where the Mauna Loa Hotel was located. The cove is flanked by fringing reefs but affords a good anchorage once you enter. We sailed in through the wide pass and, dropping our spinnaker, rounded up and dropped the hook in thirty feet or so of the clearest water I have ever seen. You could see each grain of sand that the anchor kicked up.

Then we saw the natives! They were swimming out, laughing and calling to us. As they approached, we saw that the "natives" were the sons and daughters of the golfers who make up the main clientele of the hotel. Our appearance had apparently sparked a rash of home movie-taking, and these youngsters, bored absolutely stiff by a hotel that offered only golf as its main pastime, were full of questions: Where are you from? Do you mean you crossed the ocean in that tiny little boat? Can we see her?

We were instantly invaded by dozens of laughing, chattering teen-agers, who looked with wonder at our little ship and were properly impressed with our feat of seamanship! When they all departed, swimming happily for the shore, which was about a third of a mile away, we felt like the crew of one of the explorers' vessels, come to a new land. I put on my fins and mask and had a good look at the anchor to see that it was well set, and we swam ashore, dragging our rubber dinghy behind.

The lesser management of the hotel was apparently not too happy about our presence, for they gave us looks of thinly veiled distaste as we swam ashore, changed into our shore duds behind a convenient clump of trees, and visited the bars and restaurants of the hotel. I guess they were resentful that we didn't have to pay sixty dollars a day for the privelege of viewing the scenery.

Each night, a "native" boy would blow mightily on a conch shell and then run about in a most incredible manner, lighting kerosene-powered "tiki" torches. This was advertised as an ancient Hawaiian lamp-lighting ceremony. I imagine the true Hawaiians turned over in their graves! When we could stand no more of the place, we sailed (much to the relief of the management, I suppose) down to Kailua-Kona, where we hoped to take on fuel. The swell was heavy, and we were forced to fend off with tires and boathooks all the time we were at the pier. In spite of our precautions, *Laguna* looked as if she had been clawed by a giant tiger before we had put aboard our twenty gallons of fuel.

We decided that Lahaina Maui was the next stop, so we set all plain sail and headed back for the Alenuihaha Channel. As we made our way up the coast the weather was bright and sunny and we reveled in the sights and smells of the coastline.

As we reached the northernmost point of the island we saw the wind line. Where we were sailing the water was untroubled and relatively smooth, with a gentle swell and ten to fifteen knots of wind. Up ahead we could see what looked very much like the roistering, boiling waters of rapids on a great river. We quickly downed the jib and put a double reef in the main, for we knew we would have to beat in order to make the south point of Maui, some thirty-five miles away.

When we reached the wind line, I was absolutely incredulous! It was like being thrust suddenly into another world. The wind struck with unbelievable force. The yacht heeled far over until her spreaders touched the wave tops. Pots, pans, my chronometer, and the contents of a few cupboards that we had failed to secure bounced and banged their way around the cabin. Tons of water poured over the weather side, and all around us was the most incredible display of water being thrown straight up into the air and tops being torn off waves, coupled with a howling shriek of wind through the rigging!

Laguna slowly righted herself and took off. We sailed over one wave and through the next. We were soaked through in a few seconds, but the water was warm and we paid it no mind. She would stick her bow under a sea and then rise desperately, causing a veritable Niagara in the cockpit. All manner of noises emanated from below, and Jim started down to try and stow some of the dislodged gear. He came quickly back on deck with the announcement that he had been hit in the head by a flying can of soup! We decided to let the cabin survive as best it could. As we continued out into the channel, conditions improved and we began to enjoy the trip again. We had a strong ship; the sun was shining; and to hell with the shambles below! Once we had reached midchannel, some three hours later, the wind came abeam and we took sea after sea over the weather rail. The water finally completely permeated my watch, which had been impervious to soakings for more than ten years. *Laguna* would sometimes roll down to an alarming angle, and we counted eleven times that the spreaders touched the water that afternoon. Later, when it was all over, I found that the chronometer had actually spun in its gimbals, breaking the cover glass. (I have never repaired the glass, but keep it there as a reminder not to go out in the Alenuihaha in the afternoon.) As we neared Maui, the wind came astern and we cracked on sail and made our way to the lee afforded by the south point of that island. By the following morning we had made our slow way to Lahaina, the old capital of the kingdom of Hawaii. A Coast Guard crew was there, and one of the members asked, in pidgin English, "Hey, bruddah. You the ones out in the Alenuihaha yesterday?"

We allowed as how we were, and he made the following timeless remark: "More bettah you don't have any trouble, cause we don't take our eighty-five footer out dere in the afternoon!"

We felt about twenty-five feet tall. The inside of the cabin was dented from top to bottom. My old surplus radio direction finder had jumped out of its heavy wooden cage and had committed suicide by scattering tubes and the like all over the cabin. It looked below as if a cyclone had hit the place. The engine had drowned and needed eight new valves, which I scrounged from a tractor shop, and everything (except a few scars of honor) was good as new (we thought).

It was only after we were halfway home that the damage really began to show up.

The trip home from Hawaii is one that is likely to repel all but real seamen. The semiannual races to Hawaii are a great sporting event, but they are all downwind. There is a lot of heroic talk among the crews after a TransPac race. They sometimes tend to look on cruising sailors as the little old ladies of the sailing fraternity, holding that it is they, the racers, who carry sail and drive boats, while the cruiser reefs at the first sign of a blow, and so on. It is absolutely amazing, though, how quiet the room becomes if one of the cruising skippers suggests a race home from Hawaii! I can remember a deafening silence at my own yacht club, which is made up mostly of racing sailors, when I modestly proposed a race, to be sailed without handicap and with a crew of one male and one female. The race would leave Los Angeles in June; the Hawaiian Islands would be left to starboard; and the race would finish back at Los Angeles!

Few of the racing crews sail home from the TransPac, preferring to go by plane and have one of the "little old ladies" sail the yacht home. The cruising sailor will usually have for crew only his wife or perhaps a returning college student.

The only tough part of the trip home is the long beat north through the trade wind belt to the horse latitudes, usually at about 40 degrees north. It is a bitter slog, hard on the wind, and is often wet and miserable if the trades are whooping it up.

We left Nawiliwili, Kauai, under a reefed main and our smallest jib and settled down for a good bash to weather. Nothing drastic happened until one day when the mate was using the head. I heard a loud thump, followed by curses, then by laughter and calls for help. I hurried below to find the mate flat on the deck with the head itself attacking from all directions! All four lag bolts that held the thing down had failed as we jumped off the face of a sea, dumping the mate unceremoniously flat on the deck with the head on top! It took three days before we could get the boat to stand still long enough for the head to be rebolted.

As we approached the higher latitudes, the trades lost force and we were in the gathering influence of the Pacific High, the area of high pressure that is the center of the circulating trades. Its position is not really all that stable; it moves east and west and sometimes breaks up into smaller cells of high pressure. Sometimes it disappears altogether for a time. I always like the High, because it is a gathering ground for all manner of flotsam, notably those beautiful Japanese glass fishing floats. The collection of glass fishing balls is the highlight of the trip back home from Hawaii!

As the weather becomes lighter, the seas go down, and the sailing becomes much like that along the West Coast of the U.S.—light breezes, not more than fifteen or twenty knots at the most, and a lot of calms, when the ocean looks like a great bronze mirror. The sunsets are dramatic—blood red and gold one night, purple and blue

Given proper conditions, almost any vessel can cross an ocean. This 18-footer
was capsized on the way to Hawaii, but made it none the less!

Astrea anchored in Nawiliwili.

the next, but always spectacular. The sun at noon scorches the decks, and temperatures below hit well over 100 degrees. The crew sit around trying to keep cool by sloshing buckets of tepid water at each other or trying out new shower baths made from plastic jugs.

Then someone with eagle eyes spots a small glint on a distant swell, and the chase is on. All hands turn to, getting out the large bait nets and any manner of device that may serve to pick up a slippery, round ball of glass. One must keep careful watch that the prize doesn't get out of sight during the maneuvering. When the quarry is close at hand, it requires a delicate hand to round up and approach slowly. If the approach is too fast, the bow wave will push the ball too far away and the crew cannot get it into the nets. Too slow and the yacht falls off and another run must be made! Some of the balls are two feet in diameter and are covered with netting. These can usually be grasped by hand or with the boathook. The smaller ones (and I have caught one that was the size of a golf ball) usually have no netting and are slippery as the very devil.

You can judge the amount of time the ball has been adrift by the number of goose barnacles and pelagic crabs attached. These form a "beard" that may reach thirty feet in length if the floater has been adrift for a few years. The accumulated growth may sink the ball in time, and it may go so deep that all the sea life deserts it. It will then surface, but it may then contain sea water, forced in by the tremendous pressure without any sign of a crack! You can't imagine the stink that a thousand tiny crabs can cause when they crawl out of the netting and die on your decks—in spite of valiant efforts to flush them over the side with buckets of water!

Once through the area of calms and squalls, we struck the northerly flow again, and it was here that our afternoon escapade in the Alenuihaha began to make itself felt. Jim was on the foredeck raising the big genny when the winch simply disintegrated! It broke completely in half, showering him with fragments and bruising his arm badly. The next morning he quietly told me that the lower aft shroud on the starboard side had let go. We borrowed a piece of spinnaker sheet, passed it around the spreader, and set it up taut with a handy-billy taken to a winch.

At about two in the morning I was on watch, drowsing along, lying flat on my back with an idle toe to correct an occasional luff, when I heard a great bang. I called out to Jim to look under the floorboard to see if we had been holed, for we had been seeing large balks of timber lately, castaways from the great log rafts common in the Northwest. He could find no water beyond the ordinary, and

I looked aloft to see the mainmast bending alarmingly to starboard above the spreader. I instantly put the boat about and hove to on the opposite tack to relieve the strain and ran forward, letting fly the main and jib halyards as I went by. I arrived on the foredeck with a sickening thud as my trick knee came into devastating contact with the anchor winch. I hauled down the jib and found that I could not stand because of the pain from my knee, which I had broken so many times before that I dreaded any further trouble from it.

I hopped back to the cockpit just as Jim came on deck wanting to know what all the fuss was about. We had broken the port upper shroud! How the mast stood up I will never know, but I suspect that my use of a running backstay is all that held the rig in her. We stopped and took stock of the situation.

We were about one thousand miles from the nearest land. Still, we had about twenty gallons of water left, and gangs and gangs of canned fruit, as well as plenty of other food. Obviously starvation was not imminent should we be unable to fix the shroud.

The yacht, shorn of her canvas, was possessed of devils and tried in every way to chuck us off into the Pacific. We saw that the shroud had broken in its lower reaches and that we could get at it from the cabin top. I thought of the anchor windlass, that malevolent machine, and then of the anchor rode. It had a large galvanized iron thimble. I hopped or drug myself forward and hauled out chain until I came to the thimble. We used it to make a big loop in the lower end of the shroud, securing the loose ends of the wire with three bulldog cable clamps. What to use for the rest of the shroud? I quickly came up with what remained of our shattered wire topping lift and made several turns with it through the thimble and through the turnbuckle. We secured it all with a mess of cable clamps and gingerly set up on the turnbuckle. It held! We made sail again, under the main alone since we were not sure exactly how much our battered rigging would stand. I found that I still could not put any weight on my leg, but I had done all right with just the one!

The following morning dawned bright and cloudy and we surveyed the rig and found that, except for the two broken shrouds, it was apparently all right. If anything else broke, we were in for big trouble, for we had no other repair materials left!

At that time a vessel hove into view, and we were in a dilemma as to whether to just let him pass by or ask for assistance. He was a large power boat being delivered to Hawaii for the purpose of hauling tourists to Pearl Harbor. He obviously had nothing in the way of rigger's supplies, so we kept our counsel. How has the weather been?

"Been just fine!" Any problems? "None at all!" Good sailing! And he was gone. By the afternoon we had ceased to worry about our unsteady spar and again put up our largest genny, making tracks for home.

When we finally made our slow way through the coastal calms and arrived at the entrance to Marina Del Rey, we were terrified by the huge numbers of yachts in the channel. Our engine was of course out of commission again, and we were nearly hit by some ass in a small boat who was demanding right of way over a drifting cruising boat.

When we slipped into our mooring space I got the strangest feeling. Panic gripped me, and I only wanted to get out of there and back to the open sea! Now I would have to go back to the petty political intrigues that a college professor must contend with; I must go back to those dreary acres of dull faces, totally uninterested in what was being taught; I must return to Marina Del Rey where you were not allowed to etc., etc., etc.; I must contend with the dull and uninteresting life of modern man in the city. In short, I must contend with the land.

The very thought of it appalled me.

Postscript

It may be of some interest to the reader to see the route by which I came to my present philosophy about the best hull and rig for ocean crossing. Perhaps a description of some of the yachts I have owned, together with their strong and weak points, may be helpful.

I began sailing in the early thirties in American Samoa where my father was a ship's sawbones on the old seagoing tug, *USS Ontario*, affectionately called *Mungwaa* (man of war) by the natives. I sailed in outrigger canoes that the natives built and I sailed in my own first boat, endemic to the south Pacific area, a "tin boat." These were simply a section of corrugated roofing tin, folded like a paper boat with pieces of wood to form a sharp bow and stern. We would paddle around inside the fringe reefs, much to the terror of my mother and to the secret delight of my father. Tin boats were a lot of fun, but they were most difficult to raise from a bottom more than five or six feet deep, because there was no buoyancy of any kind in them. Consequently at an early age, I learned to look for stiffness in a boat and also for buoyancy tanks in small ones!

I often went fishing with my father and other members of the *Ontario* crew in 26-foot Navy whaleboats. These had Buda diesel engines in them and more than once we would drag anchors while fishing outside the fringe reefs. The fact that the engines were very often hard to start led to some apprehensive moments. All hands would take to the oars until the engine would at last start, or expire entirely. Lesson: never depend entirely on an engine.

Several cruising yachts stopped by Pago Pago during my years there, among them *Idle Hour*. Her skipper, Dwight Long, was young and made quite an impression on me. His idea of sailing around the world took hold of me and has never let go. Since that time my goal has been the acquisition of a vessel that would do the job properly.

After the beginning of World War II, which I chanced to observe at close range due to my father's transfer to Pearl Harbor, we were sent to Portsmouth, Virginia. There I spent my free time on boyhood projects such as building dinghies made of piano boxes and raising sunken naval shore boats with dreams of returning to far off islands.

I learned about skipjacks, sharpies, bugeye ketches, pinkies, and the rather varied lot of antiquities that the oystermen used on the Chesapeake Bay. These were easily built and were surprisingly fast for work boats. They were fantastic while reaching but would not really go to weather with any authority. I learned a lot of tradition from the oystermen, though. I learned that a vessel must be strongly built if it is to resist the effects of sea and time. What I did not learn, however, was that every area has special preferences and special needs, and the boats that have developed over the years in specific areas may not be necessarily right for any other area.

When I had finished my military service, where I saw little of the sea except from airplanes flying over it, I again began to think seriously of a yacht that would serve as an ocean-going home.

My first serious cruising vessel was *Laguna*. She was canoe sterned and had a beam of 9 feet. She drew 5 feet 5 inches and was 35 feet overall. Her hull was of Honduras mahogany, copper riveted to bent oak frames. Her stem and keel were a little strange, being laminated up from one-inch pieces of white oak. She was fitted with a conventional trunk cabin with a low doghouse, a design popular in Europe in the early fifties. She was built by Cornu, et Fils, in Antibes, France, just a stones throw from the Riviera. She was launched in 1950, and came to U.S.A. on her own bottom. She was apparently one of the first yachts on the west coast that had the high aspect ratio main so characteristic of the modern I.O.R. yachts. She had a large fore triangle with a "J" measurement of over fifteen feet. In spite of the large fore triangle, she was $\frac{7}{8}$ rigged and thus suffered when it was time for spinnakers.

In general, her form and characteristics were moderate. With her canoe stern, she had about as much room in her as does an average thirty footer. She was not of high freeboard, and thus could not hold stores for a large crew on long passages. We could, however, load her with enough stores for three for as long a period as 100 days, including emergency rations for another thirty days. She would compare reasonably well with such yachts as the *Pearson 28*, the *Herreshoff 28*, or the like in hull form. She suffered from a narrow run aft, which made her begin to suck up huge quarter waves when she was running hard. The bow would begin to get up on the bow wave but the stern was so busy digging a giant's trench in the ocean that she would become unstable. Perched up on her own bow wave with no support aft, she would begin to roll rhythmically from side to side. If the helmsman tried to correct for these rolls, he would actually accentuate them and *Laguna* would often broach to. These broaches were sometimes spectacular, if a good sea was running, going sometimes through 180°! If the helmsman was of good courage, however, he would center the tiller and shut his eyes tightly for two wild rolls and she would peacefully resume her normal downwind antics. The amount of water that she would scoop up during one of these demonstrations was astounding, but to our surprise, not dangerous. On any course other than a dead run she was a perfect lady, and never gave me anxious moments.

I raced *Laguna* for several years. She was always in the top 10 percent of finishers, winning more than her share of trophies. As a cruiser she was more of a challenge than most because her hull was easily driven and she carried a lot of sail area for her weight. Her main mast was fifty-two feet high. I never figured her total sail area, but her measured area for racing was 710 square feet. She weighed fifteen thousand pounds. Her motion at sea was not alarming, except when running. In 1967 I beat all the way home from Hawaii, partly because I did not want to endure the rhythmic roll on the way home.

Her accommodation was cramped, having two semi-quarter berths in the main salon. There was not room for a table except a small folding one. Forward of the salon was the head to port, and the galley to starboard. The galley was smaller than the head and had only a two-burner stove and a small sink. There was no refrigerator or icebox. Just forward of this was the forward cabin containing a V berth, a hanging locker, and a small dresser. This may seem spartan by today's standards, but it served well for many thousands of happy miles. *Laguna* was a lot like a horse I once owned during my vagabond days. She would bite, kick, and stomp. She would try in every way to buck you off every time she was saddled but she would go like the wind, and no razorback could make her back down.

I once sailed *Laguna* to Hawaii in eighteen days under working sails alone, and her best day's run was 185 miles. Not bad sailing when you consider that her waterline was only 24.5 feet.

I don't believe I would ever have sold *Laguna* but for the fact that her cabin was of African mahogany which became soft with age. She leaked like blazes and I could just never get the cabin tight. I also felt at the time that I should try a large ketch that could be lived aboard. In that way I would soon have the means to go off on my often-postponed world cruise. How often we are in error when our hearts rather than our heads make decisions!

Astrea was my great mistake as far as voyaging yachts go. Perhaps if I had not first sailed *Laguna* and crewed on several fine racing yachts I would have been more satisfied with her. *Astrea* was of conventional wooden build, 40 feet on deck, 11.5 feet of beam, and drew 6 feet. Her waterline was approximately 33 feet. She measured from the tip of her bowsprit to the end of her mizzen boom over 52 feet. She carried 1000 square feet of working canvas, which was not nearly enough for her in light airs under force four. She never leaked a drop during the time I sailed her, and her motion in a seaway was serene. Her forward progress was also serene, unfortunately, unless a fresh breeze piped up. She had a diesel engine, a radiotelephone (it never worked), a refrigerator, a pressure water system, a hot water heater, a shower, and all the fillups one could imagine. She nearly forced me into bankruptcy just keeping up with the repairs! I made a few cruises in her but something was sorely lacking and that was any semblance of thrill. While she was a beauty (she won several concours while I owned her), she was a dowdy sailer. She suffered the same ills as do all fat ketches. She simply would not put up much of a show to weather. I sailed her to Hawaii in eighteen days and never got my feet wet. I also used two days worth of fuel because of her rotten light air performance. The trip home from Hawaii took longer than any other I have made in spite of four days use of the engine and a tropical depression that gave her an incredible 1250 miles in six days. As you may well imagine the balance of the thirty days of the journey were spent cursing her lack of weatherly ability in light airs. When I was forced to sell her because of personal reverses, I felt a great deal of relief. She will remain a fine coastal cruiser but will never make it as a long-range voyager.

Dawn Treader, 27 feet long, 10 feet wide, drew 4.5 feet and weighed just over 4,000 pounds dry. She had no engine and was a marvelous little cruiser, Joanne and I built her in just eight months from drawing the first line to launching for a cost of just over $6,000.00. She was a rocket in light airs and would begin to surf to weather when we had force four or over. She carried sixty-five gallons of water and needed no engine of any kind. The amount of gear that could be carried was severely limited. In spite of this, we could carry provisions for sixty days, and our wet suits, tanks, rubber dinghy, guitars and typewriter. We spent a very happy summer on her, relishing the thought that we could leave Los Angeles under sail while the other cruisers motored and still beat them into San Diego by hours. We would laugh with great glee as we charged by some traditional crab crusher with acres and acres of canvas spread in light air. I have never felt more independent than with *Dawn Treader*. She had only one fault, if it could be called that. She lay ahull well, she hove to steadily, her motion was surprisingly mild in spite of her speed, but if there were a five-knot increase in wind force, it required an instant sail change or she would be overpowered. We never broke anything on her and indeed never spent a dime on repairs.

We could come to an anchorage in the afternoon and then in the dusk, up anchor for an evening sail! How different from trying to get underway with a huge anchor and a many-masted rig.

Joanne and I are now in the process of building *Dawn Treader II*. She is designed to the same philosophy as was D.T.I. She will be 42 feet long because she will be our only home. She will weigh about 20,000 pounds, 10,000 of which will be ballast. She will spread approximately 1100 feet of working canvas in a modern cutter rig. Her engine will be only enough to move her around anchorages. Her beam will be 11 feet, her waterline 33 feet and her draft 6 feet. She has a narrow fin keel and a spade rudder. She is designed by Bill Lapworth and the fiberglass hull is being made by Islander Yachts in Costa Mesa, Calif. I will do the interior accommodation, set the engine, and build the rig. Her sails will be by Baxter and Cicero of Costa Mesa and she will carry a full complement of genoas and spinnakers.

Perhaps some explanation is needed for her rather large size. I do not think we need anywhere near such a size to cross oceans but we will welcome the space when living along shore. When we decided to build D.T.I, we had no plans to live aboard but wanted only a good stout yacht in which to cruise. She turned out so well that another sailor promptly bought her from us. The fuel shortage and inflation quickly stopped plans to buy another yacht as prices were sky-rocketing. We searched and searched for designs to build, looking even into Australia. I was a little timid about building a mold for such a large yacht.

I have owned Lapworth-designed yachts before and have sailed in many others, so I have the highest regard for his expertise. We finally found Islander Yachts who had a mold for a Lapworth design. It was a 44 footer but we were able to plug the mold and shorten her to 42 feet. I will, of course, make some small changes to suit my sailing style but she will remain a Lapworth design. As I write this *Dawn Treader II* is out of the mold and receiving her plug of lead ballast. I have at the ready enough teak to build her interior and the engine waits in the shop to be installed. How fine it will be to see her go together as the winter comes and goes.

When a year has passed and I am immersed in nearly terminal fiberglass rash, we hope to launch her. Until then, we will think of little else.

Bibliography

Atkin, William, *Of Yachts and Men*, New York, Sheridan House, 1949

Baader, Juan, *The Sailing Yacht*, New York, W. W. Norton & Co., 1965

Barton, Humphrey, *Vertue XXXV*, London, Adlard Coles Ltd, 1950

Bowditch, Nathaniel, *American Practical Navigator*, U.S. Navy Hydrographic Office

Chapelle, *Boatbuilding*, New York, W. W. Norton & Co., 1941

Chichester, Sir Francis, *Gipsy Moth Circles the World*, New York, Coward-McCann, 1967

Coles, Adlard, *Heavy Weather Sailing*, Tuckahoe, N.Y., John de Graff, Inc., 1968

Coulson, Morris, *Racing at Sea*, New York, D. Van Nostrand, 1959

Dumas, Vito, *Alone Through the Roaring Forties*, London, Adlard Coles Ltd, 1960

Duplessis, *Fibreglass Boats, Fitting Out, Maintenance and Repair*, Revised, John de Graff Inc., 1973

Guzzwell, John, *Trekka Round the World*, London, Adlard Coles Ltd., 1963

Hiscock, Eric, *Beyond the West Horizon*, New York, Oxford University Press, 1963

——, *Voyaging Under Sail*, New York, Oxford University Press, 1959

Howells, Valentine, *Sailing into Solitude*, New York, Dodd Mead & Co., 1966

Kinney, Francis, *Skene's Elements of Yacht Design*, New York, Dodd Mead & Co., 1927

Long, Dwight, *Sailing All Seas in 'Idle Hour'*, London, Hodder & Stoughton, 1938

Mixter, George W, *Primer of Celestial Navigation*, 5th Edition, New York, Van Nostrand Reinhold Co., 1967

Pye, Peter, *Red Mains'l*, New York, Dodd Mead & Co., 1952

Scott, Robert, *Fiberglass Boat Design and Construction*, Tuckahoe, N.Y., John de Graff, Inc. 1973

Slocum, Joshua, *Sailing Alone Around the World*, New York, Sheridan House, 1954

Smeeton, Miles, *Once is Enough*, New York, W. W. Norton & Co., 1959

Tambs, Erling, *The Cruise of the Teddy*, London, Jonathan Cape Ltd., 1949

Index

HB7E